A *Titanic* Love Story: Ida and Isidor Straus

Endowed by
TOM WATSON BROWN
and
THE WATSON-BROWN FOUNDATION, INC.

A

TITANIC

LOVE STORY

Ida and Isidor Straus

JUNE HALL McCASH

Mercer University Press
Macon, Georgia

MUP/ H840

Second Edition

Books published by Mercer University Press are printed on acid-free paper that meets
the requirements of American National Standard for Information Sciences—
Permanence of Paper for Printed Library Materials.

Mercer University Press is a member of Green Press Initiative
(greenpressinitiative.org), a nonprofit organization working to help publishers and
printers increase their use of recycled paper and decrease their use of fiber derived
from endangered forests. This book is printed on recycled paper.

Library of Congress Cataloging-in-Publication Data

McCash, June Hall.
A Titanic love story : Ida and Isidor Straus / June Hall McCash. -
- 1st ed.
p. cm.
Includes bibliographical references and index.
ISBN 978-0-88146-277-7 (hardback : alk. paper) -- ISBN 0-88146-
277-2 (hardback : alk. paper)
1. Straus, Isidor, 1845-1912. 2. Jewish merchants--United States--
Biography. 3. Titanic (Steamship) I. Title.
E184.37.S77M33 2012
338.092'2--dc23
[B]
2011050843

Contents

To Jill, Leah, and DeLynn—
with thanks to my sons Michael, Bren and Rodney
for choosing these wonderful women to be their wives
and become my daughters

Set me as a seal upon thine heart,
set me as a seal upon thine arm:
for love is strong as death.
Many waters cannot quench love,
neither can the floods drown it.

—Song of Solomon 8:6-7

Preface

It's hard to reconstruct the beginnings of my interest in the story of Ida and Isidor Straus. It may have been when I first learned of their deaths on the *Titanic* and discovered the amazing expressions of admiration and awe that poured in from people all over the world. Or perhaps it was when I saw the elderly couple who chose to die in bed in the 1997 film *Titanic*—surely *not* intended to be Ida and Isidor who stood on deck as the ship sank, wrapped in one another's arms, dressed to the nines. In fact, a brief scene depicting the real Ida and Isidor had been shot, but wound up on the proverbial cutting room floor. Fortunately the Broadway version, *Titanic the Musical*, which also opened in 1997, did portray the Strauses and gave them a moving duet. But they were utterly neglected in a film that shouted about the love and loyalty they embodied, a love that sealed their memories in our national lore, but recast it in a young, impetuous couple untested by time, who had little more in common with Ida and Isidor than their passion (in the truest sense of that word) for one another.

Twelfth-century writer, Andreas Capellanus, once began a Latin treatise on love with the words "Amor est passio" (Love is suffering). While most of us would agree this is not always the case, perhaps a modern rendition would be that love is willing to suffer and endure all for the beloved. I recall an incident that occurred in early 1991, a heart-rending time when my husband was dying of cancer. One day, as I did what little I could to give him love and comfort, he asked, "Is there nothing you wouldn't do for me?" If there was, I hadn't yet found it. But few of us ever have the need or opportunity to test the absolute limits of love as Ida Straus did when she chose not to get into a lifeboat, but to remain on the deck of the sinking ship, rather than leave her husband to die alone.

Perhaps it was this question that first drew me to the Strauses' story. As my interest began to deepen, I discovered that both Ida and Isidor also had interesting connections to the state of Georgia, where I have a home and about which I have written three books (one with my late husband). Everything seemed to draw me toward their story, to make me want to find out more about them. Many people seemed to know about their deaths, but few knew much of anything about their life together. Their births had occurred on the same day, their shared birthday of February 6 (though in different years) and ended on the same day, symbolizing their oneness.

As my interest in the Strauses grew, it seemed inconceivable to me that there had never been a book published about these remarkable people and their life together. It became my fervent hope to remedy that omission. I began my research for a book, which became *A Titanic Love Story.* While Ida and Isidor were prominent figures in New York, in large measure because Isidor, along with his brother Nathan, owned Macy's Department Store, this book is by no means a business history. That issue has been thoroughly studied by Ralph Hower in his *History of Macy's of New York 1858-1919* and rendered for a more popular audience by Robert Grippo in his *Macy*s: The Store. The Star. The Story.* Instead, *A Titanic Love Story* is the human saga of a couple caught up in an important era of American history. Like everyone, they experienced struggle, heartbreak, grief, and even prejudice. But they steered a path straight and true to the very end, never wavering from their values and beliefs. This book chronicles their love for one another, their interests, their compassion, and the family they created together.

In a world like ours today, by and large jaded and cynical, readers may find the Strauses hard to believe. They were people who consciously molded their lives with love and service to others, who blended economic conservatism with liberal humanitarian values and who were always willing to share with those in need. In short, people who can serve as a model of reason, stability, and faithfulness to our broken world.

Acknowledgments

As always, I have many people to thank for the final version of this book. My research necessitated various trips to New York, especially to Smithtown, Long Island, where the Straus Historical Society has its extensive archival collection of letters, memoirs, diaries, photographs, clippings, etc. Its archivist, Joan Adler, is an absolute treasure who always provided whatever information I needed and who responded to my numerous questions and requests promptly and courteously. Another trip was necessary to the New York Public Library, which houses both the Straus Family Papers and the Nathan Straus Papers and where the staff was exceedingly helpful. I am grateful to my friend Beth Bean for the generous use of her spacious Manhattan apartment while I was in the city. I also appreciate the help of Scott Byers, Macy's archivist, for help in locating relevant photographs. My thanks also go to Elina Kazan for permission to use the Macy's photos and to Paul Kurzman for permission to use photos from the collection of the Straus Historical Society, Inc.

In addition, I spent a great deal of time in the Library of Congress in Washington, D.C., where the Oscar Straus Papers are located. I am grateful not only to the obliging and capable archivists there, but also to my wonderful brother-in-law Selby McCash for his liberal hospitality at his home on Capitol Hill for the duration of my visit.

Similarly I want to thank members of the staff at the Georgia Historical Society in Savannah, who have assisted me not only with this project but with so many others through the years. An additional trip to Georgia took me to Talbotton, where local historian Mike Buckner allowed me to use his collection and showed me around the town, including the locations of the Straus homes and store there. I visited as well Columbus, Georgia, where I was graciously hosted by the late Laurette Rothschild Rosenstrauch, who shared her extensive collection of materials for her Blun and Rothschild families and who took me to visit the home (still standing) where Ida's sister, Amanda, had once lived, as well as to the Jewish cemetery where one of Amanda's sons is buried. I have also been blessed to have the help and encouragement of various other family members, including Thomas Francell, also a descendent of the Blun family, a Savannah, Georgia connection, Pamela Blun, and Barbie Gurgan, a descendent of Percy Straus, whom I had the pleasure of meeting in Nasvhille.

I am especially grateful to my former university colleagues, both fine historians, Jerry Brookshire and Robert Jones, for reading and commenting on the entire manuscript, no doubt saving me from embarrassing errors I might have made. In addition, Joan Adler of the Straus Historical Society read and made helpful comments about many of the chapters. My husband, Richard Gleaves, also listened to various versions of these chapters with patience and fortitude. I appreciate as well stylistic suggestions from members of the Murfreesboro Writers Group.

In terms of assistance in tracking down various important details, I thank Garry Shutlak, senior archivist at the Novia Scotia Archives; David Dearborn of the Maine Maritime Museum; Susan Olsen, Director of Historical Services at Woodlawn Cemetery in the Bronx; Kevin J. Foster, for information concerning the running of the Union blockade during the Civil War, and my friend, Rosemary Kew, for helping me resolve a question concerning the "Common" in (or near) Oxford.

My son, Bren Martin, assisted me with various computer problems, as did the staff at Middle Tennessee State University's Instructional Technology Center. I am also grateful to staff members in both Interlibrary Loan and Reference divisions at MTSU's Walker Library for helping me to locate various obscure sources and information.

Above all, I want to thank the editor of Mercer University Press, Marc Jolley, for his faith in this project, and his assistant Marsha Luttrell, as well as my agent, Jason Allen Ashlock and his associate Craig Kayser for their advice and other aid. This book would not have come to fruition without the assistance of all these people and no doubt others I have failed to mention. I thank them all.

Prologue

New York City awoke on Monday morning, April 15, 1912, to the usual cacophony of traffic and newsboys hawking their papers. It is unlikely that Percy Straus could hear them as he breakfasted with his wife, Edith, in his parents' rambling old home place at the corner of 105th Street and Broadway where he and his family were living until they could move into their new apartment on Park Avenue.[1] But the news breaking that morning on the streets was shattering to the tranquil existence of Percy, his two brothers, three sisters, and their families. Their parents, Isidor and Ida Straus, were sailing home from the South of France, where they had spent many pleasant weeks away from one of the coldest winters in the United States. Percy's older brother, Jesse, had also left for Europe with his wife and daughter only a few days earlier, and the two ships on which family members traveled were scheduled to cross in mid-Atlantic. The Straus brothers, Jesse, Percy and Herbert had followed their father and Uncle Nathan in the family business of Macy's Department Store, and were widely regarded as the "merchant princes" of New York.[2] All were wealthy, all were happily married and life was good.

As Percy stepped into the busy city streets, if he had not already heard the news, he would have been repeatedly assaulted by the shouts of the newsboys: "*Titanic* sinking! Get your paper here!" Percy was alarmed! His parents had booked passage on the ship's maiden voyage to return from their extended winter vacation. The ship they had originally booked, the *Olympic,* another of the White Star Line, had its sailing delayed several weeks for repairs. Though his sons had urged them to stay a while longer and enjoy themselves, Isidor was eager to get home to see to matters at the store. He did not want to wait for the *Olympic* and they exchanged their tickets to sail on the *Titanic* instead.

The morning edition of the *Times* had hit the streets only a few hours after the last wireless communication from the sinking ship was received at 12:27 A.M. It reported that the situation was dire and that women and children were being put into lifeboats.[3] Family members of *Titanic* passengers rushed to the White Star Line office to get the latest information. The place was pandemonium and no one seemed to know anything more than what had already been reported. If they did, they were saying nothing.

By afternoon, however, the brothers breathed a sigh of relief when an early edition of the *New York Evening Sun* announced that "All Titanic Passengers Are Safe; Transferred in Lifeboats at Sea." The article assured readers the *Titanic* was still afloat, its touted bulkheads having held, and was in the process of being towed to Halifax by the ship *Virginian*. Passengers had been put aboard two Cunard liners, the *Carpathia* and the *Parisian*. These precise details were reassuring. Even the *Christian Science Monitor* of April 15 carried the story, adding that White Star Line officials were confident the ship was unsinkable.[4]

Percy, jubilant, immediately wired the good news to his youngest sister Vivian and her family, who were vacationing at the Carlton Hotel in Cannes, France: "Passengers Titanic transferred. Parents landing Halifax Thursday. Excellent."[5] Percy's younger brother Herbert made immediate arrangements to meet his parents as soon as they reached shore, booking reservations to leave on the one o'clock train for Boston, where he would make connections to Halifax. One of Isidor's closest friends, Jacob H. Schiff, a noted Jewish banker and director of the Union Pacific Railroad, sent a personal note to C. S. Mellon, president of the New York, New Haven, and Hartford Railway Company, asking for assistance on Herbert's behalf. "His mother is suffering from heart disease," he informed Mellon, "and he is very anxious to be in a position to reach there promptly and to take care of her on the return journey as well as possible."[6] He received a reply that same afternoon, assuring him that "everything will be done for the convenience and comfort of the passengers from [Halifax] to New York."[7] Having made every possible arrangement to welcome their parents home as safely as possible, family members went to bed that evening, still anxious about Ida's condition after all the excitement, but happy and eager to see the family together again.

Their optimism was dashed in the morning when the grim truth was reported. The buoyant account in the *Evening Sun* was a reporter's hasty efforts to make the front page on the basis of rumor alone. The story was completely false. The morning headlines of the *New York Times* of April 16 blurted the tragic, but still incomplete (and inaccurate) news: "*Titanic* Sinks Four Hours After Hitting Iceberg, 866 Rescued by *Carpathia*, Probably 1250 Perish." [8] The awful reality began to take hold. The *Titanic* had sunk to the floor of the North Atlantic, and well over a thousand passengers, more than half, were dead. A partial list of survivors also ran in the *Times*. It did not contain the names of Ida and Isidor Straus.

The Straus children, at least those who knew of the disaster, were anxious as they waited for reliable and more complete information. Jesse and his wife Irma had not received any of the wireless messages Percy had sent, and continued blithely on their voyage to Europe. Still unaware of the disaster, Irma wrote a cheerful letter to her children on the morning of the April 17, "Two days ago the captain knocked at our door at seven o'clock in the morning to tell us to come on deck and see two big ice-bergs. We only had time to put on wrappers and fur coats and go on deck."

Their sister Vivian, however, *had* received the messages and was making plans to move to Paris with her husband, Herbert Scheftel, and their children to await further news. Marconis [telegrams] filled with both uncertainty and hope flew back and forth across the Atlantic, and anxious messages from concerned friends poured into New York from all over the world. But reliable news was difficult to come by. It was impossible to get private communications to or from the *Carpathia*, which was transmitting only official messages.

Isidor's brother Oscar, who served as Secretary of Commerce and Labor under Theodore Roosevelt and only two years earlier had completed his third term as ambassador to the Ottoman Empire, sought to use his considerable political influence to access to the *Carpathia*'s wireless. This would help him learn through official communications whether Isidor and Ida had survived. Among those he contacted, all of whom were acquaintances or personal friends, were Charles D. Hilles, personal secretary to President Taft, the dapper Secretary of the Navy George von Lengerke Meyer (who had fired the valet who awoke him with news of the *Titanic*) and even the Prime Minister of Canada, Sir Robert Laird Borden, who was vacationing in Hot Springs, Virginia, at the time.[9]

That same afternoon Hilles replied that the President had requested the Navy Department to inquire via the cruiser *Chester*. The following day Oscar also received an answer from the Canadian Prime Minister, who expressed regret that an "official telegram from Ottawa" had indicated that the Strauses were not aboard the *Carpathia*. He conveyed his hope that Oscar would soon receive "reassuring tidings."[10]

A family friend, Walter Beer, had agreed to meet Jesse and Irma as soon as they reached Paris and deliver whatever recent information was available. In anticipation, Percy wired his brother, "Names of only half of the survivors known. We have been unable thus far to get any news to or from Papa and Mama." Now that their lives hung once more in the balance, Percy refers to them in these urgent and abbreviated communications (as do his brothers) as "Papa" and "Mama," rather than as the more efficient "parents" he had used in his happier message to Vivian. He seems to be holding them now as close as possible, refusing to distance them in any way, refusing to admit any possibility of losing them.

By Thursday, April 18, Jesse learned of the *Titanic* disaster. Feeling out of the loop and frantic for news, he cabled Percy, "Cannot you Marconi us [wire us] information about Papa Mamma." By then Percy had received word from John Badenoch, the grocery buyer for Macy's, who happened to be a passenger on the *Carpathia*, confirming that their parents were not among the survivors who had been taken aboard from the lifeboats.[11]

Even then Percy would not give up hope. He grasped at any straw, cabling his brother that there was an unconfirmed rumor that the *Baltic*, due to arrive that day in Queenstown, Ireland, was carrying 250 more survivors. He decided to have Walter Beer take a tender and meet Jesse in Plymouth, where the *Amerika* was due to dock on Thursday night, instead of waiting until he had reached Paris. In case the rumors were true, Jesse would be better positioned to meet their parents.

The next day, April 19, four days after the sinking, Vivian's husband, Herbert Scheftel, cabled from their hotel in Paris: "Do not lose courage some hope yet." But by the time this telegraph reached New York, all hope had vanished. Badenoch had arrived the evening before on the *Carpathia*, bringing grim news to the Straus family about their parents' final moments gathered from various survivors. Percy informed Jesse in a cable, undated but surely sent on April 19, that Badenoch's information "leaves no hope Mother refused to leave father Danger realized too late Both showed perfect courage and composure to the end."[12]

The story of Ida's refusal to leave her husband first appeared in the press that same day, and by the morning of April 20 there was hardly a newspaper in America that did not run the story. One of the most detailed was published in the *New York World* and contained a third-hand account from Ellen Bird, Mrs. Straus's maid, which had been repeated to the *World* reporter by Sylvester

Byrnes, once Isidor's personal secretary but now general manager of R. H Macy & Co. Eye-witnesses abounded who claimed to have observed Ida's heroic sacrifice, as she repeatedly refused to enter a life boat and leave her husband behind. Many claimed to recall the exact words of Ida to her husband and to have seen them go down with the ship, wrapped in one another's arms.

Although the stories differed in detail and in the exact words spoken, there was a remarkable similarity to them all, and Ida quickly became renowned as the heroine of the *Titanic*. Her actions were labeled "the most remarkable exhibition of love and [d]evotion" of the disaster.[13] Expressions of admiration and condolence from around the world flooded the Straus family homes. Drawings, poems, tributes, all meant to immortalize the Strauses in their final hour, were published in newspapers throughout the country.

The family stores—Macy's, Abraham & Straus, and L. Straus & Sons—all closed in mourning, and, as people inevitably do at such times, the Strauses managed their grief by attending to the myriad details and arrangements that death requires. Now they could only hope that their parents' bodies would be recovered and that they could be appropriately buried together.

Already formal tributes were being paid throughout the city. One of the first was that of the Educational Alliance, a charitable organization that Isidor, along with his good friend Jacob Schiff and others, had helped to found in 1889 to assist immigrant Jews, and of which Isidor had been serving as its first president. Although on the evening of April 19 the Alliance adopted resolutions praising Isidor's "nobility... [and] true manhood," as well as Ida's able cooperation "in carrying out his plans for the public welfare," they planned a more public memorial and lecture for the evening of April 23.[14]

During the weekend of April 20, emotional Shabbat services were held in various synagogues and temples commemorating the lives of the Jewish notables who had lost their lives on the *Titanic*, especially Benjamin Guggenheim and Ida and Isidor Straus. The focus was on eulogizing the deceased and excoriating the steamship company that they contended had put "greed and speed" above the safety of the passengers. Similar services were held the next day in Christian churches throughout the city. Their memorials tended to cast a wider net as a general tribute to all who had perished in the disaster. But, as the *Times* commented, "The churches were all crowded, and the congregations in many were obviously deeply affected. No greater calamity in many years has so strongly aroused the public sympathy."[15]

Perhaps the most memorable event that Sunday took place not in a church, but in the Broadway Theatre, where every seat was filled and many mourners were turned away. One of those who spoke most passionately about the Strauses was William Jennings Bryan, three times the Democratic Party candidate for the Presidency, who described himself simply as "a colleague" in Congress of Mr. Straus "some twenty years ago." In fact, Straus and Bryan, though both lifelong Democrats, had been on opposite sides of the most important political battle of Straus's brief congressional career. Yet here was Bryan proclaiming Isidor a "hero" and noting that his and his wife's actions "make us proud of those whom we know who are part of us."[16]

The mania and competition to lionize the Strauses grew in New York and around the world. While Isidor, a great philanthropist, would be missed, it seemed to be Ida's actions on that dreadful night that caught the world's imagination. Memorial efforts were made not only for the couple, but also for Ida alone.[17] Her sacrificial act, her existential moment, had ennobled both their lives in the public imagination, capturing and distilling an extraordinary love at its moment of greatest trial. Employees of Abraham & Straus in Brooklyn adopted a tribute to the couple expressing appreciation for "the lesson of their lives" and "the beautiful inspiration in their death." Throughout the country, indeed, throughout the world, the tributes gained momentum.[18]

This public outpouring of emotion rose to a peak on April 23, when the Educational Alliance scheduled a lecture on the Strauses by Rabbi Hirsch Maslinsky at its hall at 107 East Broadway, a building for which Isidor had helped raise funds for construction. Organizers had not anticipated the momentum of public reaction. The hall had a capacity of 750 people, but by five o'clock, an estimated crowd of more than ten thousand had already gathered outside. By the time the event was to begin at 7 P.M. the crowd in the streets had grown to somewhere between 20,000 and 40,000 people. The Madison Street police captain called in all his reserves in an effort to keep order. As people pushed and shoved to get close to the doors of the hall, a railing on the Jefferson Street side of the building gave way and people toppled some ten feet onto the pavement below. As an ambulance clanged through the crowd, additional police reinforcements were called in from other New York precincts. More than thirty people were taken to the hospital, though fortunately no one was seriously injured. Nevertheless, Alliance officials, in consultation with police, made a quick decision not to open the doors for fear people would be crushed, but rather to disperse the crowd by canceling the affair entirely.[19]

As these events unfolded in New York, the grim task began of recovering the bodies floating in the North Atlantic, still strapped in their life jackets. The *Carpathia* carrying *Titanic* survivors had not yet reached Halifax, Nova Scotia, when on April 17 the White Star Line sent out a vessel called the *Mackay-Bennett* to recover and identify as many of the bodies as possible. The task proved formidable. Those aboard the chartered ship were unprepared for the large number of frozen corpses they found, and a second vessel, a cable steamer called the *Minia*, was soon sent out to join the search. The *Halifax Evening Mail* of April 30 reported entries from the ship's log, one of which noted that "The sea was dotted with bodies as far as one could see."[20] The Straus family began an anxious vigil to see whether their parents' bodies would be found.

They did not have to wait long. On April 26, Percy wired Jesse, who was by then at Claridge's Hotel in London: "Papas remains recovered and identified." Isidor was labeled as body number 96 and described with an "estimated age" of 65 [He was 67], a "front gold tooth (partly)—hair and moustache, grey."[21] When the body was brought on board, he was wearing a fur-lined overcoat, grey trousers, coat and vest, soft striped shirt, brown boots, and black silk socks. Found on the body were a gold watch with a platinum and pearl chain, a pocketbook containing £40 in notes and £4 2s 3d in silver, a gold pencil case, a silver flask, and a silver salts bottle. As always, he seemed prepared for any eventuality and clearly had time to dress with forethought.[22]

The Straus children hoped against hope that their mother's body might also be found, and on April 30, Percy sent a description of Ida to aid in the search. A woman of medium height, with black hair streaked with gray, she had a "prominent flesh colored mole on right cheek" and an appendicitis scar.[23] She wore a dental plate on the upper left side. In preparing a description of her clothing, Percy obviously consulted her maid, Ellen Bird, who had helped Ida dress the night of the sinking. Since her arrival in New York, Ellen had been staying with the Strauses.[24] According to the description provided, Ida was last seen wearing a "white flannel petticoat, black silk stockings, black satin petticoat, black cloth coat and skirt, black cloth overcoat lined with grey squirrel and fox fur collar, black button boots, brown kid gloves, white shawl around head and life belt tied at back." All her undergarments were marked with her initials I.S. Not surprisingly, the only jewelry she wore was her double wedding ring and her solitaire engagement ring. But she carried with her other items in a "grey suede leather jewelry pocket attached to her person, which the maid knows she put on when dressing on the *Titanic*."[25] Among the 14 items listed was a "gold mesh bag set with diamonds and emerald on the bars" that Isidor had recently bought her at Noury's in Paris. The family offered an unspecified "liberal reward" for the recovery of her body.[26]

Percy also forwarded a description of Isidor's manservant, John Farthing, who had been traveling with them. They could provide no photograph, as Farthing's wife refused to relinquish the only one she had, but Percy wired Maurice Rothschild, the son of Ida's late sister, Amanda, who was in Halifax acting as the family's agent in the matter, the best description he could. "Farthing stood about five feet nine inches, one hundred eighty pounds—dark brown hair with no grey streaks, scar on right foot where carbuncle was removed—Wore no ring." But like Ida's, Farthing's body was never found or, if found, was never identified. All told, the *Mackay-Bennett* retrieved 306 bodies before it began its return to Halifax on April 26. Of these 116 were buried at sea. Only 56 of them had been identified. At the time of these sea burials, however, the descriptions in question had not yet been provided.[27]

Isidor's body, accompanied by James Reilly of Macy's, who had been with Maurice Rothschild in Halifax, reached New York on Thursday, May 2. In an effort to avoid publicity and crowds of onlookers, the Strauses had the train make a special stop at the 125th Street station to unload the body. Representatives of each of the four families then in New York met the train: Percy and Herbert, along with Sara's husband, Alfred F. Hess, and Minnie's husband, Richard Weil.[28]

Jesse and his family were expected to reach New York that same afternoon. Vivian and Herbert Scheftel originally had not planned to return to America. But as soon as they learned on April

26 that Isidor's body had been recovered, Herbert wired that they had booked passage on the *Kronprinzessin Cecilie*, the first fast steamer, for the following Wednesday. Percy was obviously pleased and sent back a message the following day: "Glad your [sic] coming Funeral private upon your arrival fathers house Friends plan memorial service at Carnegie [Hall] May twelfth All well."[29]

The funeral was scheduled for May 8. The Scheftels barely made it back in time. The *Kronprinzessin Cecilie* did not arrive in the New York area until the evening of May 7. Even then, an official of Abraham & Straus, Edward C. Blum, had to charter a tug and make special arrangements with customs officials to meet the North German Lloyd liner at Quarantine Station on Staten Island to expedite the arrival of the Scheftels and their baggage. The ship would not dock officially in New York until the following day, the day of the funeral.[30] The Strauses had hoped that by that time Ida's body might have been found as well and that the two could be buried together. But that was not to be the case.

It rained on the day of the funeral. The Strauses' gray-framed home at the corner of 105th Street and Broadway sat humbly among the taller buildings that had grown up around it. The family did everything possible to minimize fanfare. According to the *New York Times*, "In order to avoid a great outpouring of the many friends and admirers...no publicity had been given to...the funeral...and only the members of the Straus family attended."[31] That was not entirely true. Almost 150 people were there, including close friends of the Strauses and representatives of the Strauses' stores, all of which closed on the day of the funeral, while other department stores lowered their curtains and flew flags at half-mast at 2 P.M. when the service was to begin.[32]

As the family gathered in the flower-filled parlors, only Isidor's brother Nathan was conspicuous by his absence. He had gone to Rome to attend a tuberculosis conference, which required his presence as the American head of the World's Association for the Prevention of Tuberculosis.[33] His decision not to return home was no doubt difficult. But Nathan, overcome by grief and always emotionally fragile, elected not to put himself on public display, but rather go into seclusion. There is no question that he was profoundly affected by his brother's death, for the two had been close their entire lives. Isidor would have understood completely. Nathan and his wife Lina were represented at the funeral by their only daughter Sissie, the wife of New York Supreme Court Justice Irving Lehman.

The service was brief. Rabbi Samuel Schulman of the Beth-El Temple said prayers and read the ninetieth Psalm. Although the Rabbi's words referred to the good works of Isidor Straus, he refrained, at the family's request, from any eulogies. These would be given by friends at the public service to be held in Carnegie Hall the following Sunday. When the ceremony was over, people filed out of the house into the rain and to their waiting cars. An estimated forty automobiles formed the funeral cortege that crossed the Queensboro Bridge to the Beth-El cemetery at Cypress Hills in Queens, where the body was to be interred in the Straus-Kohns Mausoleum. As the rabbi officiated at the final Jewish committal, mourners stood in the rain and many wept.

Despite of the presence of a Rabbi, Isidor Straus was not an observant Jew. He put no stock in organized religion, which he made clear in a 1909 letter to the former president of Harvard University, Charles W. Eliot. In this letter, he expressed admiration for Eliot's recent controversial talk on "The New Religion." Speaking to the Harvard Summer School of Theology shortly after the end of his forty-year tenure as Harvard's president, Eliot had expressed the need for a religion based not on traditional authority, concepts of original sin, or formal sacraments, but rather a strict monotheism rooted in the love of God and service to one's fellow man. This philosophy expressed Isidor Straus's own essential ideas. He thanked Eliot for "the pleasure and intense satisfaction" the speech gave him. "While I was born in the Jewish faith," he wrote, "I have never belonged to any synagogue or temple, have brought up a family of six children, all now having families of their own none of whom have ever associated themselves with any religious organization."[34]

Although he was not a practicing Jew, Isidor did not spurn his Jewish background. On the contrary, unlike some who changed their names or joined Protestant churches to avoid the stigma of anti-Semitism in less enlightened circles, Isidor embraced his heritage and generously supported Jewish causes. As a consequence, even as far away as Jerusalem, 60,000 Jews were said to be fasting and mourning his death.[35]

Once again on May 12 it rained outside Carnegie Hall where close friends of Ida and Isidor had planned a major memorial event. Once again the hall proved insufficient for the 6,000 people who braved the inclement weather in an effort to attend. And once again police reserves had to be called out to control the overflow crowd filling the surrounding streets. The *New York Evening Journal* of May 13 ran a photograph that vividly captured the great crowd of people, some with and some without umbrellas, that milled in the street outside, hoping for a chance to hear the tributes. Every seat in the hall was filled, and an estimated 500 people stood at the back.

It would have surprised no one who knew the Strauses well that the eulogies were delivered by friends both Jew and Gentile. The first speaker was the popular Mayor of New York, William Jay Gaynor, who was much admired for his stand against the forces of Tammany Hall. He still holds today the dubious distinction of being the only mayor of New York to have suffered an assassination attempt, which occurred shortly after his taking office in 1910. Although the would-be assassin's bullet was still lodged in his throat, it did nothing to hinder his speaking on that day.[36]

The second tribute came from millionaire steel-maker and philanthropist Andrew Carnegie, whom Isidor and his daughter Sara had visited at his Skibo Castle in Scotland in 1901 and who, like Isidor, had first immigrated to America as a young boy. The two had seemed to have little else in common as they made their way up the economic ladder. In his younger years Carnegie appeared ruthless and cavalier toward the needs of his workers, while Isidor always showed concern and generosity to his employees. But in later years Carnegie embraced what he called a Gospel of Wealth, which Isidor no doubt admired. Carnegie's gospel compelled him "to set an example of modest, unostentatious living" and to consider his wealth "simply as trust funds, which he is called upon to administer...to produce the most beneficial result for the community."[37] In short, he set out to give away his money. Once considered a cold-hearted "robber barron," Carnegie had written to Isidor's brother Oscar about Ida's heroic sacrifice, which was "beautiful beyond words." His voice broke when he spoke of the "angelic nature" of the Strauses. Then he elaborated: "No husband and wife known to us as constituting one force have excelled them in the service of mankind. They gave not only needed funds, but, what was much more important, they gave themselves." He added simply, "They were my friends."[38]

From outward appearances the man who followed Carnegie to the podium was the most curious choice of all—the Right Rev. Thomas H. Gailor, the Episcopal Bishop of Tennessee and chancellor of the University of the South at Sewanee. Described in the press as "one of Mr. and Mrs. Straus's most intimate friends," he spoke in admiration of Isidor's accomplishments, but he was especially inspired by Ida's self-sacrificial act of love and loyalty, which he compared to that of the Old Testament Ruth.

Except for Rabbi Schulman, who once again said prayers, and Justice Samuel Greenbaum, who presided over the event, only two Jews spoke that day. One was Isidor's friend, Jacob Schiff, a co-founder of the Educational Alliance and president of the Montefiore Home, described by the *New York Times* as "the largest Jewish hospital in the world," both causes to which Isidor was deeply committed.[39] The other was Ida's friend Julia Richman, the only female speaker. She was District Superintendent of Schools on the lower East Side, the first Jewish principal, and the first woman ever to hold a district superintendent's position in New York. She had also been one of the founders of the Educational Alliance and was a much-valued member.[40]

She and Ida had much in common in terms of interests and mutual respect, and had been close friends for more than twenty years. They may have met while working together on the National Council of Jewish Women, where Ida served as a board member.[41] In a very personal talk Richman underscored Ida's public service and her extraordinary love for her husband. She recounted an incident when she had seen Ida darning Isidor's socks. Although she was a woman with servants and great wealth, here sat Ida, straining her eyes to make fine, almost invisible, stitches to close a hole in her husband's socks. When asked why she did it, she replied, "If you had a husband like mine you would do more than this for him."[42]

The gathering at Carnegie Hall, held almost a month after the sinking of the *Titanic*, while by no means the last tribute paid to the Strauses, served as a culmination for the family, a closure of sorts, to the public mourning. The Straus family now began to deal with various legal matters entailed in the estate and to undertake the sad task of going through their parents' belongings. Among Isidor's papers, his children found letters written on July 18, 1904, to his sons and to their mother, shortly after he had drawn up his first will, letters intended to be read only after his death.[43] Although he was a very wealthy man by standards of the time, his wealth was nowhere in the range of people like his friend Carnegie. He left an estate estimated by the *New York Times* in October 1912 as between three and four million dollars, though later estimates suggest it was between four and five million.[44] A final will, dated December 22, 1909, provided amply for his survivors. For his three daughters he had set up trust funds of $500,000 each. Had Ida survived, she would have benefited from a trust fund of $1,200,000 as well as their home in Manhattan and their summer home in Elberon, New Jersey.[45]

His letter to his wife is addressed to "My Darling Mama," whom he proclaims at the end "As good a wife as ever man was blessed with."[46] (Mama and Papa were the pet names they had used for each other since their first child was born.) The letter stands as evidence of how well he knew and understood her, especially her tendencies toward generosity for others, and his awareness of how she would grieve his death. He encourages her in one, but discourages her in the other. "You have an ample income, enjoy it; deprive yourself of nothing which can contribute to your comfort and happiness. I know you are fond of doing good, indulge yourself in this enjoyment without stint." He encouraged her as well to "Be a little selfish; don't always think only of others." He reminded her that, in the event of his death, her children and grandchildren could still bring her many years of happiness. Thus, he urged "instead of mourning disconsolately over our separation, be thankful for the happiness which was vouchsafed to us for so many years." Ida chose a different route that even Isidor had not foreseen.

To his sons his will left the residual portion of his estate and all his business interests. The letter he had left encouraged them to seek the wise counsel of their Uncle Nathan and to maintain "the most cordial relationship," cautioning them "never bear him any malice; his peculiarities are to his virtues as the alloy of iron is to pure gold."[47]

He underscored the importance of family unity and the need "to forgive and forget any misunderstanding," concluding, "I should consider my life's work a failure if ever there would arise any serious differences between you which would disturb the family union and harmony..." In another letter, written twelve years earlier to all his children, he had described family as "one of the greatest fountains of happiness in life."[48] It was a theme by which he lived his life.

Isidor's will made no charitable bequests. Instead, he had left instructions in the aforementioned letter for his sons, indicating charitable bequests to be made, beginning with $100,000 to the Educational Alliance Endowment, $25,000 for the Macy Mutual Aid Endowment, $50,000 to "such philanthropies and charity institutions...as you may select," and various amounts for special employees.[49] His sons would waste no time in carrying out his wishes.

What touched the hearts of the Straus children most as they sifted through the papers left by their father was an unexpected discovery of a hand-written autobiography that Isidor had begun on June 21, 1911, less than ten months before his death. Not until 1955, forty-three years after the sinking of the *Titanic*, did Isidor's oldest daughter, Sara Straus Hess, have it published privately for the family. In a foreword to the printed version, she wrote of the family's surprise in finding the manuscript: "My brother, Jesse, had often urged him to write about his life and he had always brushed the idea aside, so that until his death no one knew that he had acquiesced, in part at least, to Jesse's request." That he had advanced no further with his writing is a consequence of having begun to write so late in his life. Isidor had put it off as he commented because, "the idea did not appeal to me." But finally he decided to begin "in a sort of desultory way, jotting down from time to time, as the spirit moved me," occurrences that came to mind.[50] Only time would tell, he noted at the outset, whether anything would come of it. This document, along with the surviving letters written by his father Lazarus and by Isidor himself, is invaluable in understanding the Straus family's early struggles in America and their determination to succeed, as well as certain key moments in his later life. These were the details the children had longed for to help them understand their own heritage.

Unfortunately, neither Jesse nor the other children made the same request of their mother, whose beginnings in this country were equally difficult and interesting. Without her own account or a significant collection of letters, her story has been inevitably more elusive and the task of reconstructing her early days much more difficult. Nonetheless, the quest has been worth the effort to understand the exceptional lives, and not just the deaths, of these two extraordinary people.

Newsboy in New York hawks the *Evening News* announcing the sinking of the *Titanic*. (Author's private collection.)

Front page of the *New York Times* with details of the disaster. (Courtesy of the Straus Historical Society, Inc.)

A man resembling Oscar Straus enters the White Star Line office for news of *Titanic* passengers. (Courtesy of the Library of Congress, Prints and Photographs Division.)

Above, a sheet music cover, one of the many tributes and memorials for the Strauses. (Author's private collection.) Below, a memorial plaque for Ida and Isidor Straus given by Macy's employees. (Courtesy of the Straus Historical Society, Inc.)

Above, Isidor (left) and Oscar Straus (right) as children. Below, Nathan Straus as a boy with a dog. (Courtesy of the Straus Historical Society, Inc.)

Above, the Straus family home in Otterberg, Germany. Below, Lazarus and Sara Straus, Isidor's parents. Sara was a model of frugality to her sons. (Courtesy of the Straus Historical Society, Inc.)

Above, the Strauses' first home in Talbotton, Georgia. (Courtesy of the Straus Historical Society, Inc.) Below, Levert Hall, Talbotton, Georgia, was built to house the Levert Female College in the 1830s. In 1937 it was renamed Straus-Levert Memorial Hall. In that same year Isidor's sons opened the Davison-Paxon Department Store in Atlanta, realizing a long-standing dream to open a store in Georgia, where their grandfather, Lazarus, had gotten his start in retailing. (Courtesy of the Library of Congress, Department of Prints and Photographs, Historic American Building Survey, L. D. Andrew, Photographer, HABS GA.)

Ida Straus's sister, Amanda Blun Rothschild, with her children. (Courtesy of Thomas Francell.)

Above, Frank Rothschild, husband of Amanda Blun Rothschild. (Courtesy of Thomas Francell.) Below, the home of Amanda and Frank Rothschild, neighbors of the Straus family in Columbus, Georgia. It is known today as the Kyle-Swift Mansion. (Courtesy of the Library of Congress, Prints and Photographs Division.)

Above, Isidor Straus, 1865. This photo was taken in Paris while Isidor was in Europe during the Civil War. Below, wedding photograph of Ida and Isidor Straus. (Courtesy of the Straus Historical Society, Inc.)

Oscar Straus in 1873 at the time of his graduation from Columbia School of Law. He attributed his educational opportunities to Isidor's support. (Courtesy of the Straus Historical Society, Inc.)

Above, Isidor Straus as a young businessman, wearing his characteristic carnation.Below, Ida Straus as a young woman. (Photos courtesy fo the Manuscripts and Archives Division, The New York Public Library, Astor, Lenox and Tilden Foundations.)

Above, Ida and Isidor's daughters—(left to right) Minnie, Vivian, and Sara—about 1889. (Courtesy of the Straus Historical Society, Inc.) Below, The Straus family at tea in the garden. (Left to right) Jesse, Vivian, Ida, Minnie, Percy, Sara, Herbert, and Isidor. (Courtesy of the Manuscripts and Archives Division. The New York Public Library, Astor, Lenox and Tilden Foundations.)

Wedding photo of Nathan and Lina Straus. (Courtesy of the Straus Historical Society, Inc.)

Above, the Strauses' home at Inwood on the northern tip of Manhattan. Below, the Straus home at 2745 Broadway. Ida and Isidor owned this house until their deaths. It was sold shortly thereafter. (Courtesy of the Straus Historical Society, Inc.)

April 30 1889.

The Strauses' daughters with their cousin Sissie, daughter of Nathan and Lina Straus. Standing (left to right) Sissie, Vivian, and Sara. Seated, Minnie. (Courtesy of the Straus Historical Society, Inc.)

Above, Oscar Straus as a young man. Below, Oscar's bride, Sarah Lavanburg Straus. (Courtesy of the Straus Historical Society, Inc.)

Sarah Lavanburg Straus in formal dress as ambassador's wife. (Courtesy of the Library of Congress, Prints and Photographs Division.)

Straus family and friends at the Villa Plaisance on Lower Saranac Lake in the Adirondacks, 1891. Seated on ground (left to right) are Oscar, Vivian, Herbert, Percy (with dog), and Jerome Straus. Seated in the middle row (left to right) are Lucie Mammelsdorf with Lina's and Nathan's baby, Charles Webster Straus (later changed to Nathan, Jr.) on her lap, and Sissie Straus. In the third row, standing, are (left to right) Mrs. Charles Webster, Sara, Ida, and Minnie Straus. Those in the last row (left to right) are Philip Kuppenheimer, nursemaid in background on porch, Charles Webster, and Isidor. (Courtesy of the Straus Historical Society, Inc.)

All of Isidor and Ida's children including (left to right) Jesse's daughter, Beatrice, and his wife, Irma, followed by Vivian, Minnie, Sara, Jesse, Percy, and Herbert Straus, about 1900. (Courtesy of the Straus Historical Society, Inc.)

Lazarus Straus enjoys his retirement. (Courtesy of the Straus Historical Society, Inc.)

Above, the beach at Elberon, New Jersey, 1900–1910. (Courtesy of the Library of Congress, Prints and Photographs Division.) Below, Sunnyside—the Strauses' summer cottage in Elberon, New Jersey, completed in 1902. (Courtesy of the Straus Historical Society, Inc.)

Ida and Isidor Straus, their children with spouses and grandchildren at Sunnyside in 1905. Seated on grass, Dr. Alfred Hess; seated, (left to right) Edith Abraham Straus, Percy S. Straus, Ralph Isidor Straus, Sara Straus Hess, Ida Straus, Jack Isidor Straus, Beatrice Levy Straus. Isidor Straus, Minnie Straus Weil. Standing at rear: Vivian Straus, Herbert Nathan Straus, Irma Nathan Straus, Jesse Isidor Straus, and Dr. Richard Weil. (The source of the photograph is Paul A. Kurzman. Courtesy of the Straus Historical Society, Inc.)

Rowland H. Macy, who allowed the Strauses to open a concession in the basement of his department store. (Courtesy of Macy's Inc. Archives.)

Above, Charles B. Webster, cousin of Rowland Macy and a partner in Macy's after its owner's death. It was he who brought in the Strauses as partners. Below, Jerome Wheeler, brother-in-law of R. H. Macy, was for a time a partner with Charles Webster in Macy's. (Courtesy of Macy's Inc. Archives.)

Macy's Department Store at Herald Square in 1908. (Library of Congress, Prints and Photographs Division.)

Opening day at the new Macy's on Herald Square, November 8, 1902. (Left to right) Jesse, Isidor, and Herbert Straus. (Courtesy of Macy's Inc. Archives.)

Isidor Straus as a member of Congress with his two best congressional friends. (Left to right) Isidor, William Lyne Wilson, and Clifton R. Breckinridge. Taken August 14, 1894. (Courtesy of Special Collections, Leyburn Library, Washington and Lee University.)

Above, Isidor Straus, now a mature businessman, still wearing his customary carnation. (Courtesy of the Straus Historical Society, Inc.) Below, Ida Straus as a mature matron, a capable and intelligent partner to her beloved husband. (Courtesy of the Manuscripts and Archives Division. The New York Public Library, Astor, Lenox and Tilden Foundations.)

The Straus brothers, (left to right) Nathan, Oscar, and Isidor—probably the last photograph they had made together. (Courtesy of the Straus Historical Society, Inc.)

Above, Isidor's sister, Hermine Straus Kohns. (Courtesy of the Straus Historical Society, Inc.) Below, Isidor and Ida's three sons, left to right, Herbert, Jesse, and Percy Straus about 1920. (Courtesy of the Straus Historical Society, Inc.)

Above, the *Titanic* almost collides with the *New York,* but is stopped by the tug *Vulcan.* Below, the launching of the *Titanic* in the River Test. (Author's private collection.)

Above, the stern of the *Titanic*. (Author's private collection.) Below, *Titanic* life boats. (Library of Congress, Prints and Photographs Division.)

Jesse Straus and family, c. 1910. Left to right: Jesse Isidor, Jr. [Jack], Irma, Robert
Kenneth, Jesse, and Beatrice Nathan Straus. Jesse, Irma, and Beatrice were aboard the
ship *Amerika*, which crossed the *Titanic* in mid-ocean and warned her of the icebergs.
(Courtesy of the Straus Historical Society, Inc.)

Above, the Straus Park memorial. The model for the statue, *Memory*, was Audrey Munson. Below, the dedication of Straus Park on April 15, 1915. Left to right: Jesse Straus (in top hat), Mrs. E. H. Schifley, Irma Nathan Straus, and Edith Abraham Straus. (Courtesy of the Library of Congress, Prints and Photographs Division.)

Above, Straus Memorial Dedication, April 15, 1915.(Courtesy of the Library of Congress, Prints and Photographs Division.) Below, the cenotaph for Isidor and Ida Straus at Woodlawn Cemetery in New York. (Courtesy of Straus Historical Society, Inc.)

Oscar Straus campaigning for governor of New York, 1912. (Courtesy of the Library of Congress, Prints and Photographs Division.)

Isidor Straus. (Courtesy of the Straus Historical Society, Inc.)

Above, Nathan Straus, 1914. Below, Oscar Straus c. 1912. (Courtesy of the Library of Congress, Prints and Photographs Division.)

Ida and Isidor Straus, taken not long before their deaths. (Courtesy of the Straus Historical Society, Inc.)

1

Coming To America

In his 56-page autobiography Isidor apologizes at the outset for his account's frequent, use of the pronoun "I," for he did not wish anyone to think that had "an exaggerated sense of my own importance."[1] The statement is typical of both Isidor and Ida, who never sought public recognition and would no doubt have been quite embarrassed by the to-do made over their deaths. Isidor shared many things with his brothers, but vanity was never one of them. His youngest brother Oscar published his own auto-biography during his lifetime and declared that "To write of one's self requires a certain amount of egotism…[and] I am not entirely free from that vanity."[2] Unlike Oscar's however, Isidor's personal story was never meant to be published or read by anyone except his children.

He began the account quite simply and logically with his birth: "I was born in Otterberg Palatinate of Bavaria (Rheinpfalz), February 6th, 1845—if I mistake not in the same house where my father was born. The Straus family had resided there, or in the immediate vicinity, for several generations."[3] Although the details concerning his family background become relevant as his story unfolds, his personal saga really began almost a decade later with his voyage to America aboard a ship called the *Saint Louis* en route to his new home in America.

It was early September 1854. One can imagine Isidor, a nine-year-old boy, gripping the handrail and peering out into the black sea. He could see little beyond the swath of moonlight cutting across the restless surf, except for the stars that sparkled against the night sky, brighter than they had ever seemed in his native Bavaria. Leaning over the rail to watch the ship's hull slice through the waves, he could see lights, reflected from the portholes below, dancing in the choppy waters and cheering the darkness. Even the chilly gloom of the North Atlantic could not dampen his spirits.

This was his first time at sea. The steamship, *Saint Louis*, was fresh from her maiden voyage from New York to Cowes on the Isle of Wight and then to Le Havre. Now she was following that same itinerary in reverse, promising the boy excitement, adventure, and a whole new world. In later years, when he wrote about the crossing, his memory and imagination quite understandably transformed this leg of the journey into the ship's maiden voyage. The newness of the vessel, resplendent with burnished brass and gilt fixtures, wooden railings and oak panels varnished and polished until the boy could see his own image, mirrored his own renewed and buoyant spirit. The thirteen days at sea left ample time for him and his six-year-old brother Nathan to explore the ship's every nook and cranny and to absorb its technological wonders, which combined sails with paddles and steam. They could marvel at its two-masted topsail, its great paddle wheels, and the massive smokestack that rose arrogantly above the deck, belching smoke from the coal-run steam engines below. And they could rejoice at each mournful wail of its majestic foghorn and the throbbing of the engines running day and night to propel the ship across the great Atlantic.

During the daylight hours, Captain Asa Eldridge stood smartly on the bridge surveying the endless ocean as though it were his personal domain and perhaps occasionally smiling at the curious boys. In his blue captain's cap with the shiny bill and his navy jacket with brass buttons, he looked every bit as seaworthy as the *Saint Louis* herself. The voyage would create in Isidor a lifelong interest in the ships on which he traveled, and he carefully recorded most of their names in the autobiography he would later undertake to write for his children.

It was quite by happenstance that the Strauses found themselves on that particular vessel. The ship normally scheduled for the run between Le Havre and New York was the Havre Line's *Franklin*. Less than two months earlier, however, on just such a return crossing as this one with 160 passengers on board and 700 tons of cargo worth nearly a million dollars, she had run afoul of the dangers of the sea. Almost at her destination, on the morning of July 17, 1854, she had sailed into a dense fog. The captain, eager to reach his port, urged the vessel briskly on through the fog until she ran aground at full speed near Moriches Inlet on Long Island. Fortunately, the ship's proximity to shore allowed all passengers and their baggage to be rowed safely from the stranded ship to tugboats waiting nearby to assist. But the *Franklin* itself could not be saved. The tides rose and furious waves pounded her hull for three days, driving her across the outer sandbar on which she had been resting and stranding her fifty feet from shore, where the battered hull groaned, bent, and twisted helplessly in the angry surf. The wreckage was finally sold for salvage at auction for a mere $1,625, a pathetic reminder of the perils of ocean travel.

Fortunately, the Havre Line had been quickly able to charter from the Pacific Mail Steamship Company a brand new vessel, the *Saint Louis*, to keep its transatlantic service going on schedule. The new ship, ready to sail by August 1, had been originally constructed to carry passengers and cargo from Panama to San Francisco.[4] Designed for the tropics, the *Saint Louis* was built in the British style with the boilers aft of the engines, overhanging guards extending beyond the paddle wheels, and a dining room, where windows could be opened to let in cool breezes. After the grounding of the *Franklin*, however, the vessel was quickly modified for the cooler and stormier waters of the North Atlantic, and the projecting guards were removed to prevent damage in the waves.[5]

The *Saint Louis* provided room for 160 cabin passengers and hull space for 600-700 more in steerage. On this trip the ship carried 162 passengers in all, among them Isidor's family, with the rest of the space reserved for cargo—350 tons of French and Swiss goods bound for America. The cargo also included 150 baskets of champagne to be enjoyed in the dining room on the main deck, which gleamed in its newness of polished oak, gilded ornaments and white panels. The cabins were equally luxurious, and the vessel boasted a nursery with attendants to oversee the children, a doctor, a barber, and a baker. In short, everything needed to keep the passengers happy during the voyage from Le Havre to New York.[6]

The excitement and anticipation of their departure on such a splendid new vessel coursed through Isidor's veins, as he and the other children waved goodbye to their uncle Jacob, who had accompanied them and their mother all the way from Otterberg. The adventure of the sea and the excitement that lay ahead were no doubt boundless for a boy of nine like himself. But the greatest expectation he had of the voyage was the familiar face he knew would be waiting at its end. With him on board were not only his brother Nathan, but also their mother Sara, their eight-year-old sister Hermine, their little brother Oscar, who was only four, and their maid Joanna Franz.[7] They were all on their way to rejoin Isidor's father, Lazarus Straus, who had gone to America two years earlier to make his fortune.

Isidor and his family had left Otterberg, his German birthplace in Rhenish Bavaria, less than a week before, already in a state of high anticipation. Despite the presence of both his uncle Jacob and his maternal grandfather, the latter of whom had accompanied the family during part of their journey to Le Havre, Isidor was already beginning to feel like the man of the family, helping his delicate and disabled mother, who had suffered a recent stroke that left her with a useless arm.[8]

Never before had the boy traveled so far from home. His family had lived in Otterberg for as long as anyone could remember, and he had spent his entire life there. He knew he would never forget their house on Hauptestrasse, where both he and his father before him were born. Built in 1800, it was large and sturdy, with a row of five second-story windows that overlooked the busy street below. The sons and daughters of his great-uncles Salomon and Isaak lived close by, and the large Straus family had long played a major role in the town's life.

"Straus" was a well-respected name in Otterberg. All his life Isidor had heard stories about his great-grandfather, Jacob ben Lazar, and an honor that made him an important part of the century's unfolding history. Jacob had been selected to attend the great Assembly of Notables that Napoleon had called together in Paris in 1806. This assembly, among other things, ordered the Jews of the empire to take surnames.[9] That was when his family became Strauses. No one remembered for sure just why they had chosen that name, though they all assumed it was because *Straus* was the German word for ostrich, and an ostrich plaque hung outside Jacob's family home. This was similar to the way the Rothschild family took their name from the red shield in front of their house. Isidor fancied the story of the ostrich, and took pride in his great-grandfather's selection to attend the Assembly, for it reflected the esteem in which the small community held him.

For his immediate family, however, things had begun to change in recent years. It was hard for Isidor, young as he was, to fully understand why his father had left them behind in Bavaria to go to America. He only knew that it had something to do with the political upheavals during the Revolution of 1848. He would eventually come to understand the turbulence of those times throughout Europe in the wake of the French Revolution and the

Napoleonic Wars. As Austrian chancellor Metternich allegedly grumbled, "When France sneezes, Europe catches cold." People throughout Europe felt oppressed by the stranglehold the aristocracy still held on all their lives and the economic hardship it sometimes brought. A new spirit of revolt and independence had begun to assert itself among the middle and lower classes, a spirit that had planted itself deeply in the popular mind with the French Revolution of 1789. In 1848, people in France became dissatisfied with the control that had been regained by the wealthy classes, epitomized by Louis Philippe and his so-called July Monarchy. Once again, they rose up en masse to bring about the abdication of Louis Philippe and establish a second republic in that country.

News of these events spread rapidly throughout Europe. Within weeks after the abdication of Louis Philippe in France, a series of popular revolts broke out not only in Germany, but all over Europe. It seemed unstoppable. As one of the German leaders, Carl Schurz, described it, the "revolutionary spirit burst forth like a prairie-fire,"[10] with people loudly demanding constitutions, liberal ministries, and, above all, a unified nation. The German confederation was made up of a fragmented coalition of independent states, all tightly controlled by a complex aristocracy of petty rulers.

Like so many others of the middle class, Lazarus Straus, Isidor's father, a grain merchant who owned farmlands in the region, was sympathetic toward the revolution that called for a more representative government and a liberal constitution. He contributed heavily to the cause and even joined a local "defense committee." As a member of the town council, he was appointed to collect funds for the revolutionary cause in the nearby town of Niederkirchen. Like others involved in the effort, he fervently hoped to see the people wrest some of the control of the country from the aristocracy and establish a constitutional government.[11]

After witnessing the success of the new revolution in France, German spirits soared in anticipation. But their hopes were short-lived. The aristocracy of their country quickly quelled the rebellion and reasserted its prerogatives. Liberal members of the middle class led the revolt, but in Germany many of them were almost as terrified of the lower classes as they were of the aristocracy. As a consequence, leaders of the revolt waffled and folded before the complexities and apparent impossibilities of establishing either a German republic or a strong centralized government.[12] In the end little changed, except to increase the great flood of emigrants pouring out of the German states and into America, the very name of which seemed synonymous with freedom. Leaders of the uprising in Germany now lived in danger. These leaders included men like Carl Schurz, who would later become an important player in the American Civil War and its aftermath and who quickly escaped to America.

It was an uneasy period for the Straus family, and especially for Lazarus, who was unsure what reprisals those in power might take against him. In addition to his fundraising efforts for the rebellion, he was also suspected of having assisted in the flight of revolutionary leaders like Schurz. He had been called in and questioned by the authorities but had not been arrested or openly punished for his activities. Nonetheless, he remained cautious, and with good reason. As his youngest son, Oscar, would later describe the situation, "Having been active only locally in the revolutionary movement, my father was not prosecuted. He was made aware, however, of the suspicions of the authorities and was subjected to all those petty annoyances and discriminations which a reactionary government never fails to lay upon people who have revolted, and revolted in vain."[13]

Following the failed revolution, the financial problems that had begun to plague the family at the death of Lazarus's father in 1838, seemed to increase. The Strauses had always been, if not wealthy, at least financially comfortable. But the political unrest and economic instability made it increasingly difficult for landowners like themselves, who had no real authority, to collect rents or interest, and Lazarus, the eldest of fourteen children and executor of his father's will, had difficulty settling accounts owed to the estate. His siblings did not make matters easier. His sister Barbara, called "Babette" by her family, was particularly impatient for her share of the estate and wanted to have the matter settled quickly. She demanded that the real estate be put up for auction. Even though Lazarus complied by auctioning off at least one parcel of land, he was evidently unable to collect the money or come up with adequate funds to divide the estate as his sister wanted. He had already begun to think of emigrating to America himself, and the constant demands for money, coupled with the realization that better opportunities lay elsewhere, led him to try his luck along with so many of his fellow countrymen in the United States. Political freedom and economic opportunities were legend there.

The lure proved irresistible. Lazarus went about his plans for departure cautiously and systematically, carefully setting aside funds necessary to pay his expenses and keep his family comfortable in the care of his father-in-law, Soloman Straus, during his absence. His wife and children would wait in Otterberg until he had got his start in America. Finally on May 26, 1852, he obtained a passport in Sarraguemines, France, and set out at the age of forty-three to seek his fortune in the New World.[14]

Isidor, then seven, was surely old enough to understand at least some of the circumstances. Above all, he knew that his father would not leave them behind if it were not important and he would send for them soon. Even so, two years without the gentle strength of his father had seemed a long time to the boy, and he was eager to see him again. Lazarus had written many letters since his departure, letters that contained vivid descriptions of his adventures in America, making that country come alive in the boy's imagination.

He wrote of the opportunity he had sought first in Philadelphia, where people he knew lived, those who had come before him from their native Bavaria. He was receptive to suggestions and new ideas. Prospects of farming in America as he had done in Germany looked dim with only himself to till the land. Going into trade was a possibility, but Yankee peddlers were a dime a dozen, and the competition in large cities like New York, Boston, and Philadelphia was daunting. He listened with great interest as former acquaintances filled him with stories of business opportunities in the South, a rural region where a man could make a good start without too much competition or collateral as a peddler.

Tales abounded about German Jews like the Seligman brothers, Joseph, William and James, who had come to American in the 1830s from the Bavarian village of Baiersdorf. They had met with phenomenal success peddling in the South, finally settling in the area of Birmingham, Alabama. Only a few years of work had provided them with sufficient resources to bring the rest of their family to America, which they did in 1842, a full decade before Lazarus arrived there.[15] Henry Lehman, from yet another Bavarian town called Rimpar, had followed suit, selling his wares along a route north from Mobile along the Alabama River in a wagon, considered "the fashionable means" of peddling among German Jewish immigrants. When he arrived in Alabama's capital of Montgomery, however, he decided to set up shop there. He also soon acquired the means to send for his younger brothers, changing the name of his firm from H. Lehman to Lehman Brothers.[16]

Their success, and that of others who were hard-working but relatively poor German Jews, served as an infusion of inspiration to an ambitious man like Lazarus Straus. And even though a number of Jews had already gone to the South and made a successful start at their fortunes, there were still plenty of opportunities and many relatively untapped areas in the rural backwaters where King Cotton reigned.

After thinking it over only briefly, Lazarus heeded his friends' advice and headed for Georgia. Even there a network of German immigrants had preceded him and were eager to provide him with the benefits of their experience and counsel. Acquaintances introduced him to a group of brothers named Marx, Jacob and Julius Kaufman, who had settled in 1850 in the area of Oglethorpe, Georgia, the seat of Macon County in the southwestern part of the state.[17] They owned a fleet of peddler's wagons that circulated the countryside from plantation to plantation with an assortment of dry goods or "Yankee notions" for sale, and they were willing to give Lazarus a start. The Kaufmans provided him with a wagon and supplies, and he set out to peddle his wares along the country lanes that led to unfamiliar Georgia plantations and farms. His son, Oscar, would later characterize it as "a pioneer business in a pioneer country."[18]

Lazarus found the South to be a region still sparsely settled, where slaves labored in rural cotton fields, and unpaved roads led to isolated houses far from their neighbors. Transportation was slow, commercial centers were a good distance away for most people, and the country residents needed some of the items from the motley collection of supplies and dry goods he stocked in his wagon. But they needed even more desperately the news his visits brought from the outside world. As a consequence he was welcomed like an old friend even by the wealthiest planters as he drove up their tree-lined driveways toward the big house. As he wrote to his family, "if the peddler proved to be an honest, upright man, who conscientiously treated his customers with fairness and made no misrepresentations as to his wares," he was "treated as an honored guest" by plantation owners and small farmers alike.[19] They invited him to their table, fed his horse, gave him a room for the night, and looked forward to his periodic visits. In the true spirit of southern hospitality, they would refuse any payment for room and board, but Lazarus, an astute businessman, always brought along for such occasions special trinkets that might make a "suitable present, either to the lady or her daughter."[20]

Peddling was a trade that opened many planters' doors for Lazarus, much to his surprise. The spirit of equality with which wealthy plantation owners treated him, without any hint of anti-Semitism, amazed him. In the end he concluded that, though he was Jewish, he was also a white merchant in a slave state and thus he was accorded immediate status, "which probably did not prevail in sections where slavery did not exist."[21] He was no doubt right in his assessment. One of the Kaufman brothers had estimated in a letter to his family in 1850 that there were fifteen times as many blacks as whites in the area, but there "there is no difference among white people," for they "don't know about Jews."[22] At the time Jews were still relatively rare in the South, and consequently Lazarus did not encounter in antebellum Georgia the anti-Semitic attitudes that often prevailed in Europe.

Such good treatment from his customers made his trade more pleasant and business was good. As Marx Kaufman noted several years earlier, "the cotton is high in price, and the people are getting so much money that they don't know what they should do with it except spend it...they buy the finest clothes, gold jewelry, and other fine things."[23] Lazarus's business thrived, but he did not intend to remain a simple peddler for long.

About a year after his arrival in Georgia, his travels took him through a little town called Talbotton, the county seat of Talbot County located not far from Oglethorpe, where he was immediately struck by the contrast between that village and others through which he had already passed. Although the town was small, having fewer than a thousand inhabitants, it impressed Lazarus with its "air of refinement." He informed his family, of all the towns he had been to, this one was the first that made him feel "that he had gotten away from the uncouth, primitive and frontier-like conditions" he thought characterized the region. Here, he found houses that were neat and well-kept, gardens with "flowers and cultivated shrubbery," good schools, and fine people.[24] It was a bustling town when Lazarus arrived there.

Court was in session that week, and many farmers and cotton growers from the surrounding countryside had come to Talbotton to take care of various legal and economic transactions, bringing with them family members who were busily engaged in shopping or trading. As a consequence, the town was even livelier than usual and made a decidedly favorable impression on Lazarus. Local merchants, druggists, wagon makers, gunsmiths, millers, carriage makers and shoemakers all depended on such trade and seemed to be thriving. No doubt, he surmised, a peddler could make a good living in such an area. It was here, he decided on the spot, that he wanted to bring his family. He would not regret his decision until many years later.

At first Lazarus planned to continue plying his trade in the county as an itinerant peddler, but when he went to the courthouse to apply for a peddler's license, he was shocked by its high cost in Talbot County. He left the courthouse a bit discouraged, but still determined and interested in the town, which had impressed him with its lively and flourishing atmosphere. As he walked down the streets, he could see that there were all kinds of businesses, law firms, a shoe factory, a grocery store, even a gin maker, but only one dry goods store that sold everything from coffins to carpets and from harnesses to hats. Perhaps, he concluded, they could use a little competition.

Then he happened upon a local tailor named Bernard Curley, who ran "Curley's Corner," a spacious shop at the intersection of Washington and Monroe Avenues opposite the Franklin House Hotel.[25] It was a fine location in the very center of town. Lazarus looked about with care and astutely judged that the tailor had more room in his shop than he really needed. During an idle moment, Lazarus struck up a conversation with the proprietor and broached the possibility of renting a portion of the space. Curley was at once amenable, and Lazarus, without further ado, moved his wares from his wagon into his new store.

To his amazement, the fledgling enterprise was even more successful than his itinerant peddling had been. Sensing an important economic opportunity at his fingertips, Lazarus contacted his partners, the Kaufman brothers, and proposed that they rent an entire store and increase their supply of stock. The Kaufmans were at first a bit skeptical about the overhead costs of storekeeping in the town as opposed to working out of a wagon that could take them constantly to new customers. They were also uneasy about shifting their center of operations from Oglethorpe, where the railroad line ended, to Talbotton. But Lazarus's obvious success soon changed their minds.

Thus, in June of 1853, Lazarus Straus, now a full-fledged merchant, headed to Philadelphia to purchase stock for the store, bypassing the Oglethorpe merchant who had previously served as middleman and enhancing his own profits. Lazarus discovered to his pleasure that his good reputation in Germany had preceded him and, thanks to his Philadelphia connections, he had no difficulty at all establishing credit and good faith with his suppliers. The only problem came in purchasing "dry goods and domestics," which were absolutely essential for stocking a general store in a town like Talbotton. In these lines of merchandise he had no prior contacts. Fortunately he arrived in Philadelphia in June, before fall stocks were completely ready, so he had ample time to find friends who could smooth his path and vouch for his good name among the purveyors of the necessary goods.

Finally, when he had completed his purchases to his satisfaction and was preparing to head for home, the Oglethorpe merchant from whom he and the Kaufmans had previously bought their wares appeared. The man was "astonished and evidently displeased" at this turn of events and made threats that he would see that Straus received no credit to buy, but he was too late. Realizing his fulminations were useless, the man changed his tune and "expressed the hope that [their] heretofore friendly relations would not be disturbed."[26] By the following summer, the store was prospering, and Lazarus had managed to lay aside enough funds to rent a little house for his family and pay for their passage to America.

And here they were at last, on their way to the New World to make a new life in a little town in Georgia. The trip was hard for Isidor's mother, Sara, though she was eager, knowing that Lazarus would be waiting for her. She had not fully recovered from the stroke that she had experienced the year before his departure. Her right arm still hung limply at her side, paralyzed, as it would remain for the rest of her life. She could not even brush her own heavy dark hair and had to rely on her maid Joanna or her eight-year-old daughter Hermine to help her arrange it.

Sara had selected late August for their departure, hoping for good weather. On August 24 they said "Auf Weidersehn" to their loved ones in Otterberg and began the long journey to Le Havre, where their ship awaited. In an effort to ease the voyage, Sara's father had accompanied them south as far as Kaiserslautern, riding alongside the carriage on his horse. From Kaiserslautern, the little entourage took the train to Forbach.[27] Jacob escorted his half-sister Sara the rest of the way to Le Havre, not leaving her side until he saw them all safely aboard the vessel.

Isidor remembered the stuffy carriage ride from Otterberg to Kaiserslautern, with his mother, his Uncle Jacob, the four children, and the nursemaid, Joanna, all crowded inside. Then there were the final moments with his grandfather as they said goodbye and climbed aboard the train for Forbach, where they would spend the night. The trip by rail was smoother than the carriage ride had been and much faster. The countryside rushed by, as the children pressed their faces against the cool window glass to drink it all in while the train passed through Homberg, Sankt Ingert, and Saarbrücken. After the night in Forbach, they continued the next morning by train to Paris. They made a brief stopover in Paris on August 29 and then left the French capital for the final leg of their journey to Le Havre, where they would board the *Saint Louis*.

Their ship sailed from Le Havre on August 30, as they waved goodbye to Jacob.[28] The children could hardly contain their excitement. After a day crossing the English Channel, the vessel paused briefly at the bustling port of Cowes, on the northern tip of the Isle of Wight, for an exchange of passengers and cargo. As their ship anchored at the mouth of the River Medina, Isidor and Nathan could see Cowes Castle in the distance and colorful yachts and tugboats bobbing in the harbor. But soon their vessel was under way again for their long voyage to their new homeland.

How many times they had gazed out over these seemingly endless waters, gray in the mornings, blue under the late summer sun, and finally an impenetrable black in the nights under the stars. It seemed that they would never arrive, but fortunately, the vessel was pleasant and the crossing was mercifully uneventful. The children were delighted by the sighting of two icebergs on September 8. And there was always a flurry of excitement whenever they came in view of another ship, as they did the *Abby Brown* on September 1, the *Cosmo* on September 8, and the U. S. Mail steamer, the *Washington*, on the day before they reached New

York.[29]

Finally the new world that was to be their home for the rest of their lives was in sight and drawing closer by the minute. The *Saint Louis* docked in New York around noon on September 12. Even before it was fully secured in its berth, Sara caught sight of Lazarus, "impatiently pacing up and down," eager to see his family again. She pointed him out to the children, and they all waved to catch his eye. He waved back with exuberance. How frustrating to be so close but not yet able to throw themselves in his arms. For what seemed an eternity they waited for the docking procedures to be completed and the gangway lowered. Later in his life Isidor vividly remembered "the lengthened minutes, which seemed like hours, that elapsed between his first recognition and the time when we could be embraced in his arms."[30] But finally they were able to race down the gangway and rush into their father's open arms.

Lazarus was eager to take them at once to their new home in Georgia. But for the moment that was not to be. Although a brand-new, first-class steamer, the *Knoxville*, waited at pier number four to take passengers to Savannah on its run scheduled for the following Saturday, Lazarus decided against the trip. A yellow-fever epidemic, called the "black vomit" by coastal residents, had been raging in the port city of Savannah since its outbreak on August 12. Two-thirds of the residents of Savannah had left the city and more than a thousand people there had died of the disease. To make matters worse, four days before the Straus family's arrival, a hurricane with winds of 125 miles per hour lashed the area and killed an additional twenty-six people, leaving a devastated city strewn with debris, downed trees, and damaged buildings.[31] Though reported cases of yellow fever had begun to wane, Lazarus Straus thought it prudent to keep his young family in the north for the time being. Their first trip to Talbotton would have to wait.

2

Growing Up In Georgia

The Straus family delayed their trip to Georgia, spending the first few days in New York getting reacquainted with each other before going to Philadelphia where they remained for several weeks visiting old friends. The leaves were already turning in mid-October before Lazarus deemed it safe to take his family to their new home in Georgia. Only a few more days at sea brought them to Savannah, but even when they landed at the dock, he was wary of taking his children into the city. As Isidor described their first day in Georgia. "[T]he steamer arrived [at] Savannah in the morning, and as it was considered safer not to enter the city, we spent the day, until evening… at the shanty called the station…on the outskirts of the town."[1] There they waited for the train that would take them only as far as the little town of Geneva, where once again the family would crowd into a stagecoach for the final five miles to Talbotton.[2]

The children were excited. Isidor had never seen a house like the modest frame structure on the corner of Monroe and Jefferson Streets. After inspecting it thoroughly from all sides, which didn't take long for it was small, the boy pronounced with amazement that it was "built on stilts."[3] Like many Georgia houses of the era, it had no basement, but rather open spaces beneath the floors that allowed the air to circulate. Utterly unlike their house in Otterberg, which hugged the ground for warmth, this one was designed to keep them cool and catch whatever breezes might pass through in the sticky Georgia summers. The house had a wooden porch, the like of which Isidor had never seen before, a brick fireplace, and a huge oak tree that shaded them from the hot sun.[4] Hardly a mansion, even by the modest standards of Georgia's rural communities, it was built of logs covered over with white clapboard, but Oscar would later write that upstairs, "where we children played and slept," the logs "had no covering, which pleased us all the more."[5] All in all, it provided adequate shelter and some degree of comfort to the young family, and soon Sara would have flowers and vegetables growing in the garden. This would be Isidor's home for several years before his family moved to a larger and more comfortable house south of town, a bit farther from the store but closer to Isidor's school.

The little town was all their father claimed it to be, the seat of the fifth largest county in Georgia and a thriving community, far more so than it is today. For decades Georgia politicians had carved up their state to meet various political needs, and Talbot County was no exception, having been pieced together in 1827 from sections of Crawford, Marion, Macon, Harris, and Muscogee Counties. Chosen as the county seat, Talbotton boasted a splendid courthouse, built in 1831, and no fewer than six doctors, six lawyers, six tailors, two druggists, a dentist, two silversmiths, two carriage makers, two wagon makers, as well as sundry schoolteachers, music teachers, shoemakers, and millers.[6] It even had a Drug & Book store on the public square. When the Strauses arrived in 1854, the town was at its peak. Sara was delighted to find it adorned with fine well-built houses and carefully cultivated gardens, just as Lazarus had said. Talbotton had even been selected as the site of the first session of the Georgia Supreme Court on January 26, 1846. It seemed to be just the place for a new merchant and his immigrant family.

The Strauses quickly settled into their new community. As the oldest son, Isidor helped his father at the store in the summers and during the hours when he was not in school. A diligent man eager to earn as much as possible, Lazarus kept his store open in the evenings. When the last hoop-skirted lady had purchased her spool of thread and headed home to prepare supper, Lazarus closed the store for a brief time so that he and Isidor could go home for their evening meal. It was a short walk, just around the corner and one block away. But after supper, the two would return to reopen the store so that farmers might come in after a day's work to look for a new hat for Sunday church or men on their way home from their blacksmith shops or their law offices might stop in to buy a ribbon or a bit of licorice for their children.

Isidor enjoyed evenings with his father at the store, where kerosene lanterns provided better light than the candles at home and a better place to study. Money was still scarce, so in an effort toward frugality, the Strauses lit their home after dark only by firelight or homemade candles, while the more expensive lighting was reserved for customers. There, in the golden light of lanterns, Isidor clerked and prepared his lessons until 9:30, when he and his father locked up for the night and the two walked home together in the dark along the dusty road.

The entire family worked hard and practiced a studied economy, raising vegetables in their garden and chickens for meat. Setting aside Jewish dietary laws, they also enjoyed bacon, which they laid in at their smoke house during the annual hog-killing season, enough to last for the whole year. "Fresh meat was a rare delicacy in that part of the world," Isidor noted.[7] The town had a market place on the public square where, from time to time, during the brief winter months when the weather was cold enough, a farmer might bring the slaughtered carcass of an ox or a sheep to offer the fresh meat for sale. But ice was scarce, and meat spoiled quickly. Thus, chickens, which could be easily kept in a hen house or pen, and smoked bacon or ham were the meats of choice and necessity.

One of the Kaufman brothers, Julius, also boarded with the family, which helped to defray household expenses. Sara, always frugal, stretched her meager monthly household allowance of twenty dollars to save enough money to buy a piano for her daughter Hermine. Hidden behind her gentle demeanor was a toughness of spirit and determination to help her husband and mold her children. She had no intention of allowing her children to forget life's refinements or the value of a good education, particularly in such a relatively cultured setting as Talbotton.

Whatever other funds Sara and Lazarus managed to set-aside went toward paying tuition and purchasing used textbooks for the children's schooling, for no free public schools existed in Talbotton at the time (the public school system in Georgia was not established until 1871). Nevertheless, although it might surprise anyone who visits the little town today, Talbotton was considered a center of education, culture, and refinement in the area, and more than twenty schools, academies, and institutes had been chartered there in the two decades before the Strauses arrived. The town attracted students from all over central and south Georgia. Isidor recalled the "feeling of exultation" he had when, after advancing in his studies of Greek to the point where a dictionary was essential, his father bought him a brand-new Littell and Scott Greek lexicon during one of his buying trips to the North.[8] The book was his pride and joy.

Like many Jews in the South, the Strauses were determined to fit in and be a part of the community, and they were prepared to sacrifice many of their Jewish customs to do so. Isidor remembered his family being the only Jews in Talbotton, though historic records show five Jewish families living there only three years earlier. Still, not enough Jewish men were present for religious services.[9] But Lazarus wanted to provide some religious education for his children. He often invited local clergymen, like the Baptist and Methodist preachers, over for dinner, where they would debate the finer points of the Old Testament. And soon Lazarus, at the urging of the Baptist minister, was sending Nathan, then eleven, and Oscar, eight, to the Baptist Sunday

School. As Oscar recalled the experience, "Our teacher was a gunsmith who had more piety than knowledge, and [what] he lacked in erudition he made up by good intentions." [10]

For the first two years after arriving in Georgia, Isidor attended Levert College, a local preparatory school, where his sister Hermine also attended classes. Then he entered the more prestigious Collingsworth Institute a mile south of town. The Institute, founded in 1838, was the brainchild of a well-to-do planter and devout Methodist, Josiah Flournoy, who named it for his friend, the Rev. John Collingsworth. In 1856, when Isidor entered, the institute was enjoying its largest enrollment of about 100 boys.[11] Perhaps in sending his oldest son to school with the Methodists, while his two little brothers attended the Baptist Sunday school, Lazarus sought to show preference to neither of his two clergy friends or their faiths. But he believed that the children needed both religious training and an education, and the town had no synagogue or Jewish teachers.

Schools in the Talbotton area showed a surprising diversity of curriculum, and students were able to select such courses as grammar, rhetoric and logic, mythology, Roman, Grecian, and Jewish antiquities, algebra and higher mathematics, natural sciences, and classical languages.[12] Isidor's own classes for his first year included orthography, writing, geography, grammar, arithmetic, declamation, and composition. His grades, though passing, were not outstanding his freshman year. However, they steadily improved as he moved on to such subjects as Latin, Greek, and higher mathematics.[13] But though he remained at Collingsworth for four years, Isidor longed for something more.

In 1860, when he had reached the age of fifteen, he was seized with the desire for military training. A neighbor's son, a cadet at West Point who came home during summer vacations in 1860, filled him even further with such ambitions. The dapper uniform and the young man's sharp, military demeanor impressed Isidor.

The cadet encouraged his ambitions and suggested that, at his own graduation, Isidor should seek the congressional appointment to West Point that he currently held. Though the boy's imagination soared at such a possibility, the coming of the Civil War would put a quick end to his dreams of military glory.

On November 6 Abraham Lincoln was elected president of the United States, defeating Stephen Douglas, the official Democratic candidate, John C. Breckenridge, a breakaway southern Democrat championed by southern planters for his support of slavery, and John Bell, candidate of the new Constitutional Union Party. From that point on, events took on a life of their own, igniting a spirit of southern independence and war fever throughout the region. South Carolina on December 20 became the first state to secede from the Union. Georgia followed suit on January 19, 1861, and sent delegates to Montgomery, Alabama, for a February 4 meeting to draw up a new constitution. Four days later delegates elected Jefferson Davis as president of the newly formed Confederate States of America, and war became inevitable. Few were surprised, and many were thrilled, when Confederate troops fired on Fort Sumter in Charleston harbor on April 12, igniting the most destructive war in American history.

On the day Fort Sumter fell, Lazarus was in New York on his annual trip to purchase his spring stock. He had gone first to Philadelphia, but encountered slimmer choices than usual. Everyone had seen the war coming, and his northern suppliers had brought in fewer supplies, assuming the southern customers would not appear. Most of them did not, and Philadelphia wholesalers expressed surprise to see Lazarus on his usual buying trip, despite the war fever. When he realized that he couldn't find all he needed in Philadelphia, he made a hasty trip to New York to complete his purchases. However, when he heard of the Confederate attack on Fort Sumter in Charleston, he realized the danger he was in and rushed home, leaving behind his order for crockery in the hands of a random salesman, asking him to place it wherever he chose.[14]

After nearly seven years in the South, and for Lazarus even longer, the Strauses considered themselves southerners and sided wholeheartedly with the Confederacy. Lazarus had always made efforts not to judge his neighbors, but rather to fit in, to belong to the community, and to accept its ways. The one thing he had difficulty accepting at first was the institution of slavery. His son Oscar recalled that he discussed the subject frequently with his friends in the clergy, pointing out to them that, although many defended slavery on Biblical grounds even in the pulpit, the Bible must be read "with discrimination and in relation to the period to which the chapters refer." Even then, he argued, there was "no such thing as perpetual bondage, as all slaves were declared free in the year of jubilee."[15] At first Lazarus and Sara resisted any form of slave-owning, preferring to hire their domestic servants from other masters. But, according to Oscar, the slaves they hired begged the Strauses to buy them, for in the Straus household they were treated with kindness and courtesy. Finally, they gave in and purchased some of those they had hired from others.

Lazarus, however, was determined to prepare them to support themselves and had one of the men trained as a tailor, while another became a shoemaker.[16] Evidently the family made other slave purchases as well, for the 1860 census shows thirteen mulatto slaves in the household. One of the Straus descendants recalls an incident when Isidor and Nathan were sent to buy a slave. The two made what they thought was the clever selection of a pregnant woman, hoping to be frugal and get two for the price of one. They had not counted on the inconvenience of her confinement or the disruption that the new baby caused in the small household. When the family later moved north after the Civil War, they would take with them their two youngest servants, a boy and a girl, whom they felt could not yet live on their own.

One of those might well have been this baby born in the Straus household.[17]

The coming of the war not only cut short Isidor's dreams of West Point, now totally out of reach, it also cost the Strauses their boarder. Julius Kaufman, 38 years old, enlisted as a private in Company A of the 4th Regiment of the Georgia Volunteer Army, becoming one of the so-called "Southern Rifles," commanded by none other than Capt. Bernard Curley, who abandoned his tailor shop for the war. On April 26, 1861, a parade of young men, more than ninety in all, marched toward active service in Virginia. Isidor watched them go with mixed reactions of envy and disappointment. After Julius's departure, he found it necessary to drop out of school for a year to help his father at the store. However, a little more than a year later, in the spring of 1862, Julius Kaufman was discharged with a disability. According to his grandson, Gus Kaufman, even though his disability was based on an old leg fracture, he walked back to Talbotton, no doubt catching whatever rides he could on the back of a friendly farmer's wagon. With Julius's return, Isidor was once again free to pursue his studies.

While the most able-bodied men from Talbotton were away serving in the army, older teenage boys of the town organized their own company of soldiers. Isidor proudly enlisted among them and was elected, as was the custom, by the young men to the rank of first lieutenant.[18] The makeshift company of boys "offered their services to the Governor of Georgia," but Gov. Joseph E. Brown declined the offer, noting that the state did not have enough arms to equip the men, and that, "to accept boys as soldiers was out of the question."[19]

His dreams of West Point dashed by the coming of the war and the withdrawal of southern cadets from its ranks, Isidor set his sights on another military school. Many high schools and colleges in the area had suspended operations because faculty members and older students had joined the Confederate army. But the Georgia Military Academy in Marietta, north of Atlanta was thriving with its training of future Confederate officers. Isidor set out for Marietta to take entrance exams at the Academy.

Unfortunately, he knew nothing about the tradition of hazing at such institutes, though he was soon to learn, to his profound humiliation and disgust, in the rudest of manners. While waiting for his interview with Academy authorities, he was invited into the dormitory room of a boy he apparently knew from Talbotton. While he was in the boy's room, others made ready a new "invitation." The cadet and Isidor were invited into the room of another cadet, and, as Isidor later told the story: "the gallantry of my friend bade me, when reaching the door of his room, to precede him in entering. I failed to discover until it was too late that the door was a little ajar, enough to enable a tin pan full of water to be perched over the opening, which came down on me as soon as I pushed it open. I was so thoroughly drenched that I was compelled to return to the hotel and change my attire from head to foot." He felt humiliated and betrayed by his friend. It was enough to convince Isidor that he wanted no part of the Georgia Military Academy. "This disgusted me so utterly that I never returned to the Academy, and to what extent this episode changed the course of my life is speculation."[20]

Speculation or not, the incident probably determined his future career as that of a merchant and businessman. Still stinging with chagrin, he left the Academy never to return, but he was determined not to go home empty-handed. Considering how he might salvage the trip from fruitlessness, he decided to put to immediate use the lessons he had learned from his father. Hiring a buggy and driver, he made his way the next day to a nearby mill in the area and placed an order. Then he went into Atlanta the following day and sold at a profit and for future delivery the goods he had ordered the day before from the mill, a procedure he evidently repeated several times. Thus, he was able to return home to Talbotton, not as a failure, but rather as a young merchant and successful entrepreneur, which in his own words "appeased the disappointment which an utter failure of the purpose of my trip would have caused."[21] No doubt it provided his parents with a source of pride in his unexpected accomplishment. Such business talents would prove infinitely more useful in the years to come, both to his family and to the Confederacy, than learning to march, shoot, and bark orders at enlisted men could ever have done.

The Civil War and the blockading of southern ports by the Union navy brought both scarcity and opportunity to enterprising merchants. Supplies that had been previously imported from northern states were suddenly unavailable. Oscar remembered his mother "cutting sweet potatoes into little cubes, drying them in the sun, then roasting and grinding them together with grains of wheat" to substitute for the coffee they could no longer get.[22] To make matters worse, merchants from larger cities, who received the news of the shortages first, quickly scoured the countryside and smaller towns like Talbotton buying up their stocks of merchandise before local citizens got wind of the situation and before prices skyrocketed. They resold them at a considerable profit. Such profiteering was publicly denounced as extortion, and Georgia citizens, who could not afford the higher prices, particularly as the value of the Confederate dollar dropped, were outraged.

For the first time since their arrival, the Straus family felt the full force of anti-Semitism, for Jews, as Isidor observed, were "singled out" in the denunciations and "tirades" in the Georgia newspapers against such practices. Though the records show that profiteering went on among all segments of the population, the frustrations of the war and the need for a scapegoat brought out the worst in human nature—its bigotry and prejudice.

In Thomasville, on August 30, 1862, a public meeting was called to discuss the "unpatriotic conduct" of Jewish tradesmen. Citizens passed resolutions that denounced "German Jews" in particular, prohibiting them "from visiting the village, and banishing all those now resident in that place."[23] Other incidents were potentially more violent. In Milledgeville in April 1863, one such case occurred. Southern women, whose men were at war and who had reached the point of desperation, felt justified in raiding Jewish stores at gunpoint and then loudly denouncing the merchants as "extortionists" and "profiteers."[24] But in other parts of the South where Judaeophobia was running rampant, cooler-headed citizens defended the Jews. At a public meeting in Savannah, citizens passed a resolution denouncing the people of Thomasville because of their actions as "enemies of human liberty and freedom of conscience." [25]

In Talbotton, where a decade earlier no anti-Semitism had been evident to Lazarus, at the peak of this hysteria, prejudice against Jews had been aroused. In 1863, a grand jury in Talbot County, evidently in sympathy with such extreme acts as those of the people of Thomasville, issued a public presentment about "the evil and unpatriotic conduct of the representatives of Jewish houses who had engaged in this nefarious business." Lazarus was outraged. As the only Jewish business in town, he took the jury's statements as a "personal affront," declaring his intent to close his store at once and leave Talbotton.

The citizens of the little town, who had come to depend upon the merchandise of his store, as well as the man's impeccable honesty in business practices, were horrified. Every member of the grand jury came personally to visit Lazarus in an effort to dissuade him from leaving and assure him that the pronouncements had not been directed at him. Ministers from the town's

Protestant churches came to call on a similar mission, seeking to persuade him to stay. But Lazarus was adamant. He recognized anti-Semitism, and he refused to expose his family to such abuse.[26]

The Strauses packed their household goods and the store merchandise and moved to nearby Columbus, Georgia, where their friend Julius Kaufman had settled the previous October. Although it was only about forty miles away, it was a ten-hour distance by wagon, according to Julius.[27] Nevertheless, some of Lazarus's Talbotton customers, sympathetic and distressed by his departure, made it a point to shop at his new store for their purchases whenever they could travel to Columbus. But, in spite of all efforts to bring him back, Lazarus Straus never returned to Talbotton. His sons, however, in their later lives remembered with fondness their growing up there. All three brothers would return at least once, each at different times, to their childhood homes in both Columbus and Talbotton, where they were met with warm welcome and admiration. Isidor returned in 1889; Oscar, in 1908; and Nathan, in 1915.[28] And in August 1906, the three brothers donated $20,000 to equip and furnish a new industrial school building in Columbus.

However, the Strauses clearly understood the dangers of prejudice at that time, and they knew their vulnerability as the sole Jewish family in Talbotton. They had seen it before. Lazarus was simply taking no chances with the safety and dignity of his family. Although he expressed surprise over the equality of treatment he had received from wealthy white planters when he had first arrived in Georgia, he was never naïve about its racist underpinnings, and only as a white man did he merit such status in their eyes. But, he also understood, as the war continued to threaten the institution of slavery, that bigotry could be displaced to other groups as well. The incident made all too clear the fragility of his family's status in a small southern community.

In many respects life was better for the Strauses in Columbus, a much larger city that lay on the eastern bank of the Chattahoochee River. The Strauses found there a fine, new home, a receptive Jewish community, and an established synagogue. And with eighteen thousand residents as potential customers, Lazarus's mercantile trade thrived.

The move to Columbus also gave Isidor a new opportunity to exercise his own entrepreneurial instincts. His educational ambitions thwarted, he quickly turned his abilities in another direction in an effort both to serve the Confederacy and to use his business skills. In 1863, not long after the Strauses' arrival in the city, a distinguished group of Columbus businessmen organized the Georgia Importing and Exporting Company "for the purpose of opening and carrying on direct trade with foreign countries."[29] The participants were a virtual who's who in the city's business world. They had conceived the idea of sending an agent to Europe to buy steamers in hopes of running the Union blockade. They intended to export their cotton and negotiate importation from England and elsewhere of the necessities they could no longer bring in from the North. Their collateral for the steamship purchase would be almost eight thousand bales of cotton, for which European manufacturers were clamoring. These were currently stored in the warehouses of southern ports. If the company could only obtain the necessary vessels, load their cotton and make it through the Union blockade, then they could sell the cotton in England and return home loaded with the necessities required in Georgia, thus fulfilling a need and making a handsome profit on both sides of the Atlantic.

They hired a man named Lloyd G. Bowers to act as their agent, and with the labor shortage caused by the war, Isidor was able to secure a position as his secretary. He was young, only seventeen years old, but viewed by others as "clever and down-to-earth more than his years would indicate." The venture was risky, but it brought high hopes not only to the stifled business community, but also to Isidor. His arrangement with Bowers was to pay his own expenses, and in return he would be given the privilege of purchasing merchandise in England to be sold in Georgia, thereby sharing in the profits of the enterprise.

One more incentive encouraged Isidor's parents to be eager for him to participate in the undertaking. As he would later write to one of his uncles, "The war in the South...has called into requisition from time to time all the resources within her command, men were called out from 18 to 35 & I approach the age faster than circumstances looked favorable. This made the climate a little too hot & I began to look around for a cooler spot." Not only had he lost some of his fervor for garbing himself in military glory to defend an increasingly anti-Semitic South, but his father also "was very anxious for me to accept... this position, as it was one of the few chances... offered wherewith I could so honorably bid farewell."[30]

Bowers and the young Straus left Columbus on June 16 1863, bound for Charleston, South Carolina, to explain their plans to General Roswell S. Ripley, post commander at Fort Sumter. However, they discovered after a lengthy conversation with the general that the port of Charleston was blockaded by no less than twenty-one armored Union steamers, making the probability of running the blockade out of that city, even on a moonless or foggy night, extremely hazardous.

A Savannah man, a notorious figure by the name of Charles Augustus Lafayette Lamar, who had been a well-known slave trader before the war, was in Charleston on a similar mission. On June 18, Isidor wrote his family of his safe arrival in Charleston and of his meeting with Lamar, whom he described as "the celebrated african [sic] trader...a very fine man."[31] Lamar had always been a colorful figure on the Georgia Coast. He had outfitted his own personal yacht, the *Wanderer*, as a slaver in

November 1858, gutting its insides to hold a maximum number of captives in the hull, and spearheaded the last major shipment of slaves from Africa into the United States. The vessel had landed at Jekyll Island off the Georgia coast near Brunswick to unload his illicit cargo of 409 men, women, and children. Many were sick; others had died and been cast overboard en route. It was an ugly affair. To be arrested with Charlie Lamar would be a signal to any savvy Union officer that one was up to no good. Nonetheless, Lamar was a man who knew the coastal waters like the back of his hand, and he could be of use to Bowers.

The two older men decided that, rather than risk a run out of Charleston, it would be best to go farther north and try to run the blockade from the less heavily guarded port of Wilmington, North Carolina. However, Bowers decided to send Isidor on ahead through the blockade at Charleston, arguing that the Yankees would not harm him or suspect him, a mere boy, of any illegal intent. In short, they abandoned the young man to his own devices and wits.

Blockade running was an extremely dangerous activity under the best of circumstances, and only the most daring and the most desperate would undertake it. The southern ports as well as all 3,550 miles of Confederate coastline had been under blockade by Union vessels since July 1861. They had learned most all the tricks used by southern vessels to elude them. In the end, the outcome was often determined by which vessel was faster and how foggy the night might be. Nevertheless, even in the heavily guarded port of Charleston, Confederate ships still successfully ran the blockade on a regular basis.

Passage on such vessels was understandably expensive and hazardous. Undaunted by the danger and well supplied with funds, Isidor easily booked space the following day, June 18, on the steamer *Alice*, headed for Nassau. He had chosen his vessel well, for the *Alice* would become one of the Confederacy's most successful blockade runners, making some twenty-four evasions through the Union Blockade. She was owned by the Importing and Exporting Company of South Carolina, better known as the "Bee Company," for its manager, William C. Bee.[32] But passage on such a vessel did not come cheap. Isidor was obliged to pay $160 in gold, or 1,120 Confederate dollars, for his ticket. Confederate currency on the South Carolina coast was running at an exchange rate of seven-to-one for gold, though only three days earlier in Columbus, on June 15, he had been able to make the exchange on a five-to-one ratio.

Only two passengers beside himself had booked passage on the *Alice*. One of them was Elias Haiman, a young Columbus man, "whose family" Isidor noted, "had been well acquainted with ours for several years." Isidor had some reservations about his traveling companion, judging that both he and another traveler stood "too stiffly upon the size of their purses," but as he told his parents, "I stand equally as stiff, upon something more valuable & more lasting, my honor & due respect."[33] Haiman was a part of the Columbus Jewish community, but unlike the Strauses, his family had already acquired considerable wealth in the city. While Isidor obviously considered Elias a bit overly conscious of money, he would have to deal with it, for there were not many others on the vessel with whom to associate.

The ship waited for dark before making its effort to slip through the blockade. At the appropriate moment, passengers were sent below the water line and asked to remain quiet in their bunks. Isidor understood the necessity for such action. Should the Union ships fire on the boat, he said, "we would be away from the danger line and the probability of becoming panic stricken." Like other blockade-runners, the *Alice* was painted to blend with the water, and the ship's crew had taken all possible precautions to assure a successful run. All lights were extinguished, and passengers "were compelled to lie prostrate in a temporary bunk below the water line, out of sight, and possibly out of sound, of everything that might be going on on deck."

Isidor obeyed the order without protest but soon found himself in great discomfort. His mother had sewed the twelve hundred dollars in gold into an undergarment he wore tightly around his body. He sweated miserably in the June heat below deck, breathing the fetid air of the close quarters. Tension mounted as the vessel got under way, as quietly as possible sailing out of the crowded harbor. As time crept by, the vessel kept moving. The men listened intently, muscles clenched in anticipation, waiting for the dreaded cannon fire. They heard nothing.

Finally, after what seemed like hours, a crewman came below to set them free. It was 1:00 A.M. before they were able to go on deck and breathe the fresh and welcome night air. The passengers who had lain so long sweating from fear and heat in their cramped bunks looked, as Isidor described them, "as though we had been in a Russian bath with our clothes on." But they were overjoyed to have made it to safety. Always interested in the ships on which he traveled, Isidor commented: "There were a large number of other vessels, sailing ships as well as steamers, which tried to run out of Charleston harbor that night. Ours was the fastest craft of the lot and therefore we were the first to run the gauntlet of danger." But he reported with a sense of pride that "we were the only ones to escape past the blockaders. All the rest had to put back into Charleston harbor."[34] They had slipped past seventeen Union vessels, "Iron Clads & monitors," as Isidor described them, without discovery.[35]

Three days later they docked in Nassau, fortunately "without any further excitement." Isidor's ultimate destination, however, was London, where he was to rendezvous with Lloyd Bowers. In view of the dangers of United States ports, he hoped to find a route that would keep him far away from American ports. In Nassau, he was advised to head for Cuba, and from there, perhaps, he could get a ship to England. Taking the *Corsica* from Nassau after only a few days there, he steamed to Havana. But prospects looked slim for getting quickly to London, and Isidor finally decided that the fastest way to achieve his goal would be by way of New York. It was a risky route, he knew, but he saw no other logical way.

As chance would have it, a notorious Union admiral by the name of Charles Wilkes sailed with him from Havana to New York. Wilkes had become well known for his role in the *Trent* Affair, when, as commander of the San Jacinto, he had stopped the British mail packet *Trent* and removed Confederate officials, creating a diplomatic crisis between the United States and England. He had been cruising in Cuban waters in search of a Confederate privateer, the *Alabama*. In fact, during the voyage Wilkes spent much of his time on deck, perusing the waters with his spyglass.[36]

During the trip, Isidor struck up a friendship with another Georgian, a former bank cashier from Macon named A. H. Powel. The two men "drifted together" in a common bond that would continue when they sailed together for London later in the month.[37]

They arrived in New York on July 5, 1863, in the wake of a battle around the small Pennsylvania town of Gettysburg that would prove to be the turning point of the war.[38] Early news of the battle that reached them aboard ship proclaimed a Confederate victory. That news, as Isidor described it, "produced such elation on the part of the two rebels on board that we had great difficulty in restraining ourselves from jubilation." However, given the dark gloom of other passengers, particularly Admiral Wilkes, and recognizing under the circumstances that, "discretion was the better part of valor," they suppressed their joy. By the time they reached New York, however, where Isidor checked into the Astor House, the news had changed dramatically. Newsboys were "on the streets with extras announcing Robert E. Lee's retreat and the complete victory of the Federal forces," under the command of General George G. Meade.[39] The losses had been heavy on both sides, and the anger against the South was growing as news of Union casualties was released. The fury reached a fevered pitch when the United States announced that it planned to begin a draft of young men for the army. The two young "rebels" realized that their presence in New York was growing more perilous by the hour.

The Civil War

As tensions grew in New York and the two young southerners began to contemplate how they would get to England, Isidor busied himself with making social calls. He had made clear in a letter to his family written on June 22, while he was still in Nassau, that one of the people he intended to visit upon his arrival in New York was Nathan Blun, the father of his future wife, Ida. "I will take the liberty of going to see all my friends [sic] friends such as Mr David Kohns, Nathan Blun etc."

Before his departure from Columbus, Amanda Blun Rothschild, the daughter of Nathan Blun and the wife of Frank Rothschild, whom Isidor describes in his autobiography as "a friend of our family and a close neighbor," had written a letter to her parents to be delivered by Isidor should he pass through New York.[1] As Isidor describes the letter, she "recommends me so highly to her parents that when I come to New York...they will consider me as home folks. Mrs Frank Rothchild [sic] furthermore writes that whatever favor they will show me she will feel under the same obligation to them as if they would show the favors to herself."[2] When he displayed Amanda's letter to a Mr. Friedenberg, a former Columbus friend, who had grown rich in Nassau and who had looked Isidor up as soon as he heard that a son of Lazarus Straus was there, Friedenberg's reaction was that, if he had received such a letter, "he would have felt attached to me on the strength of that recommendation."

Unfortunately, we have no surviving description of Isidor's first meeting with the Bluns. Although he was a prolific letter writer, sometimes sending his parents more than one letter about specific events, for he never knew which communications they would receive, none of the letters he wrote while he was in New York have survived.[3] The Bluns, however, must have been delighted to have first-hand news of their daughter Amanda, who had married Frank Rothschild in 1860 and moved South, first to Eufala, Alabama, and then to Columbus. She had since given them two grandsons, Simon and Elias, whom they had never seen.[4] Whether Isidor met Ida herself during his initial visit to her home we can only speculate. She was only fourteen at the time and perhaps too young to attract the notice of an ambitious and precocious eighteen-year-old boy on his own for the first time. But she too would have wanted to hear all the news of her sister Amanda, who was ten years older than she, and who had been like a mother to her for most of her life. It is tempting to surmise that Isidor *did* notice her—her long, dark hair that fell below her shoulders and her inquisitive air—and that it was his curiosity about her that later encouraged him to want to return to New York. Whatever the case, the meeting with Ida's parents was important, for it provided a positive introduction to her family that would stand him in good stead when he later sought Ida's hand in marriage.

During the week Isidor spent in New York, he and Powel, well aware of their danger as southerners in a Union city, tended to be on their guard. But despite the risks of prolonging their stay, they toyed briefly with the idea of booking passage on the steamship *Great Eastern*, which did not leave New York until July 21. Never losing his boyhood enthusiasm for ships, Isidor as a mature man still recalled their reasons for wanting to sail on that particular vessel. Of the *Great Eastern*, he said, "We chose this boat as she was the wonder of the age—the largest boat ever launched."[5] The ship had been built in 1858 for the purpose of laying cables on the ocean floor. Her maiden voyage, however, had not been until June 17, 1860. She was 680-feet long, with six masts and five funnels over a double iron hull—mammoth by comparison to the *Saint Louis*, which had first brought him across the sea. So great was the ship that she could carry up to four thousand passengers and had been originally dubbed the *Leviathan*.[6] The temptation to wait for the *Great Eastern* was strong, but Powel was especially nervous.[7] A friend and former bank correspondent in New York had warned him that it would be dangerous for them to remain longer in the city, given the growing anger against southerners and anticipated riots in the wake of a recent announcement of an impending army draft.

With a mind to caution, the pair decided to book passage instead on the less impressive and less expensive *City of Baltimore*, an older iron-hulled vessel with only three masts and one funnel. Its greatest advantage was that it was bound for Liverpool on July 11, ten days earlier than the *Great Eastern*, and it would have to do.

As it turned out, their decision proved wise, for the predicted riots indeed took place only two days after their departure. On the Saturday they sailed, the *New York Times* carried the headline, "The Draft. It Begins Today." The article made clear that "All able-bodied male citizens...and persons of foreign birth who have declared on oath their intention to become citizens...between the ages of 20 and 45" would be subject to the draft. Names would not actually be drawn for the draft until Monday morning, and over the weekend preceding, anger among men of draft age rose to a fevered pitch.

The demonstrations that followed on July 13 quickly degenerated into some of the worst riots New York has ever seen. On Monday morning, unruly mobs attacked not only the draft office and a police armory, they also targeted blacks throughout the city for their particular wrath. One black man was attacked by a group of about 400 boys and men, beaten and lynched, and his body burned. The mob even attacked the Orphan Asylum for Colored Children on Fifth Avenue, looting the building and burning it to the ground. Hundreds were injured and at least seventy-four people killed during the riots that raged, out of control, for three days.[8] Finally, the army was called in, and units fresh from the Battle of Gettysburg were able to bring the riots to an end. Learning of the terrible events of that day, Isidor noted with understatement, "I had every reason to conclude that our leaving New York was a prudent step."[9] They had escaped just in time.

Once aboard the *City of Baltimore*, however, things were different. The ship's captain, realizing that he had two very nervous southern passengers on board, sought out Powel and Straus to inform them personally that they could now relax. He assured them, that they "need not be bashful or reticent about giving vent to our feelings" aboard his ship, which belonged to the Liverpool, New York, and Philadelphia Steamship Company, for they were now under "the protection of the Union Jack." English sympathies in the war clearly lay with the South, which supplied the cotton they needed for their manufacturing concerns.[10] The two young men breathed a sign of relief at the friendliness of the captain.

When the steamer docked in Liverpool on Friday, July 24, Isidor did not tarry there, but made his way immediately to London. Before leaving Charleston, Bowers had given him a London address, 40 Albemarle Street, where the two would rendezvous. News of the Confederate loss of Vicksburg greeted Isidor upon his arrival, making negotiations for a steamship even more difficult than before. Bowers and Lamar had also quickly perceived that they were not going to be successful in purchasing steamers on the basis of collateral in the form of cotton bales warehoused in scattered locations throughout the Confederate states. They needed to return home and make arrangements to have the cotton shipped to a port city, ready to be loaded on vessels, and they needed to do it soon, before the South suffered any more defeats.

Bowers recommended that, during their absence, Isidor visit relatives in Germany. It seemed a good idea, for Isidor's funds were limited, as he had not anticipated such a long stay. He was determined to live as frugally as possible, a habit he had learned from his parents who contended that "saving was the basis of providing against want."[11] Besides, he longed to see again his grandparents, aunts, uncles, and cousins, whom he had not seen since he was a boy of nine. Thus, he set out at once, informing his family by mail on July 29 that "I will leave for Otterberg to night [sic] & will write to you soon after my arrival."[12]

From Paris, where he lingered "only a day or two," to Kaiserslautern, he followed in reverse the same route he had taken with his family as a boy. Arriving at the very train station from which he had departed almost exactly nine years earlier, he was obliged to make the final lap of the trip to Otterberg by stagecoach, just as he had originally begun his journey to the New World. The accommodating coachman delivered him directly to his grandfather's house.

It was an emotional moment, for he had not notified them of his coming. Nor had they received notice from his parents. The mail between the Confederacy and European cities since the blockade had become unreliable, and for many months letters between his parents and grandparents had been interrupted. Thus, the Strauses in Otterberg had no knowledge of his presence in Europe.

Inside the house he found his grandfather sitting just as he remembered him. In Isidor's own words, "it required no stretch of the imagination to believe, although it was nine years since I had last crossed that threshold, that I had left him there an hour before." Soloman Straus had changed very little, and his grandson recognized him instantly, finding him "as youthful & lively as ever."[13] Isidor himself, however, had changed a great deal, growing into a deep-voiced young man who looked nothing like the child who went away. His grandfather stared at him in bewilderment when he said "Grandfather, it's Isidor—Sara's son!" The old man had long since given up hope of ever seeing his daughter or grandchildren again, and he had difficulty understanding what Isidor was trying to tell him. When he finally grasped who Isidor was, his excitement knew no bounds. It did not wane for days thereafter, and he kept asking over and over, as if to reassure himself that he was not dreaming, "Are you really my daughter Sara's son Isidor!"[14]

Only Isidor's grandfather, his step-grandmother, Sara, and their twenty-three-year-old daughter, Augusta, resided in the house now. As Isidor would learn, Jacob, their son who had accompanied Isidor and his family to Le Havre so many years ago was now living in London, where he had established a business. They insisted that Isidor must look him up when he returned to England. Now that his mission for Confederate Columbus seemed distant, if not almost impossible to carry out, Isidor took two leisurely months to reacquaint himself with his family and his boyhood home, a time spent "most pleasantly" basking in the attention his German relatives lavished on him. His grandparents "treat me like their own children, Augusta like a brother & in short the whole family tries to do everything to make me as happy as possible & to make me feel like at home."[15] He told them all the latest news about the Strauses in America and tried to explain to them as best he could the dreadful war between the Union and the Confederacy. He had grown unaccustomed to speaking so much German, and at first the words did not come as easily as they once had but, with his eagerness to answer all their questions, it returned by leaps and bounds. It was good to be back, though he realized clearly that Otterberg was no longer "home." He was now an American — a son of the South.

He remained in Otterberg for two months before setting out once more for London. There, one of the first things he did was to look up his Uncle Jacob. He did not write much of their reunion, though Jacob must have been as excited as his father had been to see the young man, and Isidor would maintain in steady contact with him throughout his time in England, using his uncle's firm, Straus & Co., 20 St. Dunstan's Hill, London, as his primary address.

Despite the contact and warm welcome he received in London, Isidor decided he needed to be in the seaport city of Liverpool. Upon his return there, he met up once more with Elias Haiman, the Columbus banker with whom he had run the Union blockade out of Charleston. Although while they were on the ship together Isidor had found Elias to be a rather haughty young man, overly impressed with his family's wealth, he soon learned to enjoy his company. With Elias was a man named H. L. Daughtry from Wetumpka, Alabama. The three young men lived together for several months at Birkenhead, across the Mersey River from Liverpool. They were part of an expatriate community who found themselves unable or unwilling to return to their war-torn country.

With his funds rapidly diminishing, Isidor knew that he must quickly find a means of livelihood. Therefore, when a gentleman named Ashbridge from New Orleans offered him a post of clerk, he readily accepted, at least for a limited time, during which he learned double entry bookkeeping from the head office man. But he found little in the position to challenge him and was soon casting about for other opportunities.

In the late summer of 1864, Isidor encountered a fellow Georgian named Henry Blun, who was a nephew of Nathan Blun and, thus, a cousin of Isidor's future wife. Henry Blun was a blockade runner from Savannah who had first set out on April 1 in a little sloop he called the *Maggie Blun*, named for his baby daughter, to deliver thirteen bales of cotton to Nassau. Eleven years before, he had "unceremoniously" left his parents' home in Worms, Germany, to settle in Georgia. When war broke out, Blun had entered service in the Confederate army and served as quartermaster in the German Volunteers. Because of failing health, although he was only thirty-one, he had obtained a six-month furlough, during which he made his way to England, where he met Isidor.

Isidor does not record the meeting in either his auto-biography or his surviving letters home. Fortunately, however, Henry Blun mentioned it in a pamphlet he penned called *Reminiscences of My Blockade Running*, though his recollection seems a bit uncertain, for he mentions encountering "friends" in Liverpool, naming both "Nathan and Isadore [sic] Straus." Nathan, however, was not in England during the war. Blun may have met and mistaken Isidor's friend Elias for Nathan, though we can't be certain. In any case, the meeting was only a brief one, for Blun soon returned to Savannah to take up his life as a captain in the Confederate Army once again.[16] How well Isidor and Henry Blun had known one another before this meeting is uncertain, although Blun's reference to him as a friend suggests that they had indeed met before. Neither of the young men could have foreseen their future family ties, nor did they apparently spend much time together. Blun stayed in Liverpool but a short time, leaving soon after their meeting for Holyhead to board a steamer bound for Wilmington, North Carolina.

The Union navy had so strengthened its blockade forces that fewer and fewer Confederate vessels were successful in getting through. Thus, the blockade-running endeavor, Isidor's original reason for being in England, had little prospect for success, yet going home to be recruited into a losing army seemed pointless. He felt that he could help his family more here in England than he could in Georgia. For quite a while he had been trading

Confederate bonds for fellow Georgians in the European markets. He was especially successful in England, where sympathy at the time he arrived and for much of the war, "was entirely with the Southern cause" because the cotton the South produced was essential to so many of Great Britain's manufacturers.[17] Here, at least, he could accumulate funds that would be useful to his family after the war, for he knew the hardships they were all now suffering in the South. He set out to do just that.

The most frustrating part of his life in England and his efforts to help those at home was the difficulty he had in communicating with his family. Although he wrote almost every day, asking his father's advice on sundry business matters, he seldom received a response. Even more annoying to Isidor was the fact that Elias Haiman, whose family was also in Columbus and no doubt using similar delivery methods, received letters from home on a regular basis. Isidor complained to his family, "Elias who is living here with me receives letters by every mail & why I dont receive them also I can attribute only to your want of providing."[18] Isidor himself wrote them long, newsy letters, usually several about the same incidents, in the event that one or more might not reach them, but he had cautioned his family, in a letter written on June 24, 1863, "dont feel uneasy if you should not hear from me in longer time than you anticipate, as I might write a dozen letters & not one would reach its destination."[19] He promised to write about all business matters and urged them as well to write to him "often & explicitly." True to his word, his letters became increasingly concerned with business issues at hand and how the family might best preserve its capital until the end of the war. He was far less anxious about with southern cause than he had once been and was instead intent on finding a way to keep himself and his family from ruin.

On his own for the first time in his life and eager to succeed, it was clear that he hoped for his father's counsel and wisdom.

However, few letters reached him or them in a timely manner. Sometimes he didn't receive a letter for months at a time and he was frustrated that so few of his letters seemed to reach their destination.

In the most recent letter that had arrived from his family, his father had urged him, in light of the apparent failure of the importing/exporting venture, to use his time in Europe to continue his education, but Isidor responded: "It is impossible for me to follow father's advice of going to school as I prefer to continue in the business life. At present I am in business here & about making my expenses; I will remain in the situation until I find something, more profitably, to do." But the one thing he made most clear was his longing to hear from them. "I do wish that this war would come to an end so that Son would have no longer to be separated from his parents. Do write me & write me often as it is so much comfort to hear from home." He had also learned in the letter he had received from them about his sister Hermine's recent marriage to Lazarus Kohns. He wrote: "I hope that the new step which you have taken in life may prove one only of pleasure & happiness. I congratulate you all, my dear ones, upon the change in the family."[20]

In his own letters, he begged them to send him money and advice. As his confidence grew, he began to send advice of his own, urging them to "Buy good lands, R.R. stocks, houses & lots, all kinds of real estate, but no Shwarze [blacks]."[21] From his perspective in England, so removed from the war effort, he could foresee very clearly the end of slavery, which had already been proclaimed by Abraham Lincoln, and the decline of Confederate currency and bonds, though he considered "old state bonds" still a good investment. He urged his parents to send any bonds they might have to him quickly. He had begun a modest trade in Confederate bonds and urged his father to help "throw some business in my hands."[22]

His well-being, always of concern to his family, was solid, he assured them. "I never was as healthy in my life, looking as robust as a rail splitter & have stretched myself to the heighth of 6 feet."[23] By January 16, 1864, however, he had completely given up on his Confederate mission and informed his parents that he "will now try & make a living on my own hook, which I no doubt will be able to accomplish. Elias & myself will act together in everything."[24]

Finally, at the end of February, Lazarus Straus heeded his son's request to throw business his way. Bowers returned to England and brought with him a package of twenty-three thousand bonds from Isidor's family as well as letters from home and news from Frank Rothschild that he was also forwarding to the young man another twenty thousand bonds. Isidor was elated for, in addition to the bonds, there had been letters from Hermine, Nathan, Oscar, and Julius Kaufman, as well as from his parents. Though he playfully chided his new brother-in-law, Lazarus Kohns, for not including a letter as well, he wrote back enthusiastically, thanking them all for writing and sending his respects to the Frank Rothschilds. He also urged his father to send him even more bonds without delay, for he believed that they would sell well for the next three months or so.[25]

From this point on, once more in contact with his family, Isidor's self-confidence and success soared. As he wrote his parents on April 2, "Accidentally, through the kindness and diligence of Uncle Jacob I found out the market for them & hope to make in fact already have made considerable profit on account of it. Few people know the market and I charge a commission for selling same which parties have been very willing to pay since I always obtain the top of the market." He cautioned his father to send only 8% bonds *"plainly and legibly stamped."* He underscored this point, for all others he deemed unsellable.[26]

Nonetheless, though he was receiving letters more often now, all of the correspondence from Isidor to his family was not getting through. In early July he received a letter from home that clearly stung and angered him. In his own words, he rebuked his family:

In your letters you reproach me most awfully & blame me with actions that I have never previously heard of, much less committed. You say that I am carried away by the busy world around me & acting careless and unpremeditatedly. You charge me with wild speculation & feel uneasy about your money in my hands. You say that I will lose all my & your money through my heedless enterprises...But most of all you charge me with having transgressed your instructions & advice when in fact I have never received a word. To all these charges I have simply to say, that were they true I would not feel or care about your reproaches, for I don't believe that any one who would be fool enough to commit all these charges had sufficient sense of honor or conscience to feel at all; but as they are, thank God, not true...I can assure you that I don't pass over them as easy as you wrote them, but that they sting me, sting me like a yellow jacket, very like a snake; that my reputation or that the confidence you formerly placed in me has dwindled to such a stage, that even you have felt uneasy about the funds in my hands. Your money has been laying at interest from the day of my arrival & not one farthing has been touched.[27]

Not only had he received such a letter from his parents, but he had also received letters from Frank Rothschild and David Kohns complaining about

the heavy expenses I charged in the sale of their bonds. I charged them just what I paid & did not make a farthing myself. I charged them no commission because I was thinking they were going to assist you in getting out bonds...Is this not outrageous? Attending to this business without a penny of profit & receiving such letters...Had it not been for the high esteem I have for Simon R[othschild] I would have written Frank to go to h—l with his bonds & send them to whom he pleases.[28]

Fortunately for his future, he refrained from such actions.

Evidently Isidor's letter reassured his father, for he continued to send him bonds to sell. In August, Lazarus sent eight-five thousand bonds, ten thousand of which were lost on the *Tristram Shandy*. By October 20, Isidor had received only sixty thousand of them, with fifteen thousand still unaccounted for. By then Atlanta had fallen to the Union Army, and the price of Confederate bonds had fallen.

Isidor, in Germany on business, kept his spirits high by spending Rosh Hashanah, the Jewish New Year, which fell in early October, with his grandparents in Otterberg. He then went on to Karlsruh, Baden Baden, and finally to Lichtenau, where he visited the parents of Julius Kaufman. They were delighted to see him and get first-hand news of their son, and Isidor found them "in perfect health & in better spirits."[29] On that same day, Isidor wrote his parents to congratulate them "upon the ascendancy to the title of Grandparents." His sister Hermine had just given birth to her first child, a little boy named Lee to honor the Confederate general. To his mother in particular he asked, "How do you my dear mother feel in the shoes of a grandmother, perhaps as awkward as I in those of an uncle."[30]

The original purpose of Isidor's visit to Germany was "to arrange some business with Mr. Lafone connected with Rosenberg's contract." David Rosenberg had partnered with Elias Haiman of Columbus in obtaining a Confederate government contract to provide supplies for the army to be delivered to southern ports, with payment in low-priced cotton, which could then be resold at higher prices in England. A Liverpool man, Henry Lafone, had agreed to undertake the financing and provided Rosenberg "a letter of credit for twenty thousand pounds sterling."[31] Rosenberg had quickly exhausted his credit without purchasing the supplies for which it was intended and demanded more. Lafone quite understandably refused. Rosenberg argued that Lafone had agreed to provide additional funds when those were exhausted and he considered Lafone's refusal a breach of contract. He would, therefore, consider the funds he had already received as "damages." When his Columbus partner, Elias Haiman, received the news, he was, "distressed," to use Isidor's word, and came personally to England to try to locate Rosenberg and straighten out the matter. Haiman sued Rosenberg in an effort to make him use the funds for the purpose for which they were intended. However, at this point in the controversy, Rosenberg disappeared.

Henry Lafone offered nineteen-year-old Isidor a position paying fifteen pounds per month. His assignment was to track down Rosenberg and get the money back if possible. His search took him first to Germany. He traced Rosenberg to Cologne and Düsseldorf, where he had last been seen. At first, officials of the German banks that still held some of the funds were reluctant to talk to a nineteen-year-old boy. But when Isidor threatened them with legal action, "they gave me more respectful attention," and he was able to reclaim "a few thousand pounds sterling for Mr. Lafone."[32]

Several months later Isidor learned that Rosenberg had been seen in the streets of New York, so in December 1864, Isidor set out for New York. He took the opportunity to call once more on Nathan Blun, who as it turned out "knew Rosenberg's where-abouts and directed me to his address in Philadelphia."[33] Isidor indeed found Rosenberg where Nathan Blun had said he would be. Rosenberg, not happy to see him, threatened to turn him over to Union authorities as one who was giving "aid and assistance to the enemy of the United States." However, Isidor, resolute even as a young man, stood his ground and reasoned with Rosenberg, persuading him to return two thousand pounds "in full settlement."[34] He then returned to London, where once again he made his Uncle Jacob's office his headquarters for the duration of the war.

In March 1865, shortly before the war ended, Isidor received a telegram from Lafone, asking him to make one more journey on his behalf to oversee the disposition of steamships that had formerly been used as blockade-runners into southern ports, but which were now lying idle in Havana harbor. He was to go to Liverpool and from there take a steamer to Halifax, Nova Scotia, the quickest route to his ultimate destination of Havana, Cuba. He was so tied up in his bond trades on the day he received the telegram from Lafone that had to leave without having time to pack and was compelled to buy clothes in Liverpool. Lafone's instructions took so long that he missed the steamer from Liverpool and had to catch the Irish Mail Train to Queenstown, where he boarded the Cunard Line's *Canada*. He suffered frostbite in Halifax and from heat in Cuba, where he remained only a few days before returning to England. He had concluded that the only solution was to sell the steamships in question, for their usefulness as blockade-runners was over. During this trip the war came to an end, and shortly after his return to England, Isidor learned of the assassination of Abraham Lincoln.[35]

His bond trade had taken a big loss during his absence, for he had, prior to departure, purchased Confederate Erlanger bonds that he had not had time to resell and which had become virtually worthless with the defeat of the Confederacy. A second loss was the result of "inside information" that didn't pan out. "The two losses I sustained…proved a blessing in disguise for me; they cured me of all speculative tendency, and I profited thereby afterwards."[36] Isidor was never a man to make the same mistake twice.

His last letter from London was written on June 16, 1865, exactly two years to the day since he had left his home and family in Columbus. It was written to his mother and sister, expressing gratitude to God that, "after a period of four long successive years of bloodshed and civil strife, a bright star is once more seen in the distance." The war had ended in April, and Isidor began to think of the possibilities of going home. He had not heard from his family for four months, with the exception of a single brief letter from his brother-in-law, Lazarus Kohns, written on May 3, which had arrived in record time. He had, however, heard rumors of a battle that took place in his family's city of Columbus, but knew no details. When he finally learned that Columbus had fallen and that Union forces had ransacked the city, he wrote "Sad indeed was the news of the fights and hardships to which you my dearest ones were exposed in consequence of the armies and battles in your very midst."[37] But for Isidor, as terrible as was the news from Columbus, his family was still alive and the war was over. His thoughts were positive and even poetic in the letter he wrote to Sara and Hermine, in which he promised that "soon very soon I trust to realize what has heretofore been only a dream." Isidor was coming home!

Early Years In New York

The battle that raged around the Straus home in Columbus, Georgia, on Easter Sunday, April 16, 1865, proved to be what one historian has called "the last true battle of the Civil War."[1] The city might have been spared altogether had lines of communication been more efficient. Wilson's Raiders, the Union forces that attacked the town, knew nothing of Robert E. Lee's surrender to General Grant at Appomattox a week earlier, nor did they know of Lincoln's assassination just two days before.[2] The commander who led the attack, Gen. James H. Wilson, viewed the city as "the last great manufacturing place and storehouse of the Confederacy."[3] As such, it had to be destroyed.

The first attack came early in the afternoon and was successfully repelled by Confederate troops under the command of Major General Howell Cobb. Cobb had served as both governor of Georgia and U.S. Secretary of the Treasury. Expecting the Yankee forces, he had rushed from Macon "to take command of whatever forces Georgia and Alabama could muster."[4] A second attack began after dark about 8 P.M. when Union troops captured the Franklin Street Bridge.[5] The remnants of Cobb's forces, members of the reserves, and local men made a valiant effort to stand them off, to no avail.[6] The battle raged on for more than six hours. Eventually, southern troops were overwhelmed, and federal soldiers marched into the city and began systematically capturing or destroying its sources of livelihood and resistance. Columbus lay in economic ruin.[7] Isidor's brother Oscar left a vivid picture of the aftermath.

As soon as Wilson's army took possession of our debilitated city general confusion reigned. Looting began by the town rabble, led by several drunken Federal soldiers; cotton warehouses were burned, the contents of which represented the savings of many, including most of my father's; all horses were seized, and among them our little pony, which I never saw again, though I still retain a vivid picture of him in my mind's eye.[8]

The pony in question was a bay named Patrick that Nathan Straus had bought for himself and his little brother with money he earned from collecting old hemp, hemp rope, and waste copper. Years later, after the wounds of war had healed, Oscar encountered General Wilson, by then an "old veteran," and "jestingly reproached him from taking from me the most prized possession I ever had." [9]

Lazarus's description of the ordeal confirmed his son's recollections: "we had to witness robberies, fires and killings and have lost very much ourselves."[10] The battle, he recalled, "practically destroyed everything."[11] Under the circumstances, he saw little hope for a merchant's future in a region so devastated by war. As Isidor put it, "he made up his mind that he did not care to waste away the time he feared would be consumed before normal conditions could be reestablished."[12]

There seemed to be two reasonable options remaining. The first was to stay in Columbus and adjust as best he could to present circumstances. This was the route his friend Louis Haiman would take when he literally beat his swords into plowshares. Haiman had made a fortune as sword maker for the Confederate Army, but after the war he converted his forges to make ploughs and other farm equipment instead. The alternative was to leave the war-torn area and go north, an example already set by the Straus family's neighbors, the Rothschilds, who had sold their house even before the war ended and gone to New York.[13] Frank Rothschild had been taken prisoner, when the Union Navy had captured a blockade-runner, on which he was a passenger, in January 1864. According to his war record, he was held prisoner for a short time in Washington, D.C., but was soon released by order of the military commander.[14]

He was evidently taken prisoner a second time later that year. This time he was not so lucky. When his wife, Amanda, had not heard from him in several months, she decided to take her children to New York, some say in search of her husband, but more likely to spend the duration of the war with her parents. Packing up her two young sons, Simon and Alfred, who was an infant between two and three months old, she set out in a covered wagon across Georgia and Alabama, finally reaching Memphis, Tennessee. From there she and her children made their way to Cincinnati and then on to New York. Her husband, Frank, was released from prison in the spring of 1865.[15] They had sold the house they shared with the family of Frank's brother, Simon, in 1864, and, by war's end, they were living in New York with Amanda's family, among them her sixteen-year-old sister, Ida.

Lazarus agreed that going north seemed the better option. The family—by then only Lazarus, Sara, Nathan, and Oscar (Hermine had married and Isidor was still in England)—arrived in Philadelphia on the morning of July 7, ready to start again.[16] Assuming that Isidor would soon be coming home, Lazarus tried every means possible to let his oldest son know their where-abouts. He wrote to Isidor directly but had no idea whether or not he would receive the letter. Thus, on the morning of their arrival in Philadelphia, he also wrote to his brother-in-law, Jacob Straus, in London, in hopes of getting a message to Isidor before he left England. The letter was written in haste so that it might make a steamer that was about to depart. As yet, the family had no address in Philadelphia, though they would soon move into a small hotel, and Lazarus gave a return address in care of the firm of Arnold, Nusbaum & Nirdlinger.[17]

It was a difficult time, for most of the family's funds had been in now worthless Confederate money. Lazarus wrote to his mother-in-law on July 17, perhaps to put her mind at rest, that they had had the foresight and "good luck" to have sent "money for storage."[18] Most of their post-war assets, however, were tied up in remaining cotton, still stored in southern warehouses. As Isidor later noted, there was great "difficulty in bringing the cotton to New York, owing to the confusion of conditions everywhere throughout the South, and the interruption of transportation facilities."[19] Lazarus would have to wait until the early months of 1866 for sufficient funds to start a new business. In the meantime, he spent his time visiting his creditors in New York and Philadelphia and making arrangements to pay his debts.

In the spring of 1861, when Confederate troops fired on Fort Sumter, Lazarus had been in the North placing commercial orders. He'd hurried home, leaving someone else to finalize his purchases, which were still unpaid four years later. Now in 1865 his creditors were astonished to see him. They had assumed that none of the southern merchants would ever be able (or for that matter willing) to meet their ante-bellum obligations, and they had already written off their debts. But Lazarus was determined to pay back every cent he owed. One of his creditors, George Bliss, offered to take a lesser amount "in view of the hardships of the war and your family obligations." But Lazarus refused his offer, stating, "I propose to pay my debt in full and leave to my children a good name even if I should leave them nothing else."[20] He paid off whatever he could at the time and arranged to pay the rest as soon as he had sold his cotton. Northern merchants were impressed by his integrity and sense of responsibility. And from that point on, his name was his bond.

Isidor, returning from England, did not discover that his family had left Columbus and moved to Philadelphia until his arrival back in New York. He immediately departed for

Pennsylvania to find them and to learn his father's plans for the future.[21] The family had not seen him for more than two years, nor did they know when to expect him. Lazarus had written of Isidor to his mother-in-law on July 17 that "We…can hardly wait for the time when he comes."[22] They would not have long to wait, for he returned sometime in late July or August.[23] When he finally found his family, their reunion was joyous, and it gave Isidor, now twenty years old, a great deal of satisfaction to be able to come home with $10,000 in gold, with which to help his family in its time of need. During his years abroad, traveling on his own, he had achieved some business success and gained self-confidence. When he learned that his father had still made no definite arrangements to start over in business, he saw it as his duty "to stay with him and add my mite to his efforts."[24] And he felt ready to give his advice about the matter. Prior to Isidor's arrival, Lazarus seemed to have every intention of setting up shop in Philadelphia, but any final decision had been delayed until he had adequate resources from the sale of his cotton. Isidor, however, was convinced that they should not begin in Philadelphia, which he considered a "secondary market," but rather in the "chief market" of New York. He later noted, "I had very little difficulty in persuading father that New York was preferable to Philadelphia."[25]

Isidor used his $10,000 in 1865 to buy and furnish a home for his family in New York City at 136 (later changed to 220) West 49th Street.[26] It was "a high-stoop, three-story brick house," where the family would live for the next eighteen years.[27] They intended to use the money from what was left of his father's cotton to open a wholesale crockery business. The sale of the cotton, eventually shipped to Liverpool, would take another six months, and prices fell in the meantime. By the time the money arrived and Lazarus had settled all his debts, only $6,000, far less than they had anticipated, remained to invest in the new business—L. Straus &

Son—in which Lazarus and Isidor would be partners. It wasn't much, but they were unwavering in their will to succeed. And it wasn't the first time Lazarus had been compelled to start with very little.

Together father and son finalized their plans and rented a store, "with basement, first and top loft, at 161 Chambers Street" for $3,000 a year. As Isidor was negotiating the lease and providing references to the owner, one of the people with whom Lazarus had settled his pre-war debts, a Mr. Cauldwell, "stepped into the shop" and greeted Isidor by name. When Cauldwell told the lessor, whose name was Cole, that Isidor's father had paid his pre-war debt and "he had no hesitancy in giving satisfactory references...Mr. Cole said that he required nothing more."[28]

Thus on June 1, 1866, the firm of L. Straus & Son opened its doors for business. The first year was exceedingly hard. Isidor remembered it as a "great struggle, which kept me awake many nights planning and calculating."[29] On multiple occasions they even contemplated selling their home to raise capital, but somehow, with thrift and hard work, they managed to stay afloat and even turn a modest profit, grossing $60,000 their first year. Isidor gave much of the credit to his mother, whose "frugal and circumspect economy" always managed to provide a comfortable home on meager resources, just as she had done during their early years in Georgia.[30]

Isidor, enjoying his new manhood and his acceptance as an equal by his father, who now judged him "an able young man,"[31] was resolute in wanting his brothers to have advantages that had been denied to him by the war. After the family's arrival in New York, his brother Nathan enrolled in what was known as Bryant, Stratton & Packard's Mercantile College, but which in 1867 became Packard's Business College.[32] There he would learn bookkeeping and gain the business savvy from formal training that Isidor had to learn from experience. Lazarus knew his three sons very well, and celebrated their individual talents. He noted in one letter that "Nathan is very valuable to me in business, only he does not have much patience to learn much, but I want Oscar to go through all schools since he enjoys learning."[33]

Oscar, still only fourteen, already showed a great deal of academic promise and would continue with more conventional schooling, as his father wanted.[34] It was Isidor, however, whom Oscar described as "my guide, philosopher, and friend," and who made arrangements in the fall of 1865 for his youngest brother to enroll in Columbia Grammar School in preparation for later admission to Columbia College. Although their private academy in Talbotton, Collinsworth Institute, was a well-respected school in Georgia, it did not maintain the high standards of what Oscar deemed a "first-rate school" like Columbia. He was compelled to work very hard to live up to the expectations of his brother and his father, and he appreciated the privilege he was being granted. He fully understood that "[m]y brother…was desirous that I should have the advantages of the college training which circumstances, notably the war, had withheld from him."[35] And he was determined to be worthy of it.

While Oscar's schooling continued, Nathan graduated from business college in 1866, and joined the family firm not long after its founding, at which point it was renamed L. Straus & Sons. He became the company's outside salesman, a role for which he clearly had a gift. He was an ambitious young man, filled with ideas and unafraid to take risks, while Isidor, perhaps because of his wartime experiences, was the more cautious of the two. He filtered Nathan's enthusiastic ideas and selected only the soundest ones to implement. Both men made significant contributions to the family business throughout their careers, though the two were quite different in talent and temperament.

The house that Isidor purchased for his family was located in midtown Manhattan, only eleven blocks north of where Nathan

Blun now lived with his wife and children at 20 West 38th Street.[36] Isidor took the time to call once again on the Blun family and introduce his own parents and siblings to them. By way of introduction, they may have looked up their former neighbors, the Rothschilds, who were living with Amanda's parents. However it was accomplished, in the coming years, Isidor found ample opportunities to visit the Blun household.

The Bluns' daughter, Ida, only fourteen years old when they might have met for the first time, had by now blossomed into an attractive young woman who would be seventeen on her next birthday. Her father, like Isidor's, was a merchant. His trade of choice, however, was not crockery, but rather men's clothing. Nonetheless, the two fathers had much in common. Both had come from Germany in the early 1850s, shortly after the failed Revolution of 1848. Both had preceded their families to make certain they could succeed in this new country, and both had prospered.

Their wives also had many common experiences. Nathan's wife, Wilhelmine, whom most called Mine (pronounced Mina), arrived in America with her six children and her brother Isaac Freidenberger in 1851 aboard a vessel called the *Seine*.[37] They followed the same route from Le Havre to New York that Sara Straus and her children would take three years later aboard the *Saint Louis*. And both women were in poor health. As previously noted, Sara had suffered a stroke shortly before they came to America and needed much help from her children and her maid during the trip. Ida's mother had given birth to her sixth child, Moritz, shortly before the family set sail, and was not well throughout the fifty-three-day trip on open sea. She had to rely heavily on her oldest daughter Amanda to help with the younger children. Since that time Mine Blun had never fully recovered her health. She gave birth to her last child, Abraham, in 1853, after their arrival in America. In 1858, she grieved over the death of her seven-year-old son Moritz. Although Sara Straus had no more children after coming to America, she continued to suffer from the effects of her stroke, and her husband Lazarus had to write most of the letters to her family since her right arm was still useless.[38] Finally, both women had lost their daughters to marriage during the war years. Amanda Blun had married Frank Rothschild in 1860 and moved South with her husband, while her sister Augusta had married Emanuel Eising in 1864 and no longer lived at home. Similarly, Hermine Straus had, in 1863, wed Lazarus Kohns and set up her own household in Columbus. At the end of the war, Amanda and Hermine had both come to New York to be closer to their families.

Unfortunately, Sara Straus and Mine Blun would not have long to compare these similar elements of their lives. On November 11, 1866, Mine died leaving several young children, the youngest, Abraham, whom the family called Aby, still only twelve.

By the time of Mine's death, the Strauses were well settled in their new home not far away. They were present to offer their condolences to their former neighbor, Amanda Rothschild, to her father, and to the other Blun children, including the youngest daughter, Ida.

Ida had been a child of only two when her family first arrived in New York. Now she was a young woman of seventeen, and certainly attractive enough to have caught the eye of twenty-one-year-old Isidor. During the next five years, the two young people would come to know one another well. They were drawn together, like their parents, by common bonds of background, interests, and as they would discover, even a common birthday. Both were born on February 6, Isidor in 1845 and Ida in 1849.[39] As their friendship deepened, both families approved heartily. Isidor knew that L. Straus & Sons was now on solid footing. In fact, when their lease was up on Chambers Street in 1869, the partners felt they had grown sufficiently to move to better a location, signing a new lease at double the price on an entire building one block north on 44 Warren Street.[40] Isidor, in his mid-twenties, had reached the time in his life when he began contemplating marriage and starting a family, which he could now well support. When he and Ida discovered their common birthday, they made an effort henceforth to share the celebration. By the beginning of 1871, it was clear to Isidor that their relationship was a serious one.

In January of that year, he made a business trip to San Francisco, where his uncle Emanuel, his father's brother, was a partner in a crockery and glassware firm known as Helbing & Straus. The firm's New York representative had resigned in 1869, and Emanuel had asked L. Straus & Sons "to attend to their purchases in the eastern market."[41] The increased buying volume would be an advantage to both houses, and Isidor and his partners were pleased to accept. His five-week trip to San Francisco was for the purpose of studying "their market conditions on the spot." He had been "anxious to be in New York on February 6th," for, as he notes, "I had lately learned that there was another person in whom I took some interest at that time who also had the same birthday."[42] However, to his dismay, he did not make it home until February 8. At the insistence of his brother Nathan, he stopped for a time in Fort Wayne, Indiana, a stopover, he believed, that was a factor in his brother's later marriage, though unfortunately he never explains why.

Nevertheless, the delay caused him to miss the birthday in New York with the woman he had come to love. Isidor had turned 26 and Ida, 22. She evidently forgave him for his absence, for he was happy to announce that it "did not prevent my becoming engaged on April 24th following, and married on July 12th."[43] The day after their engagement, Isidor wrote with pride and delight to a cousin named Gabe: "I take pleasure in acquainting you of my engagement with Miss Ida Blun, which happy event took place last evening."[44]

His family was equally overjoyed. Lazarus wrote to his in-laws: "my dear Isidor got engaged yesterday with the daughter of Nathan Blun....My dear wife and I and Isidor are very pleased indeed with this match, since it is in every respect an outstanding one.... My wife is so beside herself with joy that she is not even capable of writing her own name."[45] We have no record of the Bluns' reaction, but there is no question that Isidor was an exceedingly promising young man. He was from a family well respected both in Germany and in the United States. His integrity was unquestioned, and he had shown himself to be a dutiful son who promised to be a devoted husband. And his prospects in the business world were bright. Above all, he and Ida loved one another with a love that would grow even more profound and passionate through the years. This was not simply a marriage of convenience, nor one that had been arranged by their families, however pleased they might have been. It was a love match.

Ida's sister, Amanda must have taken special pride in having served, in some small way, as matchmaker by providing Isidor with a letter of introduction to her father. Though she could have had no idea at the time how it would work out, she must have been pleased to be part of it all. After her mother's death five years earlier, she had become, once again, surrogate mother to her younger siblings. And she and her sister Augusta must have been delighted to help their little sister make plans for her wedding celebration.

The day of the marriage, however, which Isidor refers to in his autobiography as "*the* important and happy event of my life,"[46] did not go smoothly. The ceremony, to be performed by Dr. Samuel Adler, Rabbi of the Temple Emanu-El, who, like the Bluns, came from Worms, Germany, was scheduled for 4:00 P.M. on Wednesday, July 12. A dinner was to follow at 5:00 P.M. at the home of Ida's father at 20 West 38th Street. However, circumstances beyond their control made it difficult for Isidor to get there at all, and "prevented some of the guests from arriving at the wedding until very late."[47] Ida's nephew, Alfred Rothschild, who was almost seven at the time, recalled the circuitous route he had to follow in getting to the wedding. Because of the fighting on Broadway, "my servant walked me down from 48th Street along 8th Ave. to 38th Street and then across town to 20 West 38 where Grand dad lived."[48]

Riots were raging in the city streets. Although to the Jewish families involved in the wedding, July 12 was merely a convenient date for the ceremony, for Irish protestants known as Orangemen, it was the anniversary of the victory, more than two centuries earlier, of the Protestant King William III (William of Orange) over the ousted Catholic king, James II of England. New York's Irish Protestants planned a celebratory march through the streets, and the city's Irish Catholics, by far in the majority, were dogged in their attempt to prevent it. Anticipating the kind of violence that had occurred the year before when the Orangemen undertook a similar event, city officials issued an order forbidding the march, but were so severely criticized that the order was remanded. Instead, to protect the marchers, officials called out city police and several regiments of the National Guard. The result was one of the bloodiest riots the city had ever seen. The slow march began at 2:00 P.M., two hours before the wedding, and the riots raged on into the evening, leaving at least thirty-one rioters and two policemen dead, with many more wounded filling the city hospitals.[49]

In spite of the complications, the wedding went on as planned, with the two fathers serving as witnesses. Nathan Blun's home was a gracious haven in contrast to the chaos in the streets of New York. Young Alfred's most vivid memory of the day was going out into the yard, where he could see a church that stood at the northwest corner of 37th Steet and 5th Avenue. It was a beautiful summer day. Inside the house light filtered through the long French windows of the back parlor where guests, even those who arrived too late for the actual ceremony, enjoyed the wedding banquet. The bride had never looked finer than she did in her flounced and bustled wedding dress. Her dark hair was elegantly styled, much of it piled high on her head, but with a portion knotted loosely at the back of her neck. Isidor too was quite splendid in his elegant cutaway jacket and his long bushy sideburns.

In their wedding portrait, neither of them is smiling, which is not unusual in such nineteenth-century photographs. Still, the image suggests a sense of tension as they look into an unknown future, or perhaps an anxiety created by the events happening outside. Nonetheless, it is interesting to compare the stiff pose of the handsome young couple—Ida standing behind Isidor, her right hand at her side, her left resting on the back of the chair in which he is seated, both rigid in their demeanor—with that of the last photo they had made together. In their final portrait, the poses are reversed, with Ida seated and Isidor standing. She leans back toward him, and he leans forward toward her. One can see a softening in their faces and their bodies, as they tilt their heads toward one another. The contentment and gentleness of their smiles reflect a lifetime of affection and understanding, a tenderness and joy in being together. Had they known on the day of their wedding the lifetime upon which they were about to embark, and even had they foreseen the end they would one day face together, it is doubtful that either would have changed his or her mind. Theirs seemed from the outset a partnership of equals, in which each assumed a rightful place of reciprocal respect, support, and mutual love.

The first five years of Ida and Isidor's life as a young couple were filled with relative bounty and joy, not only for themselves, but for their entire families. The years were replete with weddings, births, and business success. They were years that formed patterns and relationships, years in which they explored their interests and lived life to the fullest.

The young couple began their married life living in the home Ida's father, where they had been wed. Eleven months later, they were delighted to welcome the birth of their first son, Jesse Isidor. Before dawn on Tuesday, June 25, 1872, Ida went into hard labor. It seems to have been an easy birth, and the baby was born shortly before 5:00 A.M., no doubt creating something of a stir and disruption in the Blun household.[50]

By early 1874, Ida was pregnant again. She and Isidor knew that they were soon going to need more room and a home of their own. That summer they found a house on 26 East 55th Street and moved in none too soon, for their second son, Clarence Elias, whom they called "Lally," was born there on August 27.[51] It was a happy time, for Ida's sister Amanda, who by this time already had six sons, finally gave birth the following December to a baby girl she would call Minnie.[52] Thus, Ida and Amanda were mothers together, bringing them ever closer as sisters.

The following year, on one of his buying trips to Europe, Isidor's brother Nathan met his future wife, Lina Gutherz, during a visit to Mannheim, Germany. Lina was an exceptionally beautiful woman who captured his heart at once. They had a whirlwind romance and were married five weeks later. When Nathan brought Lina back to New York to meet his family, she and Ida struck up a lifelong friendship.[53] Not only did Ida take an immediate liking to Lina, she would also take a special interest in Lina's sister, Lucie, who came to New York with Nathan and Lina in 1878. As Lina remembered the occasion, Ida and Isidor were there to meet them as always, and the moment Ida saw Lucie, she "made up her mind, as she afterwards told us, that [Lucie] was the girl for her youngest brother," Abraham Blun.[54] Their marriage would not take place until 1879, while that of Nathan and Lina occurred on April 28, 1875.

By early 1876, both Ida and Lina were pregnant. Lina's baby, Jerome Nathan Straus, was born on February 27, 1876. Four months later, before dawn on Tuesday morning, June 24, Ida gave birth to a third son, Percy Solomon. Percy and Jerome, whom Ida called affectionately "Puss" and "Jerry," would become almost inseparable in the future when the two families summered together.

It seemed to Isidor and Nathan, given their business success and their young families, that nothing could go wrong. Then, suddenly everything changed, and Isidor recalled in his autobiography that the year 1876 was "a sorrowful time for us."[55] Their new baby was less than a month old when Isidor's mother Sara was taken ill and diagnosed with a strangulated hernia, the symptoms of which are abdominal pain, nausea, and fever. She was compelled to undergo what he describes as a "precipitated operation."[56] Emergency surgery, even today, is necessary to correct the condition. In the twenty-first century, such operations are routine and usually uncomplicated. However, in 1876, surgery was always dangerous, and no doubt Sara's weakened condition from her stroke so many years ago worked against her. She lived only a few more days, dying unexpectedly on July 21 at the home young Isidor had bought for her and his family so many years ago. Her death was a severe blow to Isidor who admired his mother and her cheerful nature very much, even in her suffering. He wrote of her: "She was such a buoyant, sprightly and joyous disposition that she got more pleasure out of life, in spite of her great disability, than the majority."[57]

About three weeks later, even before they had time to recover from the grief of Sara's death, Ida and Isidor's middle son, Lally, also began to suffer from severe abdominal pain, fever, and nausea, symptoms agonizingly similar to those that had led to his grandmother's death. He was not quite two years old, and his parents were frantic with worry. Doctors diagnosed him with "inflammation of the colon." But they were able to do nothing. The child suffered for nearly a week until he finally died in his mother's arms at 6:00 P.M. on August 16, eleven days short of his second birthday. Isidor later concluded that the real cause of the child's death was appendicitis, which "was not known at the time."[58] Untreated, appendicitis is likely to result in a ruptured appendix and possibly peritonitis, a painful death that must have broken his parents' hearts. The toddler was buried two days later in Machpelah Cemetery on Cypress Hills in Queens, near the grave of his grandmother. He was recorded in the family prayer book as having lived "1 year, 11 months & 20 days." One has the feeling from the entry that his parents counted every one of those days as a singular blessing. These dual misfortunes, coming so close together were devastating for Ida and Isidor.

But with two other sons to care for, one of them less than two months old, they had little time to indulge their grief. Ida and Isidor shared a belief in looking for the positive in life, in being grateful for its blessings, which in their view, far outweighed its grief.[59] Thus, they consoled one another as best they could and buried their small son. Although they grieved, they knew they were luckier than Isidor's sister, Hermine and her husband Lazarus, who had lost two daughters in a period of about eighteen months in 1868 and 1869.[60]

Unfortunately the death of their young son did not end the family's run of bad luck and loss. Three years later, Ida's father died. Nathan Blun had not been doing well for several years and had been advised by his doctors to take a sea voyage. The ocean air, they contended, would do him good. Thus, in November 1879, he set out for Nassau with his son Abraham, and the young man's bride Lucie Gutherz. The young couple had married that very month. The trip was to serve a dual purpose, as both a "bridal tour" for Aby and Lucie, and the sea voyage Nathan's doctors requested. En route, however, Nathan Blun "took a turn for the worse" and died, even before the steamer reached its destination.[61] His body, which was shipped home on the *City of Austin*, did not reach New York until December 8. His funeral took place the following day at the home of Isidor and Ida, and he was buried in the Salem Fields Cemetery of the Temple Emanu–El in Cypress Hills.[62] He had become an American citizen on April 17, 1872, nine months after Ida and Isidor's marriage, and perhaps in foreboding of his death, he had drawn up his will on May 7, 1878, the year before his death. Finally, the death of Ida's brother Abraham came only two years later at Eaux-Bonnes, France, on August 10, 1881. He was only twenty-nine years old.[63]

In spite of so many family losses during that five-year period, the love that Ida and Isidor shared continued to be fruitful. Less than a year after the death of Ida's father, their first daughter, Sara, was born on May 16, 1878, followed by another, Minnie, on February 19, 1880. Twenty-one months later, on November 24, 1881, Ida gave birth to a son, Herbert Nathan. And finally, almost five years later their last child and their third daughter, was born. They named her Vivian.[64]

Although the couple would never forget the son they had lost, they took solace in their six other children, all of whom were healthy and handsome. They had all been born at the family's home at 26 East 55th Street, except for the first and the last. By the time of Vivian's birth, they had moved to a larger home farther uptown, but Vivian was not born in the family home. Not long before her birth, some of the older children came down with whooping cough. Isidor, ever cautious, was concerned that Ida should not be in proximity to her sick children so close to the time of her delivery. Thus, his sister, Hermine, agreed to take care of the Straus sons and daughters at their home, while Isidor and his pregnant wife went to live at the Kohns' residence at 220 West 49th

Street, where Vivian was born without mishap on Sunday morning, August 29, 1886, at eight minutes before 2:00 A.M. She grew up to be "incredibly beautiful" as well as lively and funny.[65] Their family was complete. And what a family it was.

5

The Family

The midtown neighborhood, where Ida and Isidor had settled their young family on E. 55th Street, grew steadily in population and changed in character over time. As neighboring buildings became larger and taller, their home and yard fell into shadow, "hemmed in so completely by high walls that we felt that not enough sunshine was admitted into the rooms for heath."[1] Ida was especially concerned that it was no longer a healthy environment for her children, who seemed to be sick far too often, even though, as Jesse would later remind the family in a light-hearted "roast" on his parents' fortieth wedding anniversary, she plied them regularly with castor oil and ipecac.[2] There was also increasing traffic in the neighborhood—hansom cabs, private landaus, and horse-drawn streetcars—that Ida felt threatened their safety.

Thus, in the early 1880s, shortly after the birth of their third son, Herbert, Ida and Isidor began to cast about for another, less crowded location.[3] One locale that seemed promising, even idyllic, for it was distant from the problems inherent in big city life, was at the northernmost tip of Manhattan. Isidor and Ida bought a country house on Bottom Road in Inwood. The area was bounded on the north and east sides by the Harlem River, and on the west by the Hudson River. It did not take long, however, for Ida to discover that it was far from ideal. While she may have enjoyed the peace and quiet, it was too isolated, too lonely for her children. They had no one to play with but each other. And it was too far from Isidor's place of business to be practical, too hard for him to come home at an early hour, and even harder to host the many guests they so enjoyed.

The final straw broke the day a goat butted their two-year-old son Herbert in the abdomen and he lay unconscious. Ida was frantic, for there was no medical help nearby. Jesse had to be sent galloping on horseback to fetch a doctor. Although Herbert recovered, the family simply could not remain at Inwood. It was too far from hospitals, doctors, friends, and civilization to suit Ida.[4] They would have to move once more.

In late 1883 or early 1884, they put the Inwood home on the market and began to search for a new place to live. As it happened, a man named Nathaniel Meyers had put his house up for sale. It was large and rambling, perfect for the Strauses' growing family, and came with several acres of land conveniently located at 2745 Broadway on the corner of 105th Street in a section known as Bloomingdale on the upper west side of New York.[5] A man named Matthew Brennan, a former New York fireman, who had become sheriff under Boss Tweed, and gained notoriety a decade earlier as the man who arrested the Boss himself, had built it in 1866. Far from being a man of principle, however, he allowed Tweed a "prison" that consisted of a luxurious suite of rooms in a hotel owned by the Boss's son. Brennan himself was later arrested and imprisoned for fraud and for allowing another prisoner to escape.[6] The *New York Times* remarked that he had preferred to ingratiate himself with the Tweed gang rather "than to perform his duty to the public, whose servant he has solemnly pledged to be."[7]

The Strauses brought a new and very different reputation to the house, which they would own for the rest of their lives. They moved in, according to Isidor's recollection, on July 24, 1884.[8] The property ran eastward from West End Avenue along 105th Street to upper Broadway. At that time the area was still relatively rural, with fields and parks where the children could play, though not so rustic or far away from the store. The new house was far more accessible, with one-horse streetcar lines serving the neighborhood. It was, however, more sparsely inhabited and with far less traffic than had been the case with their 55th Street home.

The new property struck a happy medium between city and country life, and proved to be ideal for the family. It was a virtual farm, with an apple orchard, pear trees, and grape arbors, as well as goats, chickens, cows, a vegetable garden, and a barn they used as a stable near the corner at West End Avenue. An empty field provided the perfect site for neighborhood baseball games, and a there was a rocky area where the boys loved to climb.[9] Best of all, it offered what Isidor described as "fresh air and sun-shine...beyond the power of any neighbor to interfere with."[10]

Ida settled contentedly into her new domestic life, where she reigned supreme. She refused to hire a housekeeper, who in most wealthy homes of the era, was the highest-ranking female staff member, the person in charge of the other female servants.[11] Ida preferred to instruct the servants herself. It was a big job, for the household staff was ample. There was Patrick MacDermott, their Irish Catholic coachman and the most popular staff member with the children. He was their riding instructor, a man extremely reliable and devoted to the entire family, especially the children. He did everything from nursing them through childhood illnesses to making them snowshoes out of barrel staves during the Great Blizzard of 1888. He took them to school or to railway stations when they went to college, and met them when they came home. He drove them to their weddings and was a family fixture who helped to look after Isidor when Ida was in the mountains or at the seashore with the children. He tended to help out wherever he was needed, even packing Isidor's bags when he planned a trip.[12] The only thing Patrick refused to do was drive Isidor's Rochet-Schneider Landolet, his first automobile and one of the few in New York at the time. It was made in France by a company that in the mid-1890s began producing luxury vehicles that featured brass, leather, and hand-crafted wood fittings. Although the automobile was noted for simplicity and silence, Patrick would have none of it. He considered himself a coachman, not a chauffeur. Others who worked at the Straus home included a German nursemaid they called simply "Fraulein" in their correspondence, a French tutor for all the children, a German tutor for the girls only, a gardener, and six "indoor servants" (possibly including Fraulein).[13]

The house itself was a three-storied, rambling structure as understated and unassuming as its owners. Painted a brownish-gray color with darker trim, it tended to fade into the landscape. Its wide porches were partially hidden by a huge wisteria vine that grew at the front of the house and a portion of the front porch was enclosed in glass, for use in the cooler months. An ample basement provided a place for the children to play on rainy days.

One approached the house from the street by way of a circular drive that surrounded a cast-iron fountain. At the top of the circle, high stone steps led up to the front door. Inside, a long central hallway (allegedly "at least twenty yards"), perfect for children's races, divided the house.[14] The entire downstairs was given over to entertainment for the family and the many guests who graced the Straus home for more than twenty-five years. To the right of the hallway were a drawing room and a billiard room, the latter an unusual addition to the New York home. To the left of the corridor was the library, where Isidor spent many evenings reading about economic issues. Ida would join him before the fire, reading volumes of the Jewish Publication Society of America, of which she was one of the few female members, or else engaging in more domestic tasks, such as darning Isidor's socks and just enjoying their quiet time together.[15] An adjacent dining room and pantry provided a spot for many stimulating conversations and sumptuous meals.

The house was always filled with guests, whose invitations were issued, according to one source, "solely by a possible guest's capacity for being interesting."[16] Often Isidor would invite friends at the last minute to share dinner with his family, but Ida never complained. She was a consummate and interested hostess who enjoyed the visitors as much as he did. One guest, Virginia Brooks McKelway, a graduate of the 1899 Woman's Law Class from New York University, commented, "Her hospitality was marked by generosity and elegance rather than by great elaboration. At her board one met with the finest minds of the day, people interested in the things which stand for progress, both Jew and Gentile."[17] Even when guests were not present, the house was lively with six children and all their activities. On frequent occasions the family enjoyed musical evenings, with Herbert on the cello, Sara on the piano, and the other children participating with their chosen instruments. Although Jesse never claimed to be musically gifted, he could, as he put it, "make a more or less melodious noise" on the viola or violin and the more popular mandolin and guitar.[18]

All the bedrooms were upstairs. Isidor had a porcelain bathtub, said to be the first such tub in New York City, installed in the bathroom. To be sure the floors were strong enough to support the weight of the filled tub, Isidor had the beams below reinforced, causing the bathroom floor to rise six inches above the rest of the second story. Typically, small rooms for servants would occupy the third floor, a part of which also served as an attic. The house was finished "with a mansard roof, particularly ornate dormers and a six-sided cupola...all topped with spiky iron cresting," a cupola that could be seen from as far away as the 81st Street Elevated Train Station.[19]

Ida's life, while her children were young, centered around their New York home. She seldom joined her husband in his travels outside the city, except for their summer family vacations. One rare exception occurred in 1889, when she accompanied

Isidor on what he expected to be "a short trip southward."[20] It would be his first visit to the South since the Civil War. He indicated to Oscar that is was "[w]onderful to be told my wife will accompany me." Oscar would have understood, for by this time he too was married. Isidor clearly wanted Ida with him, and he indicated to his brother that "it would not be surprising to me if in our meanderings we should land in Talbotton."[21] Ida was able to "leave with an easy mind," when Oscar's mother-in-law agreed to "take charge" of their household in their absence and because the children were "all in such good condition." They set out on February 11 with a brief visit to Washington, where Ida had never been before and where, Isidor indicated, they would stay "as long as she enjoys it." [22] It would be a special treat for her, especially since they visited President Grover Cleveland and his wife Frances during their final days in the White House.[23]

Isidor had intended to take only a week's vacation, but in fact they did not return home until March 4, when they boarded a steamer from Savannah to New York. Unfortunately we have few details from this trip, which were contained in a lost letter from Ida to her sister-in-law, Oscar's wife, Sarah. Isidor described it as "a triumphal march through the south" [sic], during which they were "treated with marked distinction." He mentions a brief stopover in Atlanta, during which they met Henry Grady, whom Isidor describes as "the most prominent figure in the whole South."[24] They left Atlanta that same day, presumably to visit Columbus and Talbotton, but soon returned to Atlanta where they were both invited to a luncheon at Grady's home. A handful of other guests included Georgia's governor, John Brown Gordon, and Atlanta's mayor, John Thomas Glenn. Following the luncheon, the mayor treated them to a tour of the city. All in all, they traveled about three weeks. It was the longest trip outside of New York Ida had ever taken, except for their summer trips to the seashore or the Adirondacks. Her first trip back to Europe would not occur until 1892, when she and Isidor spent eleven weeks on the continent, most of it in Italy.[25] But such trips for Ida were still the exception. Now, while she had a young family, her primary ambitions were to maintain a loving household, raise healthy, well-educated, and honorable children, and support her husband in all his undertakings, including his nostalgic visit to Georgia—all endeavors in which she certainly excelled.

In the summer months, however, the family, like many New Yorkers, liked to get away altogether from the unhealthy heat of the city. Although there were many resort hotels in the cooler regions of the Adirondacks and coastal areas, the wealthiest New Yorkers began to acquire their own private summer homes. It became the trend among affluent Jews particularly in the wake of a well-known anti-Semitic incident that had occurred at the Grand Union Hotel in Saratoga Springs, New York, in June 1877. A great deal of publicity surrounded the incident, for it involved the well-known banker, Joseph Seligman, who, along with J. P. Morgan and the House of Rothschild, had recently helped the United States recover from its war debt. Prior to the Civil War, there had been relatively little overt discrimination against Jews in America. Seligman's family had, in fact, stayed at the Grand Union without incident for a decade, when suddenly they were informed that they were no longer welcome, thanks to a policy recently established by the hotel's new owner, a well-known anti-Semite, Judge Henry Hilton. The incident brought on a wave of anti-Semitism among Adirondack resorts and a reaction among affluent Jews who did not wish to subject their families to the possibility of such indignation.[26]

Nathan Straus had purchased a cottage at Lower Saranac Lake in the Adirondacks, but when he, like Seligman, was turned away from a Gentile hotel at Lakewood, New Jersey, in July 1889, in response, he bought a great deal of land in proximity to that establishment to build another luxury hotel that opened its doors to everyone.[27] By January 1890, Nathan was already buying up property for his new project. Ida wrote Isidor, "he will soon own nearly all of Lakewood if he continues."[28] That same year he and Max Nathan formed a company along with multiple investors called the Lakewood Hotel Company. The magnificent Lakewood Hotel with adjacent cottages was complete and ready for occupancy in 1891, and Nathan offered the use of a hotel cottage to his friend, former President Grover Cleveland and his wife Frances, during its first season. They would return frequently.

But it was Nathan's earlier purchase of the Adirondack cottage that served as impetus for Isidor to buy a home next door so that their two families could vacation together, which they did for the next several years. Another and perhaps even more important incentive for Isidor to buy a private cottage was his expressed aversion "to these lively fashionable resorts," like the West End Hotel & Cottages at Long Branch on the Jersey shore, where his family sometimes vacationed, often with Isidor's father and sister Hermine's family. In June 1887, Isidor wrote Oscar that, while he and Ida planned to go to the shore, "our boys are up at Nathan's mountain home."[29] Isidor also occasionally visited Nathan at Lower Saranac Lake, as he did when he joined his sons, who were already there, in August 1886. Even then, he may have been considering the possibility of buying something in the area. There is no question that he liked it. As he informed Ida, "This place, the house and its surroundings as well as the temperature and pure atmosphere impress me fully as favorably as ever, and I am more convinced than ever that it is the place of places for our boys as well as for every one that seeks thorough benefit from summer vacations."[30]

Although both Ida and the children seemed "to thrive at the seashore" and even Isidor found surf bathing "exhilarating," by 1890 they had purchased a small mountain cottage of their own, which they called the "Villa Plaisance," and which stood next door to Nathan's house on Lower Saranac Lake.[31] While Ida enjoyed their Adirondack cottage and especially its positive effect on her health, she seems to have preferred the seashore. She had written to Isidor the year before they bought the Villa Plaisance that she was "giddy" with satisfaction during her week at Long Branch. Her only complaint was having to endure the unwanted attentions of boorish guests.[32] But if Isidor wanted to buy a cottage in the Adirondacks, then the Adirondacks it would be. And she would come to love it as much as he did.[33]

With six children, ranging in ages from the oldest, Jesse, who turned eighteen on June 25, to the youngest, Vivian, who would be only four in August, their summer house bustled with activity from morning to evening. While they may have thrived at the seashore, they delighted in the mountains as well.

Isidor was frequently absent, for he and his brother Nathan took turns minding the store, while their families enjoyed their mountain lake homes together. Ida was in charge of Villa Plaisance, and, though she had a firm hand in managing the household, she also took pleasure in the wilderness with her children. Together they picnicked on the sandy beach, fished, and rowed for exercise. But she and Isidor always put their children's education before their entertainment, sending them to the Sachs Collegiate Institute, one of the best and most demanding schools in New York, and setting extremely high expectations.[34] Both parents took responsibility for overseeing the children's education. Isidor set for them strict schedules and requirements. For example, a letter to Percy during his first year at Harvard was typical. He reminded his son to exercise "at the appointed hour" and adopt "the habit of a bath every morning." Isidor always held to a regular routine and recommended that his son begin his Harvard years with "a systematic course in everything you undertake."[35]

In Isidor's absence, it was Ida who supervised their activities and lessons. She urged them to write letters to their father, read every day, practice their musical instruments, and engage in constructive activities with others around the lake. When twelve-year-old Sara finished reading *Jane Eyre*, her mother encouraged her to write about the book. Sara informed her father on August 27, 1890, that she had "already written five pages."[36] In the summer of 1891, Ida hired a tutor, a Mr. Bosworth, for all the Straus children, her own and Lina's, and the young teacher began his duties on a rainy July 3. Ida wrote her husband the next day, "I hear one after another asking questions...Percy, Jerome, Herby, Sissy, Sara and Minnie are grouped around him and form quite a pretty looking picture."[37]

The children weren't always cooperative. Ida dealt with them in a loving, but firm, way. She notes in the letter cited above that "Jerome fought with all his might and main against taking part" in the tutoring sessions, "but I hear his voice now as much as any of the others, which shows that he is interested enough." No doubt, since she was writing on the fourth of July the children would have preferred to be involved in other activities. "Herby feels himself very much wronged not to have a single fire-cracker with which to celebrate the day, but will get bravely over his injured feelings," his mother commented with wry humor.

While Ida always placed the needs of the family first, as was expected of a good wife and mother of her era, there is no question that she was a sensitive woman with multiple talents of her own, though she rarely took time to indulge them. But she was a gifted artist, and several of her drawings have survived to demonstrate her remarkable ability. We also have one surviving poem, written in the 1880s in support of Russian Jews, which, judged by the standards of the times, demonstrates a clear mastery of form, meter, and language.[38] She also had a penchant for languages, much more so than Isidor or their son Jesse, who struggled with French but never gave up.[39] She also enjoyed all types of theatre and often took her children and friends with her.[40] However, while she encouraged her children to develop their talents and knowledge, even when they resisted, her own talents and creative desires were always secondary in her view.

Thus, summer vacation notwithstanding, the children were never exempt from studies and lessons of various types. And her efforts bore fruit in their lives. By the time Herbert was a freshman at Harvard, despite his earlier preference for firecrackers over study, he was not only taking upper-division French, he had also become a talented musician.[41] While he did not make the football team, he was "put right in the orchestra," Harvard's Pierian Sodality, without even an audition. "Ernest Sachs evidently saw to that—he is first cellist and Secretary and knew how I played."[42] And Jesse, despite his struggles with French, was persuaded to persist—which proved extremely useful in his later life when Franklin D. Roosevelt named him ambassador to France in 1933.

The same year Ida and Isidor began to vacation at Lower Saranac Lake, other prominent Jewish families established summer homes in the area as well. Among them was the Max Nathan family. On the other side of the lake, on Shingle Bay, in 1889, the Nathans had joined with five other New York families to build a camp complex called Knollwood, which has been described as a rustic masterpiece. Designed by William L. Coulter for the families of Nathan, Daniel Guggenheim, Louis Marshall, George Blumenthal, Elias Ashiel, and Abram N. Stein, it consisted of a large boathouse, a "casino," and six identical cottages (except for trim), each with two and a half stories.[43]

Knollwood was occupied for the first time in 1890, the summer Jesse Straus turned eighteen and the first summer the Strauses spent in their new cottage at Lower Saranac Lake. Jesse, who had just completed his freshman year at Harvard, did not come there with his family in July.[44] He spent most of the summer traveling in Europe with his cousin Lee Kohns, before finally arriving in late August at the Villa Plaisance, where his mother waited anxiously for his return. She and Isidor had received a letter from Lucie Gutherz Blun's second husband, Edward Mammels-dorff, who had seen Jesse in Paris "and left him in the best of spirits."[45] It was Jesse's first trip to Europe without his parents, and Mr. Mammelsdorff indicated that he was handling the French language quite adequately.

One can feel Ida's pride and eagerness to see her son, though she attempted to control it, writing on August 26 to her husband who went to meet Jesse's ship, "Am I not a very patient mama to wait here so quietly?" But she could not fully conceal her anxiousness:

> I confess I would like to know when he is coming, though when this reaches you, I hope he will be here...I look forward to a very interesting time with my boy, and if he relates as well as he has written his experiences in outline we will have enough to talk about...I will not be in suspence [sic] very long any more, for today or tomorrow Jesse will surely make his appearance.[46]

In fact, Jesse arrived that very afternoon, three days before his youngest sister's birthday. His mother basked in his presence. "I expected he would be more tanned and travel-stained," she wrote, "but he is like usual no stouter, perhaps a little broader. He is full of his experiences and is giving us the benefit little by little...He brought the children and each useful presents he is so practical."[47] Jesse was never frivolous, not even as a child. He was perhaps the son who was, in character, most like his father. He never had to be reminded of his duties. In fact, as a child he would leave his games with his New York pals promptly at 4:30 P.M. each afternoon to study. As a result, he took much griping and teasing at first, but he never wavered from his duty and soon silenced his friends.[48] Of all the Straus children, he was the one his parents could readily count on to go to Europe on his own at the age of eighteen and benefit from the trip. Isidor was always reminding him to relax and frequently commented: "Jesse never had to learn manners, for he was born a gentleman."[49] On his birthday the following year, his mother wrote to his father, "I think we may congratulate each other my darling for having successfully raised him thus far, and hope and pray that all our hopes and desires for our boy—for all our darlings may be realized."[50]

Jesse had arrived at their Adirondack home a day later than Ida had expected, for he had stopped overnight in Saratoga where his grandfather was staying. While Ida waited for her oldest son to appear, she had filled her time with writing to her beloved Isidor, enjoying her children, and entertaining a variety of people, including the servants. On the evening of August 24 she gave a ball for the household help in the family boathouse. "I furnished the refreshments and paid for the fiddler and they are all in ecstasies."[51]

The Straus home at Saranac Lake, like the one in New York, was often filled with guests. On September 4, Ida wrote to Isidor that "The mayor [of New York, Hugh Grant] and Judge Holme are due this morning and Oscar and Sarah this afternoon. Oscar telegraphed yesterday that they were both coming, so the place will be gay for a few days."[52]

It was never hard to keep the children entertained. There was so much for them to do at Lower Saranac Lake. Percy and his cousin Jerome, whom she called "Puss" and "Jerry" in her letters, frequently went rowing, sailing, and fishing with varying degrees of success. Both boys were fourteen that summer and eager to try their independence and manhood. Occasionally, guides would take them deer hunting, and on at least two occasions Jerome brought home a live fawn.[53] Although they had barely reached adolescence, Percy, perhaps in a desire to assert "adult" prerogatives, decided that summer to change his name from

"Percy Solomon" to "Percy Selden Straus," a name he used for the rest of his life.[54]

Even before Jesse's arrival, his mother had made the acquaintance of the Nathan family across the lake. She had written to her son about their daughters, encouraging him, as soon as he had settled in, to row over and meet them. "There are two very nice girls here," she had informed him. "When you come up, you'll like them, I think." And indeed he did. Jesse, as a college boy back from a tour of Europe on his own, must have seemed quite attractive to the Nathan girls. By the end of August, he was spending much of his free time "across the lake" and seemed to latch on to any excuse to be there. Only a few days after his arrival, the servants from the various lake families were using the Knollwood boathouse for a helps' dance. Ida wrote her husband that "Jesse wanted to remain to see the country lasses and lads swing each other, contingent of course upon an invitation [by the Nathans] to supper." The invitation came, and he made "an evening of it."[55]

By early September Jesse and the Nathan girls had become fast friends. There were many young people around the lake that summer, and he enjoyed hosting them on various occasions. His mother entertained their parents while Jesse took charge of the young folk. On September 2 Ida wrote to Isidor that "This afternoon we have the whole house from across the lake. Jesse has the younger members this morning, two daughters of [the] Nathans, the Limburgers and Borsch boys." Such steady entertaining and festivity could be arduous, and by the end of that particularly long day, Ida was too exhausted to attend a celebration of the Nathans' wedding anniversary that evening and sent her excuses. "I feel very much fatigued after today's entertainment and then the night is so dark that I felt more like being on dry land."[56] The idea of being on the water at night held no appeal for her, though, of course, Jesse attended.

On September 8, the young people arranged for an all-day picnic. "They are going to row up to the village and then drive up, and have the boats brought up by some wagon. It is a distance of thirteen miles and will take them from ten A.M. to six P.M."[57] The event was evidently a raving success, and Ida reported: "Jesse had the two Misses Nathan in his boat so you may imagine he was happy."[58] By the following year, Jesse was apparently, at least in everyone's mind, paired with Belle, the older of the two girls. Ida wrote Isidor that "Aunt Lucy's [Lina's sister] greatest delight is to tease Jesse about Belle Nathan."[59] But it was the younger of the two, Irma, a petite and bright young woman who spoke French and Italian, as well as German and English, with whom Jesse would eventually fall in love. And in July 1895, only one month after Belle Nathan's marriage to Walter Eugene Beer, Jesse and Irma announced their engagement.[60]

Although Ida enjoyed the months in their summer home with the children, her one regret was that her husband was absent for many weeks at a time. She missed him terribly. Her longing is evident in her letters, which give us an intimate glimpse into their relationship. On the rare days she doesn't receive a letter, she is anxious. "Your Thursday and Friday's letters reached me on Saturday after two days fasting from news of you."[61] He has the same reaction when a day or two passes without word from Ida and the children. Sometimes he writes more than one letter a day in order to make her always a part of his world.[62] On occasions when he is expected and is unavoidably detained as he was in mid-September, Ida's distress is palpable. "To say that I am disappointed at your not coming tomorrow as your dispatch indicates hardly expresses my feelings. Still I know that you would not remain away if it were not necessary so I resign myself."[63] When he finally arrived almost a week later, she was counting on their being together for at least a month, perhaps longer. She closes her last letter to him that summer: "goodbye I hope for the last time on paper. Let me say welcome instead is the ardent wish of your devoted Ida."[64]

A few days before Isidor's arrival in September 1890, his family closed their small summer home and moved into the larger house of Nathan and Lina next door. Lina had left the week before to return to New York in anticipation of her husband's arrival to take up the reins of the family business there, while Isidor, in turn, vacationed with his family in the Adirondacks. Ida had at first resisted moving, not wanting to impose on her brother-in-law and his wife in any way, but the children were eager and persistent. Ida informed Isidor on September 15:

> "[E]verybody has prevailed upon me to move over…to the other house and I have at last yielded to their entreaties and am doing so now. It has turned very much cooler, having rained almost incessantly for over a week and Sarah and Oscar think our house is a little damp. Lina mentioned the advisability of it as well as Nathan which promoted [persuaded] me more than anything else as I would not like to occupy the house without their sanction."[65]

In the end, everyone was delighted with the move, even Ida, who, as their daughter Sara wrote her father, "found out at last that she is a good deal more comfortable here than she was in the small cottage."[66] Sara's younger sister, Minnie, thought that the best thing about it was that "we don't have to practise [sic] any more as the parlor is going to be closed up." [67]

Once in a while Ida's letters contained a flirtatious hint of mock jealousy, as when she writes in reaction to Isidor's having received a note from an actress named Miss [Nadage] Doree, "Won't I keep detectives on your track now, if you don't come up soon?"[68] In an undated letter, most likely written not long after the previous one, she tells him that she is "following out your line of conduct and I chose no less a personage than Tony Pastor on whom to bestow my smiles which he reciprocated with compound interest."[69] However, even though she occasionally teases him about various female friends, she never doubts his fidelity, nor he hers. "Mrs. Limburger called over yesterday and told me she had seen you very often in the park and…every time she met you, you had another lady, and only upon her assurance that they were good looking ones, was I satisfied."[70] There is even a suggestion of pride in her tone that her husband can interest so many attractive women. She has no doubt, however, that he always prefers her to any other. He spent most of his time, however, with business associates and male friends, such as the mayor of New York, Nathan's good friend, Hugh Grant. "You must have had a pleasant evening yesterday, with the mayor, I am delighted with your manner of spending your grass widowhood."[71]

Ida and Isidor were determined not to be separated for such a long time the following year. Not only did he arrive for his annual summer vacation the second week in August, he also met her in Saratoga in July, where the two enjoyed a ten-day rendezvous and celebrated their twentieth wedding anniversary without the children between July 6 and 16. When Ida returned to Saranac Lake on Thursday, July 16, the "whole family met her at the station and escorted her home with eclat. Since her return we have been very busy listening to her accounts of the trip"—at least those parts of the trip she was willing to share with her children.[72] For a while afterwards she basked in the memory. Her satisfaction was perceptible even to her children. Percy wrote to his father shortly after her return, "Mamma told us that you enjoyed yourself so much in Saratoga, and she seems to feast on that enjoyment for she seems perfectly content to sit on the piazza and sew."[73] However content she may have seemed on the outside, she was already filled with desire to be with her husband again. That same day she wrote her own letter:

My own darling papa;

This place is so beautiful today one might easily stretch the imagination and dream that the whole world were a paradise like this one. After all each individual makes his own paradise and helps to prepair [sic] it for his surroundings, and no one does that more effectively than my darling.

I am in a very home-sick mood as you perceive, the recollection of our late honeymoon always awakens such a feeling of home-sickness for my darling.

We are all, mamas and babies, so well and happy up here, and I only want you to make any paradise complete.

Your own devoted

Mama[74]

Even though they had been married for two decades, their passion for one another had strengthened through the years. Isidor wrote to Ida that "the few happy days" they had spent together at Saratoga had "made a new man" of him.[75] They were both looking forward to more of the same when he arrived for a lengthy visit. "I will not take less than 4 weeks," she informed him.[76] She had another two weeks to wait, but she savored every moment of anticipation. "In no respect is my imagination so fertile as when it wanders in the direction of my darling, fertile in the picturing of the happy days in store for me." In that same letter, she informs him that his "best girl sends you back some of those imaginary kisses and hugs."[77] In her next letter she notes him that she expects "hugs and kisses with compound interest and will pay you back in spot cash," playfully teasing him in his own mercantile language.

As their days of anticipated separation become fewer, she rejoices that "our imaginary lovemaking will soon be at an end that we will not require writing paper as our intermediary any more."[78] She writes on Friday, August 7, expecting him to arrive at the beginning of the following week, "Now, my darling, I hope our correspondence is at an end, and that we are in for a good, jolly time together."[79]

Whenever they were separated, the two were always especially concerned for the other's welfare. Ida reminded Isidor not to forget his digitalis and capsules.[80] And she tells him on one occasion that "You were mistaken in supposing I was anxious to have Jesse up here—on the contrary I...feel very safe in having him with you to watch over you."[81] As much as she loved Jesse and longed for his company, Isidor's welfare was more important to her. When Nathan had a horseback riding accident in August 1890, she expressed concern that Isidor should be careful himself. "Don't ride but take a drive whenever you can."[82] She cautions him again in the very next letter to use "the horses as often as possible but for driving and not for horse-back riding. Nathan's experience should be an additional warning."[83] By the same token, he frets about her headaches and coughs, though she always assures him that she is fine, not wanting to worry him when they are apart. She seems to suffer more from his absence than anything else.

Even though her husband was often not present, the lake cottages provided a good place and pleasant times to be with her sister-in-law. Never had the two families been closer. Ida and Lina arrived with their children at the lake on June 24, 1891, after an overnight journey by train. A Mr. Ebbe, apparently a caretaker, met them at the depot with a buggy to take them to their home. But a single buggy was far from adequate: "It took three wagons besides the buggy to take up our caravan," Ida reported. It was not surprising, considering that by now Lina had not only her older children, Sissie and Jerome, but also a pair of babies—two-year-old toddler, Charley, named for then Macy's partner, Charles B. Webster, but later renamed Nathan Straus Jr., who had been born on May 27, 1889, and his nine-month-old brother, Hugh Grant Straus, born September 21, 1890, and named for his father's handsome and debonair friend, the mayor of New York. The two women clearly had their hands full.

Fortunately they found everything, houses and grounds, "in the very best order." Spreading out over the two houses. Lina and her children occupied their usual rooms; Ida and little Vivie stayed in the blue room of the larger cottage, while her daughters shared "a large room on the third floor with Sissy"; Percy and Herbert moved into their parents' bedroom in the smaller cottage. Fraulein, the nanny, occupied the girls' room next door to the boys, and the Strauses' three servants stayed in their usual room in the smaller cottage. They took their meals at Lina's, with "the two cooks working together in perfect harmony."[84]

But these happy times, which Ida and Lina shared with each other and alternately with their respective husbands, would soon come to an end. On February 22, 1893, Nathan and Lina's oldest son, Jerome, who had been such an important part of all their lives and such a close friend of Percy, died of pericarditis and double pneumonia, just six days before his sixteenth birthday. His parents were heartbroken. Memories of the wonderful times they had all spent together at Saranac Lake with Jerome were so strong that neither Nathan, with his delicate nerves, nor Lina could ever go back. They had all loved Jerome. They had fished with him, boated with him, and enjoyed so much fun together that it would never be the same for any of them again.

Two summers before Jerome's death, Jesse had gone camping with one of the lake staff guides. On July 18, 1891, he wrote to his mother, asking permission to have his brother Percy and his cousin Jerome join him on his camping expedition. "Let me assure you," he wrote, pleading their case, "that there is not the slightest danger from guns, boats or anything else. I shall be very careful & obey all instructions. Not bathe, not wash, not swim, in short I shall do nothing but eat & breathe & sleep. The only risks I can imagine could arise from these 3 activities are doing them to excess, and I shall be careful in that respect. Do not worry as there is no cause for it."[85] He was concerned that the expense was too much for one person alone, "that the other boys ought to share the pleasure with him," Ida informed her husband. His invitation "was just enough to fire those two boys brimful with longing to go." But the two mothers wanted Isidor's permission. "Neither Lena [sic] nor I wanted to take the responsibility of allowing them without consulting you," Ida told him.[86] Although he was always kind to his children, Isidor did not indulge their every whim, and he thought Percy and Jerome were too young for the responsibilities of such an expedition. Although the two boys were disappointed, both Ida and Lina were quite content with his decision. Lina even wrote him a letter of thanks. "I would have only let Jerome go with a very hearty heart," she said, "and I was wishing that you would not consent."[87] While this denied pleasure of a late-summer camping trip might later have weighed heavy on all their hearts, Jerome, as a boy of fifteen, like his cousin Percy, quickly forgot his disappointment and moved on to other pleasures.

Nathan and Lina rented their cottage at Saranac Lake the summer after Jerome's death, then put it up for sale. They would eventually buy another summer home in the Thousand Islands. Of Isidor's family, only Ida and Jesse, who had recently graduated from Harvard, returned briefly in 1893, and they did not arrive until October 12, having also rented their cottage for the summer. "One is so forcibly reminded of Jerome [on] all sides," Jesse wrote his father.[88] This time they stayed in their own Villa Plaisance, the name of which, Ida noted, "must be changed." It was no longer a place of pleasure, as its name suggested. It was, she wrote "as beautiful as ever, but how sad it makes me feel."[89] Jerome's clothes still hung in the closets of the larger house next door. It was heartbreaking, Ida thought, that "the care and forethought and heart-love, which every portion of the house bespeaks on Lina's part" should "go to strangers."[90] But Lina would not return to the house. In fact, even in New York she rarely went out. When Isidor succeeded in talking her into an outing with him, Ida heartily approved. "Tell her she is doing me a favor in going out with you, besides giving you pleasure."[91]

Eventually, Ida and Isidor also sold their cottage at Lower Saranac Lake, and within a few years, began the construction of another, larger summer home in Elberon, on the coast of New Jersey, not far from Long Branch. This stretch of Jersey shoreline had become a well-known Jewish summer colony—a "Jewish Newport," as one writer referred to it.[92] Ida's sister Amanda and Isidor's sister Hermine often vacationed there with members of their families. It was the area where Ida had been so happy during previous vacations. The house was under construction by June 1901. Ida decided not to accompany Isidor on their by-now annual trip to Europe, for she wanted to be there to oversee the progress of the new house. She encouraged her husband to go nonetheless and to take as his traveling companion their oldest daughter, Sara, who had recently graduated from Barnard College.[93] Sara was delighted.

Isidor had been tired when they left in early May, and Ida thought "the prospect of your eight days of complete rest on ship board" would do him good.[94] It was an exciting trip for Sara. Her only disappointment came at the hand of the British royal family. Her father was scheduled to attend a reception given by the new king, Edward VII, at Windsor Castle, and she thought she was going to be able to accompany him; however, at the last minute, the ladies were excluded. Since the court was still in mourning for the death of the king's mother, Queen Victoria, royal protocol determined that female attendance would be inappropriate. While Sara was crestfallen, she was determined to find pleasure in the rest of the trip. She and her father enjoyed London together, and she accompanied him to Oxford where they lunched at what

Isidor referred to as "the Common" with one of the professors.[95] Then they went on to Scotland in a week or so to visit Andrew Carnegie at Skibo Castle. Not a bad trip after all.

During their absence, Ida busied herself with social engagements, theatre outings, tending to family interests, and, above all, the new summer cottage. She took her sister-in-law Lina to see it on May 13. "She was delighted with the house," Ida wrote to Isidor and Sara. She "thinks it grand, but she says that except the main hall, her rooms are every bit as large as ours, including her dining room." At first, the work seemed to be going very slowly, but Ida was encouraged by the visit with Lina: "I begin to see daylight in the work and hope I will be able to carry out my plan of having all workmen out of the house by June 15."[96] On another occasion she took her daughter-in-law, Irma, who was less enthusiastic about the house, though it was growing on her, she admitted. Irma "was very much pleased with the babies['] rooms and thinks on the whole it is a very fine place."[97] Jesse and Irma had had their first child, Beatrice Nathan Straus, on September 27, 1897, and their second, Jesse Isidor (called "Jack"), on January 13, 1900.[98] The new house was much larger and more comfortable than the old one at Saranac Lake and was ideal for gatherings of their growing family.

Before the beginning of 1902, the new house was complete. Always determined to look at the positive aspects of life, Ida and Isidor decided to name it "Sunnyside." It would indeed be the site of many joy-filled family occasions, including the marriages of their two oldest daughters, Sara and Minnie, both to physicians. Sara would marry first on October 12, 1904. The groom, Alfred Fabian Hess, son of a New York publisher, Selmar Hess, had received his M.D. from Columbia University's College of Physicians and Surgeons in 1901 and would eventually set up practice as a New York pediatrician. A special train brought 200 guests from New York to Elberon. After the ceremony, performed by Dr. Schulman, Alfred and Sara traveled to Europe where the young physician was continuing his medical studies[99] The wedding was very much a family affair, with Minnie serving as Sara's maid of honor and Vivian as one of her bridesmaids. Jesse, Percy, and Herbert were among the groomsmen.

Another groomsman, who would soon become a member of the family, was Dr. Richard Weil, son of the real estate broker, Leopold Weil. He and Minnie would be married seven months later, like Sara and Alfred, at Sunnyside. Their wedding took place May 30, 1904, "in the great hall of the Straus villa, which resembled a rose garden."[100] This time Vivian was the maid of honor.

These joyful occasions were only a small sampling of the happy days Ida and Isidor would spend with children and an increasing number of grandchildren in the coming years. Sunnyside would definitely live up to its name.

The Macy's Story

L. Straus & Sons had boomed with success in the dynamic economy of New York City in the late nineteenth century.[1] Isidor and Nathan each had his own special role within the firm. Isidor took care of matters with his father on the home front and minded the necessary details of the store, while Nathan, whose creative mind and entrepreneurial spirit flourished best in roles outside the confines of the office, expanded his sales territory into the western states. He was so successful the firm needed to hire a second salesman.

At first the Strauses' wholesale business had specialized in the type of articles one would find in the "general country store," the type of stock that Lazarus had carried in his store in Talbotton, but as its owners grew more sophisticated and aware of the tastes and needs of New Yorkers, they began to specialize in "china, imported glassware and bric-a-brac."[2] This specialization is not surprising, for as early as 1869 they had been handed an account to handle purchases for the crockery and glassware company of Helbing & Straus. The latter was Lazarus's brother, Emanuel, who had also left Otterberg and settled in the United States. Heibling & Straus was the San Francisco company to which Isidor had traveled in 1871, not long before his marriage, when he missed the celebration of his and Ida's birthday.[3]

As L. Straus & Sons evolved, they soon ceased to purchase their wares from New York agents, as they had done at first; instead, they began to shop European markets and import their own wares. Nathan became their buyer abroad, as well as the outside man who helped the firm find new customers and markets. It was one of his buying trips in Germany that had led to his meeting and marrying Lina. In the process of making these changes, the Strauses converted their former suppliers into either customers or competitors.

During the 1870s and 1880s, L. Straus & Sons became one of the most successful importers of china, crystal, and crockery in New York. By the time Oscar graduated from Columbia Law School in 1873, he was obviously not interested in the business world. It may have been a consequence of his decision to set up a law practice that Lazarus, in 1874, had new articles of co-partnership drawn up for the firm of L. Straus and Sons. They did not include Oscar, but they did include for the first time, along with Isidor and Nathan, Hermine's husband, Lazarus Kohns, who had become like a brother to them. In fact, when the Straus brothers wrote to him over the years, they addressed him as "dear brother." The family was so closely knit that any significant disagreement was rare. And somehow, in spite of personality differences and tastes, their activities and interests meshed for the most part, for they all shared mutual respect, ambition and a desire to succeed.

In March of 1874 their best salesman, Nathan Straus, only twenty-six years old at the time, and weary of the constant travel his job required, showed up in the office of Rowland H. Macy, carrying a package containing two china plates under his arm. He was there to urge Macy to allow the Straus firm to open a concession in his store, where they could sell their china and crockery.[4] Using his always-persuasive charm, he managed to convince the well-established department store owner to permit the Strauses to lease a 25-by-100 foot area in the basement of Macy's. It was a major coup, though at the time neither Nathan nor Isidor had any idea where it would ultimately lead. They would soon have similar arrangements at stores in other cities, like Wanamaker's in Philadelphia, R. H. White in Boston, and

Woodward & Lothrop in Washington, D.C.[5] But it was the Macy's connection that would take an unexpected turn toward a success no one could have foreseen.

Nathan took on the new department as his special project for a time. It did not take long for the fledgling space at Macy's to prove itself. By the following autumn it was this new "department devoted to china ware" that was particularly touted in an article about a new "opening" of R. H. Macy & Co. that appeared September 24, 1874. Customers were advised "to seek the good offices of Mr. Nathan Strauss [sic], who has special charge of this department" and who "has just returned from Europe with extensive purchases, having traveled through France, Germany, Austria, and Italy in quest of the finest specimens."[6] It had not taken long for the small crockery section of the store, as well as a silver department for which they also provided the inventory, to catch on. The Straus concession soon became the most profitable part of the store.

The following year, Rowland Macy, whose son had disappointed him in many ways through the years, accepted the fact that Rowland Jr. had no interest in the store, and took in two younger partners. One of these, Abiel T. LaForge, said to be Macy's "surrogate son," had become his real son's commanding officer during the Civil War after Rowland Jr. ran away from home at the age of seventeen, joined the military, then deserted, and was subsequently court martialed. LaForge took the boy under his wing and looked after him as best he could, but in the end, the senior Macy recorded in his will that "I am grieved to say...that I cannot trust him [my son] with the care or management of any property."[7] In the end, it was LaForge, not Rowland, Jr., who became the elder Macy's partner.

Macy also took in his sister's son, Robert Macy Valentine, as a second junior partner shortly thereafter. Generally speaking, Valentine was less well liked than LaForge, and he trusted no one, not his employees, and evidently not the Strauses. Lazarus and his sons, however, had the full confidence and friendship of Rowland Macy and his wife Louisa. Their "families had Thanksgiving dinner together, celebrated the Fourth of July together, and even spent the summer at Rowland Macy's country home."[8]

Unfortunately, Macy's health had not been good for several years. He suffered from Bright's Disease and died unexpectedly in Paris on March 19, 1877, at the age of only fifty-four. Straus family sources contend that he was on a buying trip in Europe with Nathan Straus. His obituary, however, states that he and his family had gone to Europe at the recommendation of his doctors, leaving his store in the care of his two partners.[9]

Abiel LaForge was not in good health either, having suffered for more than a decade from tuberculosis he had contracted during the Civil War. The year after Macy's death, he too died unexpectedly from a sudden series of lung hemorrhages.[10]

The remaining partner, Macy's nephew Robert Valentine, took on a new partner, a cousin named Charles Webster, who was then a buyer at the store, having worked his way up from floor-walker.[11] For reasons that are not completely clear, though they may have stemmed from his general lack of trust, Valentine was not happy about the Strauses' rapid advancement and success at Macy's.[12] He may have seen them, and Nathan in particular who was well liked, gregarious, and two years his senior, as potential rivals. It was rumored that he did not plan to renew the Strauses' lease. Thus far, however, he had not informed them of that possibility. Fate would intervene. Valentine planned to sail to Europe on February 5, 1879, but took ill two days before his departure and was compelled to cancel his trip. Less than two weeks later, he too died unexpectedly on February 15, of what his obituary described as "congestion of the lungs."[13] He was only twenty-eight years old. His death was part of an uncanny series of events that significantly impacted the lives of the Isidor and Nathan.

In his will, Valentine left the bulk of his estate to his young wife, Ida, his sister's husband, Jerome B. Wheeler, and his cousin Charles B. Webster. He gave them, as his executors, the prerogatives to either continue his business or dispose of it.[14] Webster, already a partner, was pleased at the outset to have Wheeler's managerial skills alongside his own. With assurance that he would become a partner, Wheeler resigned his position at Holt & Co., commission merchants, to join Charles Webster at Macy's. Together they deemed it in their best interest to continue the business and not to oust the Strauses from their basement location, particularly in light of their obvious success, which brought many people into the store and accounted for about 20% of its sales. It was a wise decision.

Webster and Wheeler tried to run the store together for more than eight years, but they were difficult and unsettling times for them both. The two men had irreconcilable management styles, with Webster preferring a distant, top down style, while Wheeler liked to deal directly and in a more personal way with the employees. In addition, Wheeler was taking some of his assets from Macy's to invest in various enterprises out West, which did nor at all please Webster.[15] One final disagreement caused animosity between the two men. Webster had taken a special interest in an attractive floorwalker named Martha Toye and promoted her to superintendent after the death of the then-current superintendent. Because of her allegedly "arrogant manner," she was disliked by many of the employees, and when Webster was on a buying trip to Europe, Wheeler took the opportunity to fire her.[16] Webster was, of course, furious.

Before the end of 1887 it had become obvious to everyone who knew them that the partnership of Webster and Wheeler could not endure, so great were their conflicts. On October 15,

Isidor wrote to his brother Oscar that the two men "have such serious differences that they [have] very little personal intercourse with each other." They have, he noted, "agreed to separate, it is now a question as to which will buy the other out."[17] The matter was finally settled in mid-November. Although the Webster-Wheeler contract ran until the following May, Isidor notified Oscar on November 18 that "Charley has bought out Jerome to take effect the 1st of January." Isidor confided to his brother, "It is not known to any one excepting them and ourselves."[18]

The ink was hardly dry on the agreement before Charles Webster had second thoughts about whether he had taken on more than he could handle. Webster had asked Nathan's advice before buying out Wheeler, but Nathan insisted that he must make the decision "of his own accord, and it seemed to lay a little heavy on his stomach." Just one week after he had signed the contract for the buyout, Charley had dinner with Nathan and Lina. After dinner the two men drove together to the store and on the way he offered to let Nathan "have the whole business, as he was tired of it all." Nathan was definitely interested, but he asked Charley to sleep on it until the next day, and if he still wanted to sell, Nathan agreed that he would "either take half of it or the whole of it," but he made it clear that he preferred half.[19] Isidor too was concerned, that when Charley "got over the blues, being that he was not of an age, nor of a turn of mind, to content himself doing nothing, [he] would regret such a step." After thinking it over, Webster "concluded our advice to be sound" and offered the two of them Wheeler's share of 45% which they accepted without hesitation. They would later acquire an addition 5% from Webster to make up a half-ownership.[20] "This is about the whole thing in a nutshell," Isidor concluded. When he and Nathan bought Wheeler's interest in the business together, the two agreed they would only "contribute what is equivalent to one man's services in the cause."[21] They signed the contract on December 1, with the new arrangement to take effect January 1, 1888, the date of Wheeler's departure. "[A]ll the negotiations were conducted so rapidly & pleasantly that there is great rejoicing all around," Lee Kohns, the Strauses' nephew, wrote his uncle Oscar. Isidor took over new duties at Macy's the first of the year, and it was Lee who would "shoulder Uncle Isidor's duties" at L. Straus & Sons. Things would go on as usual with the exception that Isidor would be "obliged to remain uptown constantly."[22]

By this time, Jerome Wheeler had announced that he would devote his time to his western interests, which included several banks. On January 2 he gave a dinner at his home to say goodbye to the buyers and heads of the various departments and to assure them that the success of Macy's was attributable largely to their efforts. In saying his farewells, he told his guests that he had "endeavored to treat employes [sic] as men and women, and not as mere machines," a not-very-subtle dig at Webster, and that he thought his departure would be "softened by the knowledge that the two gentlemen who were to enter the firm–Messrs. Isidor and Nathan Straus–were possessed not only of business foresight but of kindly hearts."[23]

Thus it was that Isidor and Nathan became half owners of Macy's. Their father, Lazarus, for the first time in all their business dealings, was not involved. In fact, he was beginning to take less and less responsibility even in L. Straus & Sons. Even though he still went to the store every day, he was slowly withdrawing from active business.

Isidor wrote his first letter from his new Macy's office on January 7, 1888, to his brother Oscar. It is a particularly interesting letter that clarifies many aspects of their new undertaking. "I am now located uptown and will spent [sic] the most of my time up there. Matters are so organized downtown [at L. Straus & Sons] that my absence will not be noted." Even though Nathan would spend "a good deal of time uptown, [he] will, however, devote fully as much time downtown as he has heretofore done." It appears, therefore, that from the very first, Isidor would be the mainstay in the Macy's operation, but he noted that "this new move on the part of two of the members of the firm of L. Straus & Sons will form no change in the composition of that firm, nor in the relationship of Nathan and myself with the firm of L. Straus & Sons."[24] It was to remain, as it had always been, the family business.

At one point in his life, even Oscar had been briefly a partner in L. Straus & Sons. In 1881, six years before Isidor and Nathan became partners in Macy's, Oscar had abandoned his law practice to become a merchant. As Isidor would later describe the reasons: "On account of the condition of his health...his brothers, now his partners in business," made him "a tempting offer" to lure him away from "a profession which was fast undermining his health."[25] Oscar was growing weary of the demanding role of a trial lawyer. As he acknowledged in his autobiography, " the law is a jealous mistress," which left no time for marriage.[26] But as a young businessman, it was a different matter, and on January 22 1882, he became engaged to Sarah Lavanburg, the only daughter of Louis and Hannah Seller Lavanburg. The Straus family had not previously known the Lavanburgs, but Nathan wrote Oscar from Mannheim on February 19, after having learned of the engagement, that he had heard from a Mrs. Gutterman that Oscar's bride-to-be was "the handsomest, sweetest, smartest, etc etc etc in N.Y. If all this is true, then you have drawn the prize sure."[27] The young couple was married the following April 19 at the home of the bride's parents on West Forty-Sixth Street, near Fifth Avenue.

Unlike his brothers, however, Oscar was never really interested in business. He had originally chosen law as his vocation, in preference "to a business career because I disliked the idea of devoting my life to mere money-making, as business appeared to me then." He knew that he could always count on "the benefit of their [Isidor and Nathan's] brotherly interest and economic protection…should I need it."[28] At one point in his youth, he had fancied the life of a poet and continued, even as a lawyer, to write and publish some of his poems.[29] Thus, though he made some effort to join his brothers in the business world, his heart was never really in it. And the future would soon lead him in another direction.

Oscar had landed his first legal post when the firm's senior member, John E. Ward, "took me into his office largely out of friendship for Isidor."[30] It was in that position with the firm of Ward, Jones & Whitehead that he experienced his first glimpse of politics. John Ward had presided over the Democratic National Convention that nominated James Buchanan for president. He also served for several years as minister to China. Oscar did not remain long in that firm, and soon formed a partnership of his own with James A. Hudson in the firm of Hudson and Straus (later Sterne, Hudson & Straus and, finally, Sterne, Straus & Thompson). But the example of Ward evidently stuck in his mind, for he would soon find himself interested in similar activities. The year Oscar and Sarah were married, he made what he called his "debut in politics" as secretary to the executive committee of an independent group organized for the re-election of William R. Grace as mayor of New York.[31] In his first term Grace had shown himself too independent for Tammany Hall, which refused to support him for a second term. But the efforts of Oscar's group were successful. Grace ran as an independent and was elected. Oscar was bitten. Politics seemed to flow in his blood.

He took part in Grover Cleveland's presidential campaign in 1884, where he worked with Senator Arthur P. Gorman of Maryland, who chaired the Democratic National Convention and who would soon play a significant role in the life of this youngest Straus brother. During the campaign, Oscar, then thirty-four years old, helped to organize an impressive parade of forty thousand people representing the Merchants' and Business Men's Association, who marched from lower Broadway to Thirty-Fourth Street, thus fully engaging the business community in such an election activity for the first time. The election was close, but Cleveland won, and Oscar was further energized by the victory. His efforts had impressed various National Committee members, who indicated "they would be glad to further any ambition I might have."[32]

His foray into the business world would, thus, be brief. He was already gaining a reputation as a speaker and writer and, in fact, expanded a speech he had made to the Young Men's Hebrew Association into a book entitled *The Origin of the Republican Form of Government*, first published in 1885 and republished two years later and then again, in a revised edition, in 1901. It was even translated into French and published in Paris and Brussels.

Quite by chance in the fall of 1886, Oscar encountered Senator Gorman once more at the Palmer House in Chicago. Still impressed by Oscar's work in the Cleveland campaign, Gorman indicated that he would like to recommend him for an appointment as minister to the Ottoman Empire. In the end, it was not Gorman who made the recommendation, for he soon fell out of favor with the new president, but he was an important factor in planting the seed of diplomacy in Oscar's mind. There had never been a Jewish minister or ambassador from the United States before. But Oscar was undaunted.

He knew that he needed to talk it over with his father and brothers, who had so graciously and without question taken him into the business only a few years earlier. Ministerial posts demanded expenditures well beyond the salary level offered. To do the job properly required a gracious home, perhaps even two, one in the city and one in the country, and a great deal of entertaining that could not be covered by the small stipend the minister received. Oscar knew that, if he were fortunate enough to be selected, he would have to depend on his family's generosity for assistance. His brothers were delighted with the possibility and encouraged him to pursue the appointment. Such a distinction could only bring honor to the family, and they had faith that Oscar would be a superb ambassador for his country. He had no difficulty in finding enthusiastic supporters, including George Jones, proprietor and one of the founders of the *New York Times*; American statesman and former German revolutionary, Carl Schurz, who had known Oscar's family since the Revolution of 1848 in Germany; A. S. Barnes, a publisher and member of he American Board of Commissioners for Foreign Missions; and Henry Ward Beecher, whom Oscar described as the "most admired and best beloved American preacher of his time."[33]

Oscar Straus was a bold choice on the part of Grover Cleveland, but he was pleased to make the appointment. Not only was Oscar the first Jew ever to serve as an American minister (and later ambassador), he was also being sent to a largely Muslim country. In his letter of support to the president, Henry Ward Beecher praised Oscar for his many good qualities, and then went on to say, "But I am interested in another quality—the fact that he is a Hebrew. The bitter predjudice [sic] against Jews, which obtains in many parts of Europe, ought not to receive any countenance in America."[34] Cleveland was receptive to the argument. He had previously named A. M. Keiley, whose parents were Jews, as minister of Austria-Hungary, but the Austro-Hungarian government, allegedly because of his Jewish background, rejected Keiley.[35]

By March 24 1887, Oscar began to receive congratulatory letters from people all over the country. The official letter from the Department of State informing him of the appointment and enclosing "a blank oath of office," which he was asked to execute, was not written until May 26.[36] His new official title was to be

Envoy Extraordinary and Minister Plenipotentiary of the United States to the Ottoman Empire. He received the letter in Atlantic City where he and Sarah were vacationing.

It proved to be an excellent appointment. Not only was Oscar so successful in his mission that he would serve in that capacity under three different presidents, both Democrats and Republicans, he was also a popular ambassador with Muslims, Christians, and Jews alike. He was viewed as a champion for religious liberty and a man of justice and integrity. Among his many avid supporters were the Christian missionaries in Turkey, who, as Isidor later informed him, "seem to take a delight in availing themselves of an opportunity to blow the trumpet for you."[37] Isidor was proud of his younger brother.

The family business did not suffer from Oscar's abdication. On the contrary, his diplomatic appointment brought favorable publicity to the Straus name. His brothers were both encouraging, and urged him to use family resources to further his career. Nathan, writing from Loon Lake House in Franklin County, New York, a resort in the Adirondacks, reassured his brother that business that year [1887] was excellent, equal to the best they'd ever had: "To be real candid, & not bombastic either, our business has reached a point where making money is simply play, & I propose to start nothing more, for as far as business goes I for one am contented. I purposely give you these points as I want to impress it firmly on your mind to have a good time, & not stint in any way."[38] Both his brothers knew Oscar's and Sarah's frugal ways. Isidor likewise urged his brother not to "stop short of any expenditure" he needed to make. "Whether it will cost you 15 or $20,000 a year more than your salary we will guarantee to you that your income will cover it—in short, money is no object for you to allow it to stand in any way between your pleasure and the success of your mission."[39] But Oscar had learned frugality from his mother, and it was a hard habit to break. Four months later,

Isidor wrote again, "I have wondered…how you managed to get along with so little money. I hope you do not stint yourself in any way; there is no reason why you should. Rather the contrary."[40]

Isidor and Oscar corresponded on a regular basis, at least once a week, letters that provide a wealth of information, and Isidor assured his brother that "I never fail to write you by Saturday's Steamer," (even listing the steamers' names at the top of each letter (*Etruria, Fulda, Servia, Umbria,* etc.).[41] He kept him informed on political issues, public reactions to various matters, deaths, marriages, and the general business climate. And he never hesitated to give his advice to anyone in the family, whether to his wife, his children, or Oscar. In one letter to his brother he noted that various members of the family had received letters from Oscar's wife, Sarah, in which she "appears to be very nervous about her ability to suit you as a housekeeper" and not to be living up to his expectations as an ambassador's wife. Isidor urges him to reassure her, pointing out that since she was separated from family and friends, it was incumbent upon her to see him "as her counselor, and not as her critic."[42]

Sarah's apparent feelings of inadequacy may have also stemmed in part from the fact that she and Oscar had left behind in New York their four-year-old daughter Mildred (Milly) to live with Sarah's parents, the Lavanburgs, though they had taken their younger daughter Aline, with them to Constantinople. There is no explanation in the letters as to why they made this decision, though it may have been because Sarah's mother was so distraught to see her daughter and grandchildren leave the country for so long. She and her husband loved having little Milly live with them, and the child apparently did quite well in her parents' absence. Hermine's son, Lee, wrote Oscar and Sarah in December 1887 and let them know that he had recently dined with the Lavanburgs, with little Milly at the table. "I will not begin to tell you about her brightness & exceeding loveliness, for if I did I fear I should be about as bad as her Grandpa Lavanberg [sic] is when you get him wound up on that subject. Suffice it to say that she is beyond all question—the best & loveliest child one can imagine."[43]

Oscar relied heavily on his older brother's advice and asked for it fairly frequently, especially on matters of utmost importance. Writing on April 22, 1888, he wanted to know, if Grover Cleveland were reelected, whether Isidor wanted him to continue as minister to the Ottoman Empire. "If you can aid me by your advice or suggestion, on what is [the] preferable decision in this matter I will be much relieved and very grateful and cheerfully accept your conclusion as my own."[44] Isidor made every effort to keep his letters coming on a consistent basis "to avoid the possibility of your being uneasy in case you should be an extra long time without advice from me."[45]

Isidor's advice to various members of the family was always given in a positive spirit and with a motive to help the other person. While Oscar clearly sought his counsel, Isidor was equally forthcoming with guidance to his wife and children. He sometimes informed Ida about political issues she did not thoroughly understand, and in one letter she thanked him for his information about the Alien and Seditions Act. Sometimes he corrected her spelling and that of his children, even those who were students at Harvard at the time. He set their study agendas and repeatedly encouraged them in his letters to be diligent. But they all accepted his counsel in the positive spirit in which it was given, and they learned from him.

While Isidor's letters to Oscar were steady and regular, Nathan's were more sporadic. He wrote only when he had something he considered particularly important to convey. He had planned a trip to Europe that first year his brother was in Turkey, but he wavered on whether or not to go and changed his mind frequently. As he informed Oscar, "When I first took passage for Europe I did so because I did not want to be here to advise Charley what to do in his settlement with Jerome; still I could not make up my mind to leave here while matters with Charley and Jerome were in such an unsettled state." Both he and Isidor remained on good terms with both men. Nathan even encouraged Oscar to invite Jerome to Constantinople for a visit, "as he is good company," though six weeks later he wrote again that he had made the request only "to have him [Jerome] away from here," considering the intensifying animosity as his time with Macy's drew to a close. "Charley detests him," Nathan wrote, "and I do not blame him, for he really treated both Charley and his wife shamefully."[46] In terms of business, Nathan focused his letters largely on their success outside of New York, noting that things were going either "remarkably well" or "tolerably well" in other cities where they had business interests— Philadelphia, Brooklyn, Providence, and Chicago. He urges Oscar to "Take care of the Turks & the dollar will be looked after in N.Y." Again he urges him to enjoy himself and not to hold back on expenses, for, as he contends, "Money is made to spend."[47]

The exchange of letters among the brothers is revealing in terms of their different personalities and interests. Nathan was the freer spirit, enjoying horseracing and travel. He was a man of passion who sometimes wore his feelings on his sleeve and was more easily offended than either of his brothers. He tended to hold grudges and sometimes sought to punish those who had offended him. But when he believed in something, he believed ardently. Once he had latched on to an idea, he was zealous in its pursuit. For example, his profound belief in the health benefits of milk pasteurization, even in the light of staunch opposition from some in the press, created in him a determination that children should no longer drink raw milk. His efforts to create milk stations in New York and around the world are credited with saving the lives of hundreds of thousands of children. If he had accomplished nothing else in life, his fight for pasteurization would have cinched his place in history.

Once turned away, like Seligman, from an Adirondack resort, Nathan bought a luxury hotel at Lakewood and welcomed all people. And after his first visit to the Holy Land in 1904, he became an ardent Zionist to the consternation of his two brothers, who did not share his enthusiasm for the cause. The energy and emotion he expended on his passions often brought him down with bouts of nervous exhaustion. His wife, Lina, protected him like a mother lion at such moments, substituting for him wherever she could and keeping away anyone who might upset him.

Isidor was the steady rock on whom the family depended in times of need. It was he who held down the home front when Oscar was on the other side of the world and when Nathan was away. Isidor was the family mainstay, the man to whom everyone turned for sound advice, help, and moral support. And Isidor was fortunate enough to have his own twin rock at home, his wife Ida. As one visitor described her, "The first impression of Mrs. Straus was that of a quiet, intellectual woman of poise, but as time went on one felt in her a remarkable union of sweetness and power. She was a tower of strength to her husband, and always encouraging those about her."[48] Both were warm and outgoing people who welcomed others into their home and lives, but who never sought glory or honor for themselves. On the contrary, they supported the goals of others. They lived modestly and without ostentation. One person recalled being invited to dinner at their home, and "knowing they were people of great prosperity" dressed lavishly for the occasion. "I put on my finest gown and every jewel I possessed, to adorn the occasion. My hostess came forward in a soft black dress, wearing a string of small pearls around her neck and a tiny, old-fashioned pin."[49] Both Ida and Isidor gave generously of their time and money for causes in which they believed. Isidor bestowed time and money in particular on the

Educational Alliance and on the Montefiore Home for Chronic Invalids, while Ida not only supported her husband's efforts, she also focused her attentions on various causes for Jewish women.

The new situation at Macy's, and even the major responsibilities he had to assume there, pleased Isidor very much. He and Nathan brought a new strength to the firm. The Strauses possessed the merchandising skills and experience that Webster and Wheeler had lacked. And they were determined to keep their prices low by cutting out the middleman wherever possible, importing products directly, and selling Macy's brands. Isidor especially enjoyed working with Charles Webster and spent a great deal of time familiarizing himself with his new multi-faceted role. "[I]t is an exceedingly pleasant task as all the surroundings are happy in the extreme & Charley takes special delight to render everything rather a pleasurable pastime and not an earnest task."[50] As Isidor noted, "Charley[,] Nathan and myself ... constitute the firm, and we seem by instinct determined that we all get a lot of fun and agreeable episodes out of each day's hours."[51]

Webster could not have chosen better partners, for he grew increasingly weary of the business and depended on them, particularly Isidor. The men became friends and enjoyed each other socially as well as in terms of their partnership. Isidor was especially happy with the new arrangement and, from all indications, took more pleasure in his work than ever. He and Webster spent a great deal of time with one another, not only at work but elsewhere, even taking a two-hour break together in the middle of the day:

> [W]e go to lunch to Delmonico's, walking both ways when weather permits....Once in a while we go up to the Manhattan Club for a change, of which we are both members...we invariably walk up Sixth Ave. to 23[d] St., then, down to Fifth Ave. and along Fifth Ave. to 15th St., so that we get our full quota of exercise and

fresh air. I have never been in better condition in my life and have never been engaged in any kind of work that seems to wear on me so little. My office is quiet and away from all the turmoil and dust; when I close my desk, my mind feels as fresh as before I began.[52]

He and Charley genuinely liked one another, and Webster visited Isidor and Ida at their Saranac Lake home on various occasions and frequently dined with them at their Manhattan home as well. The mutual membership the two men shared in the Manhattan Club, an elite organization composed primarily of Democrats and founded in 1866 as a response to the Republican club called the Union League, suggests that the Strauses and Webster were compatible in their political views as well, as later events will bear out.[53] But Webster's health was not good, and he soon began to take frequent vacations, leaving Isidor with even more responsibilities. In the summer of 1889, only a year after he sold Wheeler's interest in the store to the Strauses, he took a long vacation in Europe for his health, where Oscar, returning home from his first diplomatic appointment to the Ottoman Empire, encountered him in Paris. Although he looked fine, Oscar reported that he "is nervously run down, so that he is unsteady on his legs, he can only walk the distance of 4 or 5 blocks a day without much fatigue."[54] Webster informed Oscar that he was not worried about business, "excepting only he regrets not being able to share your responsibilities."

Isidor became of necessity virtually a full-time fixture uptown at the store. He went downtown less and less often, though he installed a direct telephone line to L. Straus & Sons on Warren Street. He felt less needed there, however, for his nephew, Lee Kohns, was doing a satisfactory job and would consult him only occasionally. Isidor wrote on February 25, 1888, that he had not spent six hours at the Warren Street office since the first of the year. "I drop in there once or twice during the week for a half hour."[55] Whenever Charley or Nathan traveled, which they both did frequently, Isidor always picked up the slack. He never complained and Ida never resented his working so hard, though she did worry sometimes about his health and encouraged him to get plenty of fresh air and exercise.

Although Nathan had commented earlier that he proposed "to start nothing more" in terms of business, when the opportunity came in January 1893 to buy Joseph Wechsler's share of the Brooklyn department store of Wechsler & Abraham, Isidor and Nathan took advantage of it. They made the purchase on April 1, and the firm was renamed Abraham & Straus.[56] Among the partners were Abraham Abraham, Ida's nephew Simon Frank Rothschild (son of her sister Amanda), and Abraham's son, Lawrence, and son-in-law, Edward Charles Blum.

The purchase was especially timely for Isidor, for his son Jesse graduated from Harvard in June of 1893, and Abraham and Straus would become his training ground before his father brought him into the management of Macy's. The close association with the Abrahams would also affect the personal life of Isidor's family, for on November 27, 1902, his son Percy would marry Edith Abraham, the beautiful daughter of his father's partner Abraham Abraham.

7

Mr. Straus Goes To Washington

In 1894, Isidor Straus, who already had as much as he could handle with business duties, and who clearly had no personal political aspirations, was elected to Congress to fill the unexpired term of Ashbel P. Fitch.[1] More than a year earlier he had turned down Grover Cleveland's offer to name him Postmaster General and, thus, to become the first Jewish member of a presidential cabinet, for he had no such ambitions.[2] It was instead his brother Oscar who would have that distinction when he accepted an appointment as Secretary of Labor and Commerce by Theodore Roosevelt in 1907. Although Isidor had worked diligently for Cleveland's election, he sought neither glory nor high office. And on the eve of his own congressional term, he proclaimed, "I don't think the life [of a congressman] will prove the least bit attractive." [3] Given such convictions, why would he ever consider running for public office? The story really begins more than a decade earlier.

Until 1882, as Isidor reveals in his autobiography, he had been completely "engrossed in the daily duties of business" and his growing family and had paid little attention to politics. In that year, however, he began to take an interest in issues "related to tariff, currency reform and banking."[4] Part of it was a matter of necessity, for it was during this period that he was elected as a director of the Hanover National Bank. In addition, he became one of the founders and a member of the Board of Directors of the New York Reform Club, which had as its goal "to promote the election of honest capable men to Municipal office."[5] His interests were sound money and good government.

The following year the *Tammany Times* noted that he often spent his leisure time in his well-stocked library, which was filled with "many valuable works bearing upon economic questions....In this he finds rest from his arduous duties as a merchant."[6] His specific interest in tariff matters was heightened in 1884 when L. Straus & Sons came under investigation by customs officials, acting, as Isidor would later learn, on information from rival merchants who had accused the firm of under-valuing their imported goods. To make matters worse, appraisers appointed to review the matter included a competitor named P. H. Leonard, with whom Lazarus and Isidor had not been on speaking terms for many years. At one time the Strauses had been major customers of Leonard, but when Nathan became their buyer and they began their own importation of goods, Leonard was furious. The two firms became competitors and "rivals" instead. In his autobiography, Isidor blamed Leonard and another firm called J. M. Young as having "engineered and hatched the conspiracy against us."[7]

The Strauses objected strenuously to the selection of Leonard and brought in several witnesses to testify to his bias against their firm.[8] The witnesses gave testimony to what one of them called Leonard's "malice."[9] Typical of their comments was a sworn statement by Samuel L. McBride that in "the latter part of 1884" he had called upon Mr. Leonard to seek his signature on a document.[10] When Leonard saw the name of L. Straus & Sons on the paper he was to sign, he "broke out in a torrent of abuse...reflecting upon their creed and integrity." McBride indicated that "Leonard is so prejudiced against the said L. Straus & Sons, that he is not the proper person to act as arbitrator, or decide any matter or question wherein he may be involved in [their] right or property."[11] The case dragged on for eighteen months, but was finally decided in favor of the Strauses.

Isidor faulted his accusers with, not only business rivalry, but also a false piety (Leonard was Catholic and Young, Presbyterian) and political motives (both were Republicans, while he was a Democrat.). But, he affirmed with a sense of satisfaction in his autobiography that "both met their just deserts; the former, a few years later, I learned, died in the insane asylum, and the latter finally reached an ignominious end, for his creditors a most disastrous failure, while it was generally known that he was possessed of ample means, but placed beyond the reach of those who had trusted him."[12]

In spite of the Strauses' victory in the courts, savings to the company were short-lived, for in 1890, during the Republican administration of Benjamin Harrison, Congress passed the McKinley Tariff Act, sponsored by Ohio congressman and future president William McKinley, which imposed protective tariffs averaging more than 48% on imported goods. These tariffs were disastrous both for New York merchants like the Strauses, who relied heavily on imported products, and for consumers, who were compelled to pay higher prices. Isidor went to Washington in June 1890 as one of the so-called "Committee of 50" to appear before members of the Senate Finance Committee and speak against the McKinley bill. In a talk given in New York on June 14, he suggested that the people preferred being taxed to paying the higher prices the duty required. "Duties that are exacted purely for protection will not, in my opinion, be tolerated by the people."[13]

That same year Congress also passed the Sherman Silver Purchase Act, which Isidor considered equally disastrous for the economy and for America's standing abroad. Once again Isidor was invited to Washington to speak before the House Coinage Committee in favor of maintaining sound currency, and in opposition to even a modest expansion of silver into U.S. currency. In spite of his opposition, Congress also passed this bill as they had the McKinley Act. The Sherman Act required the government to buy 4.5 million ounces of silver each month at market rates and issue notes redeemable in either gold or silver. Most people redeemed the certificates in gold, which they considered a more stable currency, with the consequence that federal gold reserves were being rapidly depleted.

Isidor's testimony did not go unnoticed by the former and future president, Grover Cleveland. The following September, Cleveland and his wife were vacationing at Prospect House on Upper Saranac Lake, not far from Isidor and Ida's summer home on Lower Saranac Lake. Not long after Isidor's comments were presented to the House committee, his two oldest sons, Jesse and Percy, accompanied their Uncle Oscar (fresh from his first tour of duty as minister to the Ottoman Empire) when he visited Cleveland and his wife. Jesse later informed his father that, "In the course of conversation your speech was mentioned & Mr. C said it was the only clear & concise statement of facts given. That you had 'put the thing so that they could not possibly misunderstand.'"[14] When Cleveland was reelected two years later, he would not forget Isidor's persuasive rhetoric, which he would soon encounter once again.

Only a few months after his inauguration in March 1893, Cleveland faced an unprecedented economic downturn, brought on, some believed, by the two economic bills mentioned above, especially the Sherman Silver Purchase Act. Stock prices plunged in May following the bankruptcy of the large National Cordage Company. Overextended banks and railroads began to flounder. The tally of failures for the first half of 1893 was 8,000 businesses and 360 banks. Unemployment reached an all-time high. One historian estimated that a minimum of 80,000 were out of work in New York City, while another put the figure somewhere between 100,000 and 200,000.[15]

The election of 1892 had reversed the country's course and swept Democrats back into the presidency and control of both houses of Congress. The new President believed that the repeal of the Sherman Silver Purchase Act would go a long way toward restoring a healthy economy.[16] Although Isidor had not yet been elected to Congress, he played a significant role in that repeal.

He wrote to his brother Nathan on July 5 1893 of the increasing deterioration of the economy. "Matters have been pretty severe here—we have never had a money panic that lasted so long…The President has been urged on all sides to call an extra session of Congress at once [to expedite the repeal of the Sherman Silver Purchase Act], and not wait until September." At the insistence of his business partner, Charles Webster, Isidor decided to take matters into his own hands and do what he could to persuade the President. The two were having lunch together when Webster "urged me to go to Washington to try my hand at prevailing on the president to call an extra session at once." Isidor was impressed by Webster's passionate insistence. "I never saw Charley so energetically persistent about any measure and he finally prevailed on me to start immediately without any baggage."[17]

Isidor left for Washington that very afternoon and made an appointment to see President Cleveland the following morning. His meeting fell on the day the President met with his Cabinet and normally scheduled no meetings with visitors. However, he met for a quarter of an hour with Isidor Straus. After he left the President's office, Isidor had no reason to think "that I had made any impression," and yet, that very afternoon, Cleveland called the Congress into an extra session for August 7. As Isidor reported to Nathan, "The Times gives me the credit for bringing it about—I don't deserve it but I presume it was the last straw."[18]

But the economic situation still had not improved by the beginning of August, and Isidor was alarmed. "Banks are failing all over the country," he wrote Nathan. "This country has never seen anything like it before."[19] Another bill, which Straus hoped could help to right a wrong created by the McKinley Tariff Act, the Wilson Tariff Bill, would also come before Congress that year. Isidor's friend, William Lyne Wilson, a congressman from West Virginia, proposed this bill in the House of Representatives.[20] It called for lower tariffs, but also included a controversial provision for a 2% income tax. Isidor had become a conspicuous public figure because of his testimony before Senate committees and his persuasive counsel to the President. Thus, it had come as little surprise when the *New York Independent* reported on February 15, 1893, that Isidor Straus was under consideration for a Cabinet position as Postmaster General in the Cleveland administration. But, the paper announced, "Mr. Straus manifested no desire to lay aside his business pursuits, even for exalted station." By the end of the year, however, he would change his mind and conclude that public service on his part might become necessary, given the current economic situation.

Thus, when Ashbel P. Fitch, who had served since 1887 as representative from the Fifteenth District of New York, resigned his seat in Congress on December 26, 1893, and the governor of New York, Roswell Pettibone Flower, called for a special election on January 23 to fill the vacancy, Isidor allowed his name to be put forward.[21] The Tammany Hall Congress Convention met on January 8 to nominate a candidate. Congressman Fitch had planned to nominate Isidor, but he was taken ill and the nomination was made by Stephen S. Blake, who proclaimed that Straus would help "bring about tariff reform through the medium of the Wilson bill."[22]

"I at first declined even to consider it," Isidor said, but representatives of Tammany Hall and others were persuasive, and by December 19, 1893, he had made up his mind to run.[23] Writing in confidence to Wilson, his friend in Congress, he indicated: "The pressure on different sides has about overcome my objections. As yet it is a secret. The President sent me a very pressing message through Mr. Fitch and the powers."[24] Isidor accepted the nomination because he was determined to find an opportunity to "free our commerce from the shackles with which McKinleyism has inflicted it."[25] If they were removed, Straus argued, "we will enter on such a period of prosperity as this country has not experienced in many years." He believed that Democrats, as long as they remained true to the principles of the party, which he described as "honest money, the raising of sufficient revenues for the economical administration of the affairs of the Government, no class legislation, no taxation of the many for the benefit of the favored few," they would continue "to command the confidence of The People, their support, and their gratitude."[26]

His Republican opponent, Frederick Sigrist, favored the current high protective tariffs and was determined to make it the primary issue of the campaign.[27] But despite his determined opposition, Straus won handily; receiving 15,364 votes to Sigrist's 10,653.[28]

Isidor was sworn in on February 14, 1894. An article in the *Washington Post* of February 13 quoted him as saying, "What I'd like to see done in the interest of business and the Democratic Party is the speedy passage of the [Wilson] tariff bill. I'm opposed to the income tax, but I'd rather see the bill go through with that feature than to see it fail altogether." His determination and intentions were clear.

As he had predicted, Isidor did not enjoy life in Washington. Not only did it take him away from his wife and children for long stretches of time, he was also frustrated, as a man of resolution and quick action, by the slow process of legislation. He wrote to Carl Schurz on March 12th "Effects follow causes so far apart that, so far as I am concerned, I almost fail to discover the relation between cause and effect"[29]

The one bright spot during his congressional career was his friendship with two other members of the House of Representatives, who would join him in this crusade to try to set the country on what he believed was the right path. One of these was William Lyne Wilson, Chairman of the Ways and Means Committee. He was the author of the Wilson Tariff Bill, which Isidor supported from his very first day in Congress. The other like-minded man and fellow member of the House was Clifton R. Breckinridge, congressman from Arkansas, with whom he would also develop a deep friendship. These two men would become Isidor's lifelong best friends outside the family. Wilson and Breckinridge had served together in Congress for the previous eleven years, since 1883. They welcomed Isidor into their ranks with open arms. And all three would be close advisors of President Cleveland.

The friend he would miss most during his time in Washington was Ida. As their anniversary approached that year, he realized they would not be together, but as always, he wanted her to know that he would be there in spirit. He wrote to her on the eve of their wedding anniversary: "It seems to me that tomorrow is a red letter day in our Calendar—may we live together to enjoy it for many years with no more real cause for complaint than besets us today. May we always have reason to say, as we have now, that it was the birthday of our fondest hopes realized."[30]

During his brief time in Congress, Isidor sought to share his friends with Ida and frequently invited them home with him for visits. Ida had to be prepared to serve as hostess with little advance notice to some of the country's most influential people. On August 7, 1894, for example, Isidor wrote to her, giving her three-days notice that "It is possible that Secy [Secretary of State] Gresham will come with me next Friday and Mr. Wilson also if he can in any way do so. I will telegraph you when I positively know."[31] She never complained about the extra work or the short notice, but took it all in stride and seemed to enjoy their visits as much as Isidor. She was an intelligent and sensitive woman and thanks to her husband's constant stream of letters, she was as well informed as anyone in the country who was not actually a member of Congress on the sequence of events that took place in Washington. She was Isidor's most trusted friend and confidante, though she was rarely in Washington to experience events first hand.

One exception was the open house held on New Year's Day 1895, when she was invited by Grover Cleveland to help him and his wife Frances receive his guests at the White House. It was not uncommon for the President to invite the wives of cabinet members to help receive, but the invitation to the wife of a congressman was a singular honor. Ida was delighted to accept the President's invitation and Isidor accompanied her to Washington. He was as proud of her as she was of him. When he had proved to be so instrumental in encouraging the President to call a special session of Congress to repeal the Sherman Silver Purchase Act, she wrote to him from Long Branch, New Jersey: "If I ever felt proud of you it is today, that you should be singled out among so many bright authoritative men as the one who is to help tide the nation over the crisis. I think you will find me ten inches taller on your return."[32]

The bill proposed by Wilson contained lower tariff rates and provisions to allow raw materials like iron, coal, and sugar to be imported free. However, its provision for a 2% income tax on the very wealthy to replace lost tariff revenue made it controversial even among Democrats. It was not an ideal bill as far as Isidor was concerned, but it was probably the best one they could get, and it was the bill President Cleveland wanted. When the Wilson bill was delivered to the Senate, however, Arthur Pue Gorman, a

Democratic senator from Maryland, seeking to protect industries in his state, took the leadership in drafting the Senate version of the bill. He made 634 changes, virtually decimating the House bill's intent.[33] Isidor no doubt considered Gorman a friend, since he had been instrumental in Oscar's appointment as minister to the Ottoman Empire. However, he was not happy about what the Senator had done to the Wilson bill. The Wilson-Gorman bill, as it was now labeled, contained higher protective tariffs than Wilson had proposed, though they were still lower than those of the McKinley Act. And it still retained a provision for the income tax. Isidor and Wilson both fought hard for the House version of the bill, and Isidor seemed to enjoy the battle.

He wrote to Ida to share his reactions even as the final outcome was being decided in the House. "It has been an exciting day," he told her. "[I]t is 6 P.M. and the vote is being taken—I hesitated a long time about voting against the bill but finally concluded to stay with Wilson." He had been writing to her throughout the day describing events as they were unfolding, sharing with his beloved wife this most exciting time in his life. He clearly wanted her to be a part of it. He had begun the letter in the morning to tell her about the day before: "Yesterday was a busy day Conferences and Conferences—Mr. Wilson and I did not get to bed until 1:30 and we were up at 7—breakfast at 8 and around ever since up and doing. I am writing this at the House at 9:30 [A.M.]. The caucus will meet in a half hour. The tendency is to surrender." But Wilson was at that moment still in consultation with the Speaker of the House, trying to get the caucus postponed until the following day, when they thought they would have a better chance. He continued the letter at 3:45 P.M. "The deed is done[.] We are beaten but not conquered. The caucus simply stampeded and the House will of course follow the action of the caucus and the Senate carries the day, but the country will I hope hold them responsible for being traitors to the cause." As always, he closed his letter with love to all and signed it "Your devoted Isidor."[34]

He wrote her again two days later on the 15th, and one can see a new relaxation in his handwriting. It is not the tight, tense script of the previous letter, but rather a larger, bolder, and more legible hand. Now that it was over, the three allies in the struggle had taken a day to recover. As Isidor informed Ida:

> Yesterday the house was not in session. Mr. Wilson, Mr. Breckinridge and I spent the day together. We had our photographs taken in a group in several positions. I am to see the proofs this morning. Mr. Wilson is feeling very well. He slept excellently on Monday night. The load was off his shoulders, and although the first effect, when he saw that the Senate amendments would be adopted in toto, affected him very deeply, a letter which he received from the President, expressing his great satisfaction and obligation for his manly fight, helped to a very great extent in enabling him to pull himself together.

Only to Ida did he confide the impetus for Cleveland's letter, at least at the time: "Immediately after the caucus I drove to the White House, had a long talk with the President and suggested that he write this letter to Mr. Wilson and he did it at once. I am glad to say it had the anticipated effect."[35] Only after Wilson's death did he disclose publicly the fact that he had actually found Wilson in the committee room, "his head between his hands, sobbing as if he had lost one near and dear to him." Wilson confided that the President had made a remark that had cut him "to the quick." Isidor, always a man to make peace when misunderstandings occurred, went to the President and urged him to write the letter. The contents of that letter he finally shared with the world in 1902.[36]

The other issue before the country, the continued depletion of gold, would finally come to a head by February 1895, while the three men were still in Congress. In a final desperate effort to save the economy, President Cleveland brought an end to the panic by allowing J. P. Morgan to form a private international syndicate and bolster the U.S. Treasury with a loan of $65 million in gold to restore the country's gold supply. When gold reserves stood at only $9 million against outstanding drafts of $12 million, he knew the time had come for extreme measures. Either the U.S. "would have to default on its debt and destroy its credit," or make a deal with Morgan.[37] Despite the fact that the strategy worked, Cleveland and his party would pay the price in the 1894 mid-term congressional election.

Although Isidor seemed invigorated by the political battles, efforts on behalf of the tariff bill had "sorely taxed the strength" of Wilson, who planned a trip to Europe to recuperate. When he learned that Mrs. Wilson was unable to accompany him, he invited Isidor instead. They departed the first week in September to spend a month abroad.[38] During the trip, the London Chamber of Commerce honored Wilson with a dinner in September 1894.[39] Wilson, now fully rested, was ready to begin what would be an arduous campaign for re-election. All three men--Straus, Wilson, and Breckinridge—completed their terms in office when Congress adjourned on August 24, 1895. None would return to be a part of the next Congress.[40]

President Cleveland had already offered to appoint Breckinridge ambassador to Russia, and on July 18, 1894, Isidor confided to his wife that "Mr. B. has written to the President accepting the Russian ambassadorship."[41] Breckinridge was allowed to complete his congressional term only because of what the *New York Times* called a "legislative muddle," which would have to be settled before he left for St. Petersburg. He had been nominated as "Envoy Extraordinary and Minister Plenipotentiary," but the salary appropriations had been made for an ambassador. The matter would have to wait until Russia accepted the change in rank of the American minister, for there was no salary provision for the lesser rank.[42]

In the case of Wilson, in spite of the campaign funds Isidor worked hard to raise, which included a $500 donation from the President, Wilson went down to defeat in the 1894 mid-term-election landslide by Republicans. People were angry that the nation's economic problems could not be solved so quickly. But Wilson was by no means out of public office and was soon named Postmaster General by President Cleveland, serving in his cabinet until 1897 and the election of William McKinley.

Isidor had already decided not to seek another term. According to the *Commercial Advertiser* of February 27, 1895, he was "literally counting the days when he will retire from public life. No consideration within reason, he says, would induce him to accept another nomination." He preferred being at home with his wife and children and overseeing the family's business interests, and especially Macy's, of which he and Nathan would become in 1896 the sole owners.[43]

Despite their diverging careers, the three former congressmen remained friends. In January 1897, rumors circulated that Wilson had accepted the presidency of Washington and Lee University. In a letter to Percy on January 20, Isidor wrote, "I hardly think there is any truth in the report of Mr. Wilson accepting the presidency of the Washington Lee [sic] University." He was pretty sure Wilson planned to join a New York law firm instead, for he was then in Albany, "delivering the annual oration before the State Bar Association." Isidor indicated that he "will be here today or tomorrow."[44] It may well be at that meeting that Isidor learned the truth. W. L. Wilson was inaugurated as the ninth president of Washington and Lee on September 15, 1897. The two men would enjoy their friendship only three more years, when Wilson died of tuberculosis on October 17, 1900.

Two years later, when the University unveiled a portrait of President Wilson on the occasion of its 1902 graduation exercises on June 18, Isidor was invited to give the commencement address. He took the opportunity to express his genuine admiration for Wilson's integrity, honor, unselfishness, and modesty—all traits that Isidor esteemed above all others. He also valued his scholarship and his determination that Washington and Lee should have a professor that could teach the principles in which both men so ardently believed—sound economic doctrines within a political context. Toward that end, during his lifetime and brief tenure as president of Washington and Lee, Wilson himself had paid the salary of such a professor "out of his scant individual means." Thus, as a tribute to his memory, his friends, including Isidor who had spearheaded the effort and contributed to it generously, endowed a chair of Economics and Political Science at the University.[45] In recognition of his friendship with Wilson and his generosity, three years later, in 1905, Isidor would be given an honorary doctorate by Washington and Lee.

Isidor would remain interested in politics for the rest of his life, and was mentioned in both 1901 and in 1909 as a possible candidate for mayor of New York.[46] He even flirted seriously with the idea in the spring of 1911 of running for the U. S. Senate, and was encouraged especially by the Tammany "boss" Richard Croker. But in the end Isidor never again ran for public office.[47]

His brother, Nathan, also briefly considered a foray into politics in 1894 and was actually nominated in mid-October as the Tammany Hall candidate for mayor of New York.[48] But Nathan wisely realized that he was not suited by nature and temperament to the stress of a political campaign. On October 19, before his candidacy was really under way, he withdrew his name from consideration.[49]

In spite of Isidor's refusal ever again to run for public office, he continued to be interested in the country's financial affairs. He usually voted as a Democrat; however, he was also a "sound money" man. In the election of 1896, when William Jennings Bryan, a proponent of free silver, ran against William McKinley, whose tariff bill he had so despised, Isidor was compelled to examine both men and their policies very closely and to make what he labeled "the choice of a lesser evil." He chose McKinley, voting for the first time for a Republican president, even though he would remain a staunch Democrat throughout his life. He never regretted his decision, but wrote to President McKinley during his and Ida's vacation in Vienna on April 8, 1898, that as a "gold democrat," he was "proud of having voted for "one who cannot be swerved from what he believes to be his duty in the face of censure of many in his own party who will eventually be as much ashamed of their ill advised strictures as I glory in my vote."[50]

For the rest of his life, Isidor would continue to take an interest in the country's fiscal affairs and to provide counsel to high officials whenever deemed necessary. And Ida was happy to have him home again.

A New Era At Macy's

In 1893, the year Ida and Isidor celebrated their twenty-second anniversary, their first son Jesse graduated from Harvard. They were beginning to see the fruits of their labor confirmed in their children. Now it was up to Isidor to oversee Jesse's start in the family business as he would do for all his sons, while both his parents, but especially his mother, encouraged him to make a good marriage.

Isidor did not give Jesse a position at Macy's right away. Instead he helped him to get a job at the Hanover National Bank, where Isidor was a director. He wanted his eldest son to gain business experience before entering the firm at Macy's. Jesse complained to his sister Sara, his closest family confidante, that, although he was given the title of bank clerk, they had him doing such menial tasks as filling inkwells and polishing door handles.[1] But Isidor wanted him to learn every phase of the business world, from the most basic to the most demanding. While he had been determined that his sons should have the formal education at Harvard he had been denied, he also intended for them to acquire mercantile knowledge they could gain only by working their way from the ground up.

The next position which to Isidor moved his oldest son was that of a salesman in the newly acquired Abraham & Straus. During his time at Abraham & Straus, Jesse was assigned to various divisions, learning different facets of the business, as his father sought to prepare him for a successful future in merchandising. It was not until he was twenty-four, a year after his 1895 wedding to Irma Nathan, that Isidor finally said to his son, "I guess you can come to Macy's now." Jesse called it "the happiest day of all my commercial life."[2]

His move was timely, for only a year later, the Straus brothers, Isidor and Nathan, became the sole owners of Macy's. Over time, the Strauses had taken over more and more responsibility in the store's management, as Charles Webster seemed to be losing interest and energy, until finally in 1896, he gave up his partnership altogether and sold his percentage in the firm to Isidor and Nathan for $1,200,000.[3] A letter from Isidor to Percy on November 25, 1896, is written on stationery with a letterhead containing the names of C. B. Webster, Isidor Straus, and Nathan Straus, in that order. But Webster's name is marked out. Even though he no longer held a financial interest in the company, they all remained friends and the Strauses allowed him to maintain an office in the store until his death in 1916.

Isidor's younger sons did not have such drawn-out training periods as their older brother, though like Jesse, when they came to the store, they were made to start in the receiving department, working their way through various divisions before being allowed an active role in Macy's management. Percy joined the firm in 1897, though he took a leave in 1898 to act briefly as an unofficial secretary for his Uncle Oscar in Constantinople, while Herbert began his duties at Macy's after his Harvard graduation 1903.[4]

As Isidor was training his own sons to follow in his path, the footsteps he himself had followed to learn the trade as a young man came to an end. His father, Lazarus, died on January 14, 1898, at the age of 89, while two of his grandsons were just beginning their first tenuous steps in the family mercantile tradition.

Lazarus's death occurred at his home, now 23 West 56th Street, where he was living with his daughter Hermine, her husband Lazarus, and their daughter Irene.[5] All his children were at his bedside, except for Isidor, who was traveling in Europe and Egypt with Ida and their daughters Sara and Minnie. Their trip was to be one of healing and recovery. Isidor had not been feeling well, and Sara was suffering from a knee problem that made even walking difficult for her. They had sailed three weeks earlier, knowing that Lazarus was not well, but not realizing how close to death he was.

Hermine wrote to them on January 7, 1898, "Our dear father remains about the same, his condition varying from better to not so good." He had stopped eating, she told them and was "taking no whiskey at all subsisting mainly on champagne."[6] On that same day, their son Jesse, evidently not wanting to worry his parents, wrote, "Grandpa is much better than he was when you left. He eats more, drinks more, and is in better spirits."[7]

They were in Cannes when they received news of Lazarus's death. Percy softened the blow by the sweetness of his account of his grandfather's final moments, "holding Aunt Hermina's hand, and surrounded by the various members of the family, none of whom, not even Aunt Hermina realizing that life was extinct,—so peaceful was his death."[8] The entire family was especially concerned for Hermine, who had looked after her father for so many years and who took his death very hard. Ida and Isidor encouraged her to join them abroad, but she just wasn't ready. Her daughter Irene informed them on January 21, "Mamma requests me to say that she cannot as yet collect her thoughts to write nor can she cable her decision. What her plans for the near future will be—She is trying to make up her mind to go abroad but nothing definite can be settled yet."[9] Oscar seemed certain that Hermine would not "think of leaving the house for 30 days—after that she, Laz[arus] and Irene may join you abroad."[10] And Oscar's wife, Sarah, informed them that "Hermine bears up bravely but she is weak physically." Nathan noted that she was "everywhere when needed," but that now that their father was gone, she was "feeling the after effects" of overwork and grief.[11] Nathan himself, despite what Sarah called "his high-strung emotional temperament," bore up well and made it bravely through the family service as well as the funeral at the Temple.[12] It was only when they were "about to take the body from the Temple [that] he broke down and Mr. Abraham took him home."[13]

Oscar urged Ida and Isidor not to cut short the vacation they had so recently begun. "I am sure I am expressing his [our father's] wish—when I say you should continue your much needed rest and in no way abridge your plans."[14] They knew he was there in spirit, and his sons Percy and Jesse took his place at their grandfather's bedside, sitting up with his body, helping prepare him for burial, and taking on all the duties and loving care their father would have shown had he been present.[15] Lazarus was gone, but none of his children ever forgot the example he set for integrity, diligence, and family harmony. Like him, they valued education, honesty and hard work.

Certainly Isidor was highly conscious of being for his sons the same kind of example his father had been. In some ways, he even went further, setting an example of care for the welfare of others even beyond the family. Both he and Nathan were good role models for the young men as progressive managers, concerned about their employees. The benefits they offered to those who worked at Macy's were extraordinary for the times. They "would go to great trouble to visit an employee who was ill or to attend the funeral of a long-time worker....If one of the brothers noticed that a Macy's employee seemed troubled or unwell, he would enquire about the problem and then provide any assistance that was needed, whether it was additional money, a new suit of clothes, or the services of a physician."[16]

Isidor's grandson Jack later recalled that his grandfather walked the store once each week, wearing "a high hat and frockcoat, a flower in the lapel." The flower was inevitably a pink carnation, and the boy saw the high hat as "a symbol of office."[17] Nevertheless, despite such an appearance of formality, the Macy's employees evidently found both the Straus brothers friendly and personable, calling them fondly "Mr. Isidor" and "Mr. Nathan." This personal attention continued as long as it was feasible, though eventually the firm would become too large for Isidor and Nathan to know their employees so well, and they would be required to depend more upon their managers. Still, they held annual events—picnics, sleigh rides, etc.—and gave a Thanksgiving turkey to each married couple.[18] They were also the first businessmen in America to form a Mutual Aid Society for their workers, who could choose to participate by paying annual dues. The Society also hosted various fundraising activities that helped to provide employee benefits ranging from social affairs to medical care. But dues and fundraisers never paid all the bills. Annual deficits were made up by the company's management—in short, by Isidor and Nathan Straus.

In 1888 Macy's began two progressive new programs to aid their employees—a dining hall that offered low-cost lunches for workers (a full meal for five cents or less and free milk and coffee to lower-echelon workers) and a program that covered not only doctor's bills but also funeral expenses, with additional funds set aside for elderly employees who could no longer work. They even provided the option of low-cost vacations to workers, having rented for several years a summer home with 350 acres of land in Monroe, New York, where employees could vacation for $6 a week, including transportation to and from the site.[19] In 1909 Macy's purchased a large country house in Orange County from the estate of G. Estrada Palma, former president of Cuba, "as a summer home for female employees." The house had thirty rooms and thirteen acres of land, which contained tennis and croquet courts, wooded areas, and a freshwater lake.[20] As a consequence of such efforts, morale among the Macy's workforce tended to be high, and a job there was a coveted position.

Macy's thrived and grew under the management of the Strauses. By the mid-1890s the store, located at Sixth Avenue and 14th Street, had become what one writer has called "'the Mecca' of New York shoppers."[21] However, over the years it had begun to sprawl into various labyrinthine annexes spread out over 13th and 14th Streets until finally it had no more room to grow. On September 12, 1896, a new store, Siegel-Cooper opened its doors, threatening to outshine Macy's with its convenient location, larger size, and barrage of advertising. It claimed that its fashionable Beaux-Arts building on Sixth Avenue and West 18th Street was now "The Largest Department Store in the World."[22] Indeed, with its more than 85,000 square feet, it was more than twice the size of Macy's. To make matters worse, Wannamaker's, once primarily in Philadelphia, had now gained a foothold in Manhattan and began to make an even bigger play for the New York market with the acquisition of the bankrupt A. T. Stewart's.

Stewart's, Macy's and Siegel-Cooper all formed part of what New Yorkers called "the Ladies' Mile," an impressive array of large retailers where stylish New York women did most of their shopping. The advertising competition among the large stores was fierce. Macy's tried to distinguish itself by low prices, efficient services, and impressive traditions, such as their extravagant Christmas window displays, which brought people to the store in droves. The lavish decorations had begun in the 1870s through the efforts of R. H. Macy, but the Strauses maintained them with enthusiasm. Macy had even brought in the first in-store Santa Claus in 1862.

With the turn of the century and the inclusion of Isidor's sons in the inner circle at Macy's, it seemed time to make a major change. Leases were almost up on various properties, and some of the buildings were in serious need of renovation and repair. Rather than spend the money to upgrade the old establishment, Isidor and Nathan made the decision to build a brand new store.

Thus, in the 1890s, their real estate agent, Leopold Weil, the father of Isidor's future son-in-law, Richard Weil, began quietly trying to negotiate deals to acquire the necessary land farther uptown at Herald Square and West 34th Street. It was a bold move to shift their location from the well-established merchandising district to one farther uptown, which would require shoppers to form new habits.

Weil was successful in acquiring all but one tiny lot on the corner of Thirty-Fourth and Broadway. Its owner, Alfred Duane Pell, had agreed to sell the land to the Strauses for $250,000, when an agent for Siegel-Cooper & Co. got wind of the deal and offered $375,000 instead. When the Siegel-Cooper agent then offered it to the Strauses, allegedly at the same price he had paid, they refused to pay the higher price and instead built their new store around the small plot of land and with a notch at one corner.[23]

The cornerstone for the building was laid on April 23, 1902, and the new store, which boasted twenty-four acres of floor space, opened for business on November 8, 1902, with Isidor, Jesse, and Percy there to receive accolades.[24] It was definitely a move that looked toward the future of the family as well as the future of New York. Although the building of the new store did not precisely mark a changing of the guard from Isidor and Nathan to Isidor's sons (Nathan's children were younger and would not enter store management until about ten years after Isidor's), it did symbolize a new era, suggesting that a shift in responsibility to the younger generation had begun. Although Isidor would never fully retire, now that at least two of his sons were at Macy's, he felt free to take more and more time away from the office.

It gave him greater opportunity to attend to civic commitments he had already accepted and to take on others that would benefit humanity. He was already the very active president of the Educational Alliance, treasurer of the Montefiore Home and first vice-president of the J. Hood Wright Memorial Hospital.[25] Among his other activities, not only was he a member the board of directors of Hanover National Bank and the New York County National Bank, he was also president of several civic and business organizations including the Chamber of Commerce of the State of New York, the New York Retail Dry Goods Association, and the Crockery Board of Trade, which he had founded. He also became a very active member of the board of directors of the new enterprise called Phipps Houses, a nonprofit organization founded in 1905 to provide low-cost housing for those in need.[26]

With his sons at the helm of Macy's, Isidor had more time to see to his own personal needs and those of Ida, which had become increasingly necessary. In the late 1890s Isidor had started to suffer numbness and coldness in his legs and feet, a condition that had begun with a fall and was exacerbated by poor circulation. The European voyage of 1898 had done little to improve his condition, which only seemed to grow worse. He decided to seek a cure by consulting one of the world's leading neurologists, Dr. Wilhelm Heinrich Erb, in Heidelberg. When news about Isidor's declining health reached the ears of the Board of Trustees at the Educational Alliance, of which he had served as president since the organization's founding, they were highly distressed over the matter and took it as an opportunity to draft an elegant "testimonial of our regard and esteem." In the document, dated April 13, 1899, they lauded his participation as one who has led the Alliance from its "struggling infancy to its present position of comparative prosperity." In addition, they praised his "unselfish efforts," his "catholic and liberal spirit," his buoyancy, enthusiasm, and confidence in the organization's success. They expressed their hopes that he would soon return hale and robust from his "quest of renewed health and vigor" and wished him "Godspeed and a cordial 'Au revoir'."[27]

Isidor and Ida sailed on the *Etruria* in April 1899, and finally reached Heidelberg by May to consult with Dr. Erb. The German specialist examined Isidor using the latest techniques, which he had helped to popularize—electrodiagnostic testing and the reflex hammer—and gave what Ida referred to as a "favorable diagnosis."[28] He believed that, with the treatment he recommended by a young doctor in Heidelberg named Dambacher, Isidor's condition could be vastly improved. They liked the doctor and saw him both professionally and socially. "We are fortunately doomed to two weeks longer sojourn at this charming place which neither papa nor I are in a hurry to leave," Ida wrote. It was for both of them in some ways like a homecoming, "seeing all our relatives and friends." She especially relished "witnessing papa's joy—recalling old times and incidents, his pleasure at his remembering all the old places and events." With Jesse and Percy overseeing things at the store, Isidor worried less and felt that he could take more time to recover and relax while he was away. With the exception of the trip in 1898 for health reasons, Isidor had never traveled as often and as extensively as his brothers. He was always the one at home looking after the family's affairs, but now, with his sons taking charge, he felt a new freedom to enjoy the fruits of his wealth.

Oscar, who had been reappointed minister to Turkey in June 1898 by President William McKinley, urged Ida and Isidor to come to Constantinople before they returned home. "I...trust when you see Prof. Erb he will approve of your coming here after your cure is over."[29] Oscar urged his brother to take "a good long rest," one that he felt would be "more congenial and invigorating with us." Only the year before, Sarah and Oscar had hosted Percy, who had left New York in September to work briefly and in a rather casual manner as an unofficial secretary for his uncle Oscar, before settling into his duties at Macy's in earnest.[30] At the same time, Mildred, the oldest daughter of Sarah and Oscar, was also there, taking classes a few hours a day at a Greek school. The two young people seemed to be on something of an extended vacation.[31]

It was an opportunity to see Constantinople that Isidor and Ida did not intend to miss. After Isidor's leisurely cure came to an end, they headed to Turkey. Oscar and Sarah expected them to arrive before July and had decided to spend the summer and entertain their guests on the Bosporus, where it would be cooler. Although we do not have the exact dates of the visit, it is evident from entries in Aline Straus's diary that it did take place, with the best evidence suggesting that Ida and Isidor were in Turkey sometime between June and September 1899.[32]

At the end of their stay, Oscar's daughter, Mildred, decided to return with her Aunt Ida and Uncle Isidor to New York to get ready for college. They chose to begin their voyage home by way of the Orient Express, the legendary luxury train whose rails had recently been extended all the way to Constantinople. The journey started well enough. However, by the time they reached Austria, a historic flooding of the Danube resulting from a week-long rainstorm put an end to their trip on the Orient Express. By September 19 the river was still rising and their train could not continue on its designated route.[33] The Strauses detoured farther north into Germany, first to Dresden and then to Berlin. But they took it all in stride, with Ida commenting to her children that, "We are the wandering Jews, but unlike the fated one we always turn up in pleasant places."[34]

Ida was delighted to have Mildred with her, for it gave her a shopping companion, not an activity Isidor enjoyed. She relished the unexpected stopover in Dresden, where she, Mildred, and Isidor, spent afternoons at what she called "the grandest picture gallery in the world." [35] She raved especially about the paintings by the Christian painter Heinrich Hoffmann, which appealed "strongly to our sympathies as well as to our sense of the ideal."

Her taste was decidedly conservative, and she made it clear that she did not care for the Impressionists.

Ida and Isidor so enjoyed their travels of 1898 and 1899 that they began to take annual trips to escape the brutal winters of New York in favor of the balmier climate of the Riviera and to travel at greater leisure in the European spring. They usually returned home, 1899 being a notable exception, to spend the summer at Sunnyside.

It was particularly fortunate that by 1907 Jesse, Percy, and finally Herbert (who joined the firm in 1903) had taken over so many duties at Macy's and had in the process gained considerable experience, for it is hard to imagine a busier time for Ida and Isidor.

The year began with a dinner at Sherry's on January 13, given by the directors of the Educational Alliance to honor once again Isidor's work as head of that organization and to celebrate his upcoming departure for Alexandria.[36] He and Ida planned to sail on January 19, only two days after the marriage of their youngest daughter, Vivian. The groom was Herbert Adolph Scheftel, a Yale graduate, now a young stockbroker and a partner in the banking firm of J. S. Bache & Company.[37] Vivian was the last of their daughters to marry, and instead of having a spring or early fall wedding at Sunnyside as her two sisters had done, she elected to have it in the middle of winter on January 17 at the family's 105th Street house, which continued to be the center of family life.

She planned a 4 P.M. ceremony and a reception from 5 to 7. In order to lighten her mother's load, she scheduled the wedding "at an hour when no one expects a meal," although they did intend to offer a buffet luncheon.[38] However, as time drew closer and the guest list grew to more than 300, it was quickly becoming more than Ida felt she could handle. Concerned about his wife's health, Isidor insisted that the plans be changed. "[T]he excitement of the engagement and our going away has been such a strain on Ida that I dreaded the idea of further burdens, and finally prevailed upon the young couple to use Sherry's." Thus, at Sherry's it was.

The Rev. Dr. Samuel Schulman, rabbi at the Temple Beth-El officiated at the ceremony, as he had done for other Straus weddings. Vivian, always beautiful, wore what the *New York Times* described as "a severely plain white satin Empire gown with yoke and sleeves of point lace, and a long tulle veil."[39] She carried a fragrant bouquet of gardenias, white orchids, and lilies-of-the-valley. Her friend, Rhoda Seligman, dressed in blue crêpe de chine, a large plumed hat and carrying a muff of mauve orchids, was her maid of honor. Vivian's five nieces served as flower girls "in snowy lace trimmed frocks."[40] Herbert's best man was his brother Walter, and a dozen ushers seated the guests.

Isidor wanted his whole family present, but he worried that his brother Nathan would not come. Nathan had suffered from recent bouts of insomnia and had left with his wife and two sons on December 30 to go for a rest to Old Point Comfort in Hampton, Virginia. Isidor confided to Oscar, "It would be just like him to get back a day after [the marriage] to avoid the excitement, and it would not surprise me if he did not get back until two days after the wedding and thus escape the day of my sailing."[41] Whether Nathan came or not, Oscar was there, though his wife Sarah was not.

Two days after the lavish wedding, Ida and Isidor set sail aboard the White Star Line's S. S. *Celtic* for almost four months abroad. They departed from New York in a snowstorm and had a rough crossing with much rain. Fortunately, they encountered better weather in Italy. From Naples they sailed on February 3 for Egypt, planning to return for a later sojourn on the French Riviera. As always, Isidor wrote his brother Oscar on a weekly basis and informed him of their activities. Oscar was no longer ambassador to Turkey. Instead he had been named Secretary of the Department of Commerce and Labor by Theodore Roosevelt and had taken up his post as the first Jewish cabinet member, confining himself for the most part to Washington. It was now Isidor who was traveling and who seemed to be enjoying himself immensely.

As they sailed toward Egypt, still on the *Celtic*, Ida and Isidor celebrated their shared birthday. When they came to breakfast on the morning of February 6, they found "a beautiful surprise." Their table, that of the captain whom they judged a "very sociable gentleman," was "covered with flowers—as fresh and fragrant as if thy had been just cut." [42] The birthday tribute had been arranged from New York through a business associate in Naples and with the cooperation of Isidor's valet.

Vivian and Herbert, who had also sailed to Europe for their honeymoon, had expected to meet Ida and Isidor in Naples. But when the newlyweds arrived on February 4, they discovered that Vivian's parents had departed the day before. Both couples were disappointed at the scheduling snafu, but Ida and Isidor had left a letter indicating that they would meet them later when they returned to the Riviera.[43] The older couple traveled on to Alexandria and then Cairo, enjoying "most delightful temperatures...under clear and cheerful skies" and spending their days "quietly and pleasantly doing scarcely any sight seeing."[44] In Cairo, they encountered the distinguished Harvard Professor Morris Loeb, a colleague in the Educational Alliance, and his wife, and the two couples spent much of their time together.

Finally on February 27, the Strauses set sail for Marseille on the steamer *Schleswig* to rendezvous at last with the newlyweds in Monte Carlo from March 5 to the middle of the month.[45] By the end of March, Vivian and Herbert had returned to New York, but Ida and Isidor stayed on to take an automobile tour later in the spring. They were expecting a new limousine to be delivered in

Paris by a Mr. Rothschild. Until then, he had provided them with a vehicle on loan in which they were chauffeured to Paris, arriving on April 1, "having had a pleasant run from Biarritz with perfect weather all the way." Once in Paris, they encountered the Loebs once more. It was their intention to remain at the Hotel Bristol for another week "and then motor through a part of Germany and then via Belgium & Holland to reach England about May 1st." [46]

Automobiles still represented a new mode of travel for sight-seeing, and Isidor expressed their delight: "We enjoy the motoring very much. It is the ideal way for traveling when one does so for pleasure, at least in a country...which abounds in such excellent roads as this. We have a very competent chauffeur, cautious and agreeable in manner." Isidor could not resist one more trip to his birthplace in Otterberg, and on April 20 they were there. He cabled Oscar "Otterberg greets Washington." [47] Having thoroughly enjoyed their sojourn, they turned west again the following week toward Utrecht, Holland. [48]

It was not until May 18, that they finally set sail for home again aboard the *Celtic*. They were back in New York well in time to prepare for the next family wedding, for which, thankfully, as parents of the groom, they would have less responsibility for arrangements. Their youngest son, Herbert, was marrying Therese Kuhn, the daughter of Mr. and Mrs. Edward Kuhn, on July 15. Like the earlier wedding of their daughter, that of Herbert and Therese, whom the family called Teddy, also took place at Sherry's in similar style, though with only 200 guests. [49] Once again, Dr. Schulman performed the ceremony. The bride had a single attendant, and Jesse served as his younger brother's best man. The bride and groom planned a honeymoon of several months in England and on the Adriatic.

As if two weddings weren't enough excitement for one year, Ida and Isidor also had three grandchildren born in 1907: Margaret ("Peggy") Hess on March 30; Herbert Scheftel, Jr., on

November 14; and Richard Weil, Jr. on December 5. Their family cup was running over.

Unfortunately, the year was not marked solely by such happy events. Once the festivities of the weddings and the trip to Europe had ended, Ida and Isidor returned home to summer as usual at their cottage, Sunnyside, on the shore of Elberon, New Jersey. They were still in Elberon on September 24 when Ida's beloved sister Amanda, who had been like a mother to her in her youth, died unexpectedly during her afternoon walk at nearby Deal Beach.[50] Her death was a painful blow to Ida. Only three weeks later, after they had returned to New York, did she feel strong enough to write a letter to Amanda's oldest son, Alfred, to tell him the circumstances of his mother's death.[51] The two sisters had been in close contact most of their lives, including that summer. In fact, Ida and Isidor were the first family members to reach Amanda's side shortly after her death. It was hard for Ida to believe she was gone. She told Alfred that his mother's "end was as sweet and calm as her life had been; for amid all the storm and stress in which she sometimes found herself, and no matter what trouble came to her, she never allowed those around her to be affected by anything that was amiss with her." His mother had never spent a "happier summer," Ida assured him, and she had died "without any suffering and surrounded by good people."[52]

Ida was, in many respects, much like her sister. She refused to visit her own grief on her nephew and waited until she was in full control of her emotions before writing to him. For the most part, only Isidor knew how much Ida had suffered from grief and illness over the years. Her letter to Alfred was simply one of comfort, intended to alleviate any anguish her nephew may have felt over his mother's death. It is typical of both Ida and Isidor to reassure everyone else that all was well and that nothing was amiss. Only with one another were they absolutely candid, each keeping the other informed of any indisposition.

They closed their cottage at Elberon for the winter on October 7, two weeks after Amanda's death, and returned to the city. Although Isidor was reluctant to leave Ida, the Abrahams had recently arrived in New York, and Abraham Abraham, his partner in Abraham & Straus, "has left me no peace [but] to go fishing with him for a few days in the Thousand Islands." [53] He had finally agreed, and they planned to leave on October 11 and to be joined by Judge Simon Rosendale.

The relaxation in the wilderness was much needed, but by October 14 Isidor was back in the office and "very much occupied...on account of the very disturbed condition of things."[54] He is referring to the financial downturn the country was experiencing in the so-called Panic of 1907. The stock market had fallen almost fifty percent from its peak in 1906, causing widespread economic distress, runs on the banks, and a serious recession. Macy's, like other retailers, had suffered from the fiscal crisis, which Isidor blamed in part on tariff issues, especially the Dingley Tariff, which had gone into effect in 1897 to counteract the Wilson-Gorman Act of 1894. Isidor described its provisions as "absolutely brutal" in its damage to American retailers.[55] In November, he wrote Oscar, "We are certainly financially in a most trying situation." He suggests to his brother that "a reassuring word from him [Theodore Roosevelt] may do wonders in restoring confidence in the national Banks and bring out of hiding the money locked up and taken out of channels of trade by the hoarders....In other words, modern commerce is based on confidence...and unless confidence is restored soon, business will come to a stand still."[56] Once again, as he had done in 1893, J. P. Morgan would step in to quell the panic and help the United States get back on its feet.

The Panic of 1907 was not the only disturbance that Isidor had to face that year. He was also compelled to cope with disagreements and misunderstandings, unusual among the close-knit Strauses, that seemed to threaten family harmony.[57] Ever the peacemaker, he always tried to resolve any conflicts before they could ever become serious. Whenever a contretemps occurred, it was usually Isidor who made efforts to smooth it over. On June 17, 1907, for example, he informed his brother Oscar that their nephew Lee was upset by the way Oscar had treated him the last time he was in New York. "Now we don't want any family disagreements," he wrote, "and a few lines from you can, I believe, set things right." [58] He urged Oscar to write to him at once and assure him that he had not "meant any discourtesy toward him." Oscar followed his advice, and Lee responded that the matter, "while wounding me deeply at the time has been completely erased from the slate."[59]

But there were other issues that were more difficult to overcome. While all three brothers decried the persecution of the Jews in Eastern Europe, and particularly the pogroms in Russia, which had begun in earnest with the accession of Czar Alexander III to the throne in 1881, the Straus brothers had differing perspectives on possible solutions. Throughout his career, Oscar always strived for diplomatic solutions, but he also tried to view the persecutions in a positive way. He wrote during a visit to Egypt: "I look upon the Russian persecution as another one of those disguised blessings to a race that will force them out from their degraded conditions into more civilized lands, where there is some hope and every chance for their rising up to the standard of our Western Civilization."[60] But all the brothers were especially horrified by the ruthless massacre of Jews in Kishineff in April 1903.

Following a visit to the Holy Land in 1904, Nathan, on the other hand, had became convinced that the ultimate answer was Zionism—the creation of a Jewish homeland in Palestine, and he became an ardent supporter of the Zionist movement, which neither of his brothers espoused and which Isidor in particular abhorred.

Isidor championed an entirely different solution. He proposed to help those persecuted refugees, who had been driven from Russia to America and settled in the lower east side of Manhattan, by providing great effort and resources on their behalf. It was of primary importance in his 1889 effort to help found the Educational Alliance, which assisted these new Jewish immigrants in establishing a new and better life in the United States. Along with various other Jewish philanthropists, including Samuel Greenbaum, Myer S. Isaacs, Morris Loeb, Jacob H. Schiff, and Edwin R. A. Seligman, Isidor helped raise $125,000 to construct the Educational Alliance building in 1891, and he became the organization's president, working hard for the betterment of the refugees, a role in which he persisted until his death.[61]

Like her husband, Ida was deeply disturbed by the plight of the Russian Jews and the atrocities committed against them, and she tried to raise awareness of their situation by penning a poem entitled "To the Czar: A Prophecy," which underscored "the tortures...inflicted on those of other creeds, / The exilings, the pograms, the persecutions all, / Thus planned with thy minion, within thy palace wall." She calls upon the Russian people to "throw off thy shackles, strike for the right to live!" And she points to other parts of the world as models: "Bright shines the torch of freedom in every land but thine, / Illuminating every pathway that leads to Freedom's shrine." The poem was originally published anonymously in the *New York Times* on September 11, 1910, though the *Times* republished it on May 19, 1912, stating: "With characteristic modesty, Mrs. Straus did not claim literary merit for the verses, and asked that her name be not signed to them. They are reprinted here to show her broad human sympathies and give additional light on [her] character."[62] In this issue, as in so many others, she and Isidor shared a common ground and a belief in the possibility of progress.

Much of what the couple did, they did behind the scenes, never seeking public recognition. Educator and community worker, David Blaustein recalls one such instance in his memoirs. "It is not generally known what Mr. and Mrs. Straus have done for the people of this neighborhood," he wrote. He then goes on to recount a single incident involving a Jewish man at the point of death in a non-Jewish hospital whose only wish was to see his family in Russia once more before he died. It was not an easy task, but together Ida and Isidor arranged to have the family brought to New York. Unfortunately, they arrived too late, but the Strauses helped them to become self-supporting and to remain in America. Blaustein was careful to include Ida in his comments, he said, "because Mrs. Straus always shared in his noble work and was in sympathy with and encouraged him in all good work." He indicated that it was their spirit of "nobility" and "generosity" that had inspired him and "kindled" his own spirit "by their spirit."[63]

Most of the time the brothers agreed, or on occasions where they disagreed, they never let it cause hard feeling among them. Their divergence of opinion over the issue of Zionism, however, came closest to causing serious friction within the family. The Zionist Organization of America had been founded in 1897, and in the wake of his visit to the Holy Land, Nathan became a staunch and outspoken Zionist. It did not seem to become a major issue in the Straus family, however, until the fall of 1907, when a family friend, Jacob Schiff, also one of the founders of the Educational Alliance, took a firm stand against Zionism at the Jewish Chautauqua earlier in the summer and published on August 23 in *The American Hebrew* a strong letter opposing it. He argued, "I cannot for a moment concede that one can be at the same time a true American and an honest adherent of the Zionist movement."

Schiff was vehemently attacked for his letter from many sides. Oscar, who was not a Zionist, had nonetheless written him a critical letter, implying, or so Schiff believed, "that I am giving ammunition to the enemies of our people, this being also the charge the Zionists have made at their recent intemperate meeting." Schiff went on to justify his actions and suggest that he would not be keeping good faith with the American people to encourage this movement and make Jewish immigrants "look upon this country as an Asylum only and not as upon their own permanent home and [that] of their descendants."[64] Isidor, unlike his brother, was enthusiastic about Schiff's letter and fully supported his point of view. He wrote to Oscar:

> I look upon Zionism as a dangerous dogma for us in this country. If the new immigrants who arrive here by the hundreds of thousands during the course of a few years, and of whom the Educational Alliance is trying to make good American citizens, are met with the dogma that this country is only a tarrying ground for an ultimate home in Palestine, it places in the hands of the anti Semites, as well as those who are opposed to immigration, a weapon which can be used with the same force as the sentiment which gave rise to the Chinese Exclusion Act, and has raised on the Pacific Coast the trouble with Japan. I thoroughly agree with Schiff that Zionism is incompatible with patriotism....If Zionism means a home for the Jews, I am radically opposed to it. If it simply means a spiritual hope for the oppressed and persecuted people of Russia, Roumania, and Galata, then it is a different proposition. But political Zionism, or Zionism in [any] shape, manner or form, as a propaganda in this country, I have no patience with, and I am utterly and irrevocably opposed to it.[65]

By the first of November, some other unknown dissension had also arisen between Oscar and Nathan. As was often the case, Isidor was the go-between. Oscar, aware of the friction between them, had written a letter to Nathan seeking to get back in his good graces. Nathan cabled a brief reply to Oscar: "Letter pleased me immensely don't worry." However, he confided to Isidor his reluctance to write anything more to Oscar, indicating that a letter that sought to "do <u>myself</u> justice might only create new bad feeling so I will refrain from writing for the present. I was delighted to see that he is very anxious not to let money matters interfere with our brotherly affections. I have always had the <u>utmost contempt</u> for families where there was any dissension." Isidor forwarded the letter on to Oscar, as Nathan had asked him to do, but he penned a note at the bottom that said, "I don't know what this is about but I send you this letter, just rec<u>d</u>, as desired by Nathan."[66]

Even their sister Hermine was sensing unusual family tension. In a rare letter to her brother Oscar written in December of that year, she includes two rather revealing sentences, one in which she indicates that "Brother Isidor is now in very good condition, when he does not receive too many cable instructions from his brother Nathan." [67] Her second comment is that she receives occasional letters from Lina, but "from my brother not a word or line not even a recognition. Do you not think that this grieves me very much?" Furthermore, the family's "usual Friday evening reunions" had not taken place that winter, to her dismay. "Everybody seems so busy and taken up with their own affairs, that they have no time left for each other." The closeness that was so characteristic of the Straus family seemed threatened.

Nathan was deeply involved in another project that had consumed much of his attention ever since 1892. Concerned about the death rate of children in New York, he had begun to study the issue and had concluded that the problem, or part of it at least, was their drinking of raw milk. Thus, in early 1898 he built a pasteurization plant on Randall's Island and established milk stations at his own expense throughout the city to provide safe milk for children. His efforts considerably reduced the death rate among children who drank the pasteurized milk. Now he was busier than ever, seeking to persuade city officials of the importance of his mission, and in fact, he was gratified when on February 12, 1907, the New York Board of Aldermen finally passed an ordinance "requiring pasteurization of the city's milk supply." That same year President Theodore Roosevelt launched a national milk study by the Public Health Service.

Nathan's constant and unselfish efforts in this regard, which he expanded to many cities in Europe as well, coupled with his nervous condition and his propensity to write rarely in any case, had made him seem increasingly distant from his brothers. From all indications there were never (or certainly rarely) any overt disagreements among them, just a perceptible distancing as they grew older and were caught up in their own affairs and interests, Oscar's political; Nathan's humanitarian; Isidor's business-related and philanthropic. But whenever rifts may have threatened, Isidor was always eager to heal them, and none of the brothers wanted to disturb the family harmony. Still, disagreements, however slight, among the brothers who were known for their closeness, cast a shadow over the family.

Isidor and Oscar, however, seemed to maintain a close relationship even when they were unable to be together for long periods of time. Their letters flowed regularly on a weekly basis whenever they were separated by distance, and one senses in Oscar an unsurpassed admiration for his oldest brother. On December 23, 1908, while Isidor was vacationing in Santa Barbara, California, Oscar, clearly in a reflective mood, wrote him one of his many letters from his office at the Department of Commerce and Labor:

> This is my fifty-eighth birthday. I have a great deal to be
> thankful for, and I trust I am not unappreciative of the blessings
> that are mine. As I look back over my life there is no sentiment
> embedded more deeply in my heart and memory than the helpful,
> sympathetic guidance you have given me from the earliest years

of my career until now. I clearly see but for you I never could have had the opportunity of getting such a college education as my heart longed for. You have always entered into my life and its ambitions with more than brotherly interest—rather with that deeper interest that a father takes in the career of a son. I certainly would not have been able to accept my first appointment to Turkey but for your deep sympathetic interest, and it is no exaggeration when I say that you have not only been my brother, but my philosopher, my guide and my friend.[68]

Isidor valued the affection of his brothers and would do anything to preserve family harmony, except to sacrifice his own principles.

9

The Final Trip

Although Isidor's physical condition had improved following the Strauses' 1899 visit to Dr. Erb in Heidelberg, Ida's health had begun to deteriorate. In recent years she had suffered from a series of attacks, which were becoming a matter of growing concern to Isidor, who could not imagine life without her any more than she could imagine life without him. She was suffering from what he referred to as "arterial trouble."[1] Her most severe attack to date occurred in the late summer of 1909, which alarmed Isidor. Their son Jesse and his family were traveling in Europe at the time. As soon as he heard about it, Jesse wrote his father from Paris that "for the first time we realize that Mamma had been seriously ill. We had all along supposed her attack similar to previous ones and of no serious character."[2] As a result of the news, Jesse and Irma booked passage to return home on the *Kaiser Wilhelm* sooner than they had planned.

The possibility of losing his beloved wife of almost forty years weighed heavily on Isidor's heart. Several doctors, none of whom had been optimistic in their diagnoses, had examined her. Finally she allowed her thirty-three-year-old son-in-law, Minnie's husband, Dr. Richard Weil, to examine her. Isidor informed his brother Oscar on September 17, by which time Ida had recovered sufficiently to come downstairs for dinner, that their son-in-law viewed her prospects "with a great deal less seriousness than any of the doctors who have treated her." Isidor was clearly delighted with this new prognosis. "He insists that she can live for many, many years and reach a very advanced age." The greatest factor in her health was her mental attitude. "Dick says there is no ailment

[sic], in which the mind plays so important a part."[3] Isidor was encouraged by his assessment, for Dr. Weil was already gaining a fine reputation in the medical field as a pathologist and cancer researcher. Thus, Isidor was determined to follow his advice and see that Ida had plenty of rest and healthy recreation. One of the first steps he took was to move for the winter into the St. Regis Hotel, to lighten Ida's load, particularly since she "would not hear of having a housekeeper."[4] Their oldest son was enthusiastic about this plan and agreed with his father's decision. "Mama can then have no excuse for exerting herself more than is good for her."[5]

It had become time in their lives for them to begin to take it easy. They had achieved so much of what they set out as a young couple to accomplish, and they had much to be proud of. The business was on solid footing, and all their sons were working as effective team members at Macy's. All their children were happily married and settled into their own homes. And Isidor seemed increasingly willing to turn over more responsibility to the new generation and take time away from the store for a variety of activities, but especially to make certain that Ida kept her spirits high. Jesse noted in his biography for the Harvard alumni report in 1910 that business now "absorbs most of my time and attention, and because my seniors devote a large part of their time to charitable, philanthropic and municipal work, the details... devolve on the juniors, of whom I am one."[6]

In addition to charitable, philanthropic, and civic activities, they also took more time to travel, including an ambitious trip again in 1910 to visit Greece and then Turkey, where brother Oscar, who had been appointed ambassador for one final term by President William Howard Taft, was serving his last year as ambassador.[7] Ida and Isidor sailed from Athens to Constantinople on March 27.[8]

A month before their 1912 birthday, the couple set out one final time for Europe for a three-month winter vacation. Isidor booked two rooms and a bath on the Cunard Steamship Company's *Caronia* for $1300, though their servants would travel at only $77.50 each.[9] Always frugal, as his mother had taught him to be, Isidor had sought a better price for the accommodations, but he was assured that these could not be had for less, as the *Caronia* had been very popular and had "a heavy waiting list." Resigned to pay whatever it took, the following day Isidor had his secretary confirm the reservations for Ida and himself, as well as for his valet, John Farthing, and Ida's maid, Marie.

Their ultimate destination was the picturesque village of Cap Martin on the Riviera where they planned to relax and enjoy the Mediterranean air for several months. The *Caronia* set sail on January 6 under stormy skies. The sea was rough for several days, but the weather soon began to improve as they moved eastward. They sent regular "Marconis" (telegrams) to their children from the ship. On January 19 they passed through the Straits of Gibraltar and into the Mediterranean, making a brief stopover in Algiers, which left them unimpressed, before arriving ahead of schedule at Cap Martin. Obviously pleased with their hotel, they immediately sent a cable home to their children: "Excellent—what news?"

Jesse, Percy, and Herbert, in full charge of Macy's during most of their father's absence (for Nathan as well would soon leave the country), took turns writing to their parents regularly to keep them abreast of family news, social doings, and business activities. They wrote long and detailed letters and sent cables in code concerning urgent business matters. All seemed to be going as usual in New York. Jesse took a short vacation trip to Pinehurst, North Carolina, departing January 12 and returning Sunday, January 21, looking, according to his brother Percy [?], "very well indeed...and thoroughly rested."[10] The children carried on the family tradition of dining together weekly, even in their parents' absence, and gathered at Minnie's for dinner that same evening to welcome him home.

Herbert's turn for a vacation came next, though he would not leave until Thursday, February 28, for Aiken, South Carolina, where the weather was warm and balmy compared to New York and where the camellias were in bloom. During their absence, it was Percy in particular who kept his parents informed of the latest gossip, fires, business affairs, and funerals.

As Ida and Isidor read of the January snows and slippery streets in New York, they were delighted to be on the Riviera, even though the incessant rainy weather was not at all what they had hoped for. Still, there was no snow, and the temperatures were warmer than New York in January. The village of Cap Martin was charming, with its narrow streets and delightful squares. Their hotel was located on a wooded peninsula that jutted out into the Mediterranean. Nearby, perched on a rocky promontory overlooking the sea, was a recently restored tenth-century castle that dominated the nearby village of Roquebrune. During their stay at Cap Martin Isidor wrote to his brother Oscar:

> This is a lovely spot—for old people. The hotel is on a point which stretches out into the Mediterranean and in the midst of a well-wooded park. There is nothing on the point but the hotel, and this puts us in as isolated a spot as if we were in the Adirondacks. We have had lots of rain, but, notwithstanding, we have no complaints to utter. The thermometer ranges between 45 degrees at night—68 degrees on a sunny day at the meridian is the highest—usually it does not exceed 56 degrees. We are only two and a half miles from Mentone, to which we walk nearly every day, and about four miles from Monte Carlo. We shall probably remain here until the weather is mild enough to go further north. With our auto we make delightful excursions.[11]

They celebrated their birthday—his 67th and her 63rd—on February 6 at Cap Martin. Cables of congratulations poured in from their children in New York, and the "whole dam fam," as they sometimes called themselves, sent a gift from Paris on February 19. Despite the less than ideal weather, Ida and Isidor were having a wonderful time, both enjoying good health and a renewed sense of wellbeing.

They were expecting a visit from Isidor's brother Nathan, who had sailed from New York on February 3 "in the best of spirits" and in the company of Dr. [Judah] Magnes "who recently resigned his position from an uptown synagogue...to write some articles on the Holy Land for the *Sun* during his absence."[12] Dr. Magnes had until 1910 been rabbi at the Temple Emanu-El in New York, a congregation of Reformed Jews. In a Passover sermon given that year, however, he had advocated a return to more Orthodox practices, creating quite a stir among members. The subsequent disagreement led him to resign to become rabbi of a more conservative congregation, B'nai Jeshurun. Isidor had been relieved at the time of his resignation in June 1910, for he saw his views as "extreme" and "retrogressive." He had written Oscar at the time that, with Magnes as rabbi, "Temple Emanu-El stood in danger of reversing what it had advocated for more than fifty years."[13]

Before arriving at Cap Martin, Nathan and Lina sailed the Mediterranean, their ship pausing at various ports, Madeira, Gibraltar, Algiers, and Monaco, where they visited rabbis in various towns along the way. On February 17 they reached Cap Martin, where the brothers, happy to be with one another, put aside their differences and spent a delightful day together with their wives. Lina later recalled: "We found Isidor in splendid condition; poor Ida, less so, as she had had a recent attack of her ailment. But both were in the utmost cheerful frame of mind and overjoyed that we came. We remained with them from morning until night, and every minute of the time was pure happiness to the four of us." There seemed to be no overt discord from their recent disagreement over Zionism. Apparently the brothers had agreed to disagree, and this brief meeting allowed them to turn back time and revive their "youth," in Lina's words, and "with it the atmosphere of mutual love and devotion of those early years, when our existence was one harmonious whole of living and working together." Once again, she recalled, "we were contented and free from serious cares—just happy to be together with no disturbing elements between us."[14]

But the visit was all too brief. Nathan and Lina left the following day, arriving in Jerusalem at sunset on March 5. There is no evidence that Dr. Magnes played any role in the day the two brothers and their wives spent together. The four of them made plans to rendezvous once again, during Nathan and Lina's return trip, at the nearby port of Villefranche, one of the deepest natural harbors on the Mediterranean. It was a rendezvous that would never take place.

Ironically, the weather on the Riviera continued to produce only "leaden skies and rain," while family members in New York were reporting in mid-February "the most delightful Winter weather, clear, crisp and rather cold but very bracing. In fact, it has never been so pleasant," they claimed.[15]

But everything back home was not going so well, as Ida and Isidor learned in a letter from Percy in late February. Herbert, seeking to join the Triton Fish and Game Club in Canada had been blackballed because of the "bigotry" of one of its members.[16] He was not acceptable, Percy believed, because a previous guest had proved "both objectionable and Jewish."[17] Isidor and Ida, who judged people on their character, but never on the basis of religion, could only have felt hurt for their son and disgust at such prejudice. In fact, a friend had informed Herbert it was all a mistake and that he could help straighten it out and that Herbert should try again. But when he was turned down a second time, it was obvious that anti-Semitism was the primary factor.

Although the Straus family doubtless suffered less discrimination than many American Jews, the bitter taste of anti-Semitism was not entirely new for them. Isidor could still remember the incident from his childhood that had caused his family to leave Talbotton. There had also been the situation when Nathan had been denied a room at a Lakewood hotel. And in 1909, one of the Straus grandchildren had applied for admission to St. Bernard's Academy, an elite preparatory school in New York. Isidor had even written to the headmaster, Frank Tabor, in support the boy's admission. Tabor had responded on November 17, with complete candor: "I take it as a great compliment that you wish your grandchild to attend to St. Bernard's. Though it is most painful to me, it seems only honest to tell you frankly that we dare not take a pupil of Hebrew parentage. I cannot say anything in extenuation, except that we have reason to know that we should lose our Gentile pupils were we to accept Hebrews." Tabor was most apologetic about the situation and informed Isidor that "the writing of this letter to you gives me real distress."[18] He and Ida must have seen irony in the fact that they were welcomed into the homes of ambassadors, presidents, and kings, but that their grandson was not welcome in a private school in New York.

One other item of bad news marred their last days on the Riviera. Reports from the store were not good. Profits were down, and the new department on the sixth floor, known as "Old-fashioned Macy's," where they were experimenting with what they thought customers would see as old-fashioned bargains, was not catching on as they had hoped. Percy informed him: "[W]e are not attracting customers as much on the floor as we would like. There seems to be a little feeling that our regular trade do not care to be seen in the 'cheap' part of the house, and the new trade that we hope to attract has not yet learned of the existence of 'old-fashioned Macy's."[19]

Given the unsettling news, Isidor felt that he was needed at home. He had already booked passage for their return trip on the White Star ship *Olympic*, which was set to sail on April 19. However, a little more than a month before the voyage, the shipping line notified its passengers that the sailing of the *Olympic* would be delayed almost a week until April 24.[20] The ship's brief history did not encourage confidence and might have given Ida and Isidor reason to rethink their return voyage, especially given this new delay. The vessel, which had been launched less than a year before, had already been back to Ireland twice for repairs.[21] Although she was now back in service, she was running behind schedule. A coal strike in England that had begun the day the Strauses sailed on the *Caronia* had also affected the White Star Line. The company was putting more of its resources behind the launching of the maiden voyage of the *Olympic*'s sister ship, *Titanic*, which was being hyped as a larger and improved version.

Isidor, restless to get back to New York and to the store, was not happy about the delay, and the prospect of the maiden voyage of the *Titanic* had a certain appeal. He had always been attracted to the newer ships and still recalled what he had believed to be the maiden voyage of the *Saint Louis*, his first ocean-going trip. He had also sailed on the maiden voyage of the *New York*, which at the time had seemed splendid, and he had wanted to sail on the *Great Eastern* during that Civil War journey out of New York. Although it would not have been the *Great Eastern*'s maiden voyage, it was still a new ship, considered the wonder of the age at the time. He had been tempted, despite the danger of delay. Now a chance to take the first trip on the much-touted *Titanic* must have had a particular attraction. Why wait for the *Olympic*, when the *Titanic* was supposed to be even larger and better, with several new features the *Olympic* lacked?

He wrote his brother Oscar that he was considering changing his plans. Although he still had tentative reservations on "the steamer Olympic…[t]he new steamer Titanic is to start on her maiden voyage on April 10. I have written to learn whether we can secure satisfactory accommodations on her. Other than this our plans are not formed."[22] The captain of the *Titanic* was to be the former captain of the *Olympic* and admiral of the White Star fleet, E. J. Smith.

When the Straus sons in New York received news that their parents were considering an earlier return, Percy wrote back on March 16: "Just received a cable from you telling us…that you expect to leave on Friday for Paris and that you intend to sail on the tenth of April on the *Titanic*. I do not know why you are in such a hurry to return." But Isidor felt he was needed at the store, and he was impatient to get home. His sons were "all rather surprised at the change in your plans and do not understand why you are coming home so early."[23] Their message may have given him pause, for Percy wrote again on March 27 to acknowledge receipt of another letter from his father "in which you state you have not yet made up your mind whether to sail on the *Titanic* or not."[24] But the major reason for his uncharacteristic indecision was that Nathan had still not returned from his voyage to Palestine, and he had promised Isidor he would stop by and visit them once more on his return home.

The brothers had hoped to see one another again. Isidor wanted to hear about their voyage and, always the peacemaker, perhaps to further convince his brother of his continued good will. "Nathan wanted that we should spend some time together, when he gets back from the East," he informed Oscar, but "I have not heard from him since they left Alexandria." He was evidently troubled by Nathan's silence.[25] If he booked the earlier date on the *Titanic*, Isidor wrote to his brother Oscar, their plans might not work out, for he feared that Nathan might not return soon enough for them to get together.

Ida and Isidor were also looking forward to a visit with their daughter Vivian and her family, who were on their way to France. "We may, after Vivy arrives, move to Cannes, to be with her a few days."[26]

Still, no news came from Nathan, and if Isidor hoped to book himself and his wife on the *Titanic*, he could wait no longer. By Monday, March 18, they had finalized their plans. Ida wrote to their granddaughter Beatrice that they were all packed and ready to leave for Cannes, where Vivian had now arrived with her husband Herbert Scheftel and "the babies," four-year-old Herbert, Jr. and two-year-old Stuart, on the preceding Saturday. As Ida informed Beatrice, their trunks had already been shipped, but they themselves had delayed leaving until after lunch, not only because of the continuing rain, but also because they were expecting a Mrs. Oelberman, whom Ida described as "the lady with the jewels, because she has such magnificent ones," to come from Monte Carlo for lunch.[27] After a few days in Cannes, they planned to go to Paris, which would be the next leg of their journey. "We will soon be home again," Ida told Beatrice, "as we have taken passage on the steamer *Titanic* for April 10." It was the last letter the child would ever receive from her grandmother.

Their visit with Vivian, Herbert, and the children was brief, and by the end of March the Strauses had made their way to Paris, where they stayed for several days at the Hotel Bristol. While they were in Paris, Ida wrote to Rose Abraham on May 30, telling her all the news and especially of her improved health: "We women seem to grow stronger as we grow older when we have passed a certain stage. I am able to do so much more than in the past years, and but for one or two little attacks I have felt better during this trip and able to do more than in years."[28] She refers to Isidor in the letter as "my old man," complaining affectionately that he "would not allow me to go about at all" to buy presents," for "he hates to bother with the duty, and now more than ever."[29] Evidently he relented, because Ida would write to her children only a few days later asking them to meet them at the dock in New York with three or four hundred dollars, presumably to cover duty on items they had purchased.[30] Certainly Isidor's reluctance to pay duty had not deterred him on one auspicious occasion. The Strauses had gone shopping at M. M. Noury in Paris, where Ida had seen a gold handbag encrusted on the bars with emeralds and diamonds. It was just the thing for their elegant dining on the *Titanic*, and Isidor purchased it for her as a gift.[31]

While Ida and Isidor were still in Paris, their oldest son Jesse and his wife Irma made an impulsive decision to set sail for a quick trip to Europe. They planned to leave on April 11 on the *Amerika*, one day after the sailing of the *Titanic*. As Jesse informed Herbert on March 28, they would be "crossing Papa in mid-ocean." He went on to explain their sudden plans. "We came to this determination because Papa was coming home earlier than usual, and I wanted Irma to get away from housekeeping for a little while before the summer."[32] They had also decided to take their fifteen-year-old daughter Beatrice "to put her in the Beer girls' school at Neuilly for a few weeks" so that she could work on her French, and they expected to "be back here [in New York] the first week in June."[33] The next day Jesse wrote to inform his parents of his family's upcoming trip: "This is probably the last letter that will reach you before you sail, and I hope that you will both return in as good health as you appear to have been in all Winter, and that the 'Titanic' will give you a smooth crossing."[34] He would, however, write one more letter that he mailed to them on April 2, informing his father that they would try to "communicate with you by Marconi from the 'Amerika' and sending "my love to you and Mama." [35]

Before the Strauses left Paris, they saw Ida's nephew, Alfred, the son of her sister Amanda, who had changed his last name from Rothschild to Redgis. He would later write: "I was the last member of our family to bid goodbye to them in Paris."[36]

On Sunday May 31, they moved on to London arriving in the evening, where they checked in, as they always did, at Claridge's on Brook Street in Mayfair, considered the most fashionable hotel in London ever since Queen Victoria and Prince Albert had stayed there in 1860. It had been purchased in 1893 by the owner of the Savoy, Richard d'Oyly Carte, who had the structure rebuilt from the ground up in an elegant Art Deco style, and reopened in 1898.

The Strauses were surprised by how few people were staying at Claridge's. Ida wrote her children that the hotel "is very empty, as it is said are all the London hotels. We lunched yesterday at the Carleton and there it was as empty as here in the dining salon." Although the Straus family, all of whom proudly claimed Jewish heritage and supported Jewish causes, did not for the most part practice the Jewish rituals, Ida nonetheless reminded her children that "You may not know that this is already the third day of Pesach (Passover) and that you should all be eating Matzos– Claridges does not serve them so we cannot do our duty."[37]

Despite the half-empty hotel, the Strauses' stay at Claridge's was a most pleasant one, and they enjoyed a quiet, but elegant social life. On April 3, they went to the St. James Theatre to see *Bella Donna*, a theatrical adaptation of Robert Hicheus's novel. On April 4, they were invited to lunch at Dorchester House on Park Lane by the Ambassador to Great Britain (and former Ambassador to France), Whitelaw Reid. Isidor had gone to call on the ambassador the previous Monday, but he was out of town. Upon his return, however, the ambassador had invited them to be his guests. Among the party of twelve were Frank L. Brown, the Director of the Panama-Pacific Exposition, and various distinguished guests, among them representatives from Portuguese and Liberian consulates.[38]

The stopover in London was not exclusively a pleasure trip. Isidor consulted various people about the coal strike and no doubt conducted a bit of business, including in all likelihood a visit to Harrods Department Store and a meeting with its general manager, Sir Richard Burbridge, who had turned Harrods into the one of the largest department stores in the world. It is likely that the Strauses also enjoyed a social evening with Burbridge and his new wife, Lilian, whom he had married in 1910, following the death of his first wife in 1905.[39] Business or not, Isidor loved London, preferring it to Paris, as Ida noted. He "just revels in going about here," she confided to Rose.

The one unpleasant note during their time there was the necessity for Ida to replace her maid, for Marie had clearly lost favor in the Straus ménage. She had accompanied them back as far as London, but as soon as Ida could find a new maid, Marie planned to return to France. In her letter of March 30 to Rose Abraham, Ida informed her friend that Marie "has engaged herself to the barber of the Cap Martin hotel and expects to marry this spring. A chance for all old maids, when this forty or more year old one finds a man," Ida quipped to Rose. Neither Ida nor Isidor was sorry to see the woman go. As Ida informed her children in a letter on April 4, Marie "has been behaving very badly over here. When Papa sours on a girl you know there is good cause, and he is disgusted with her." Fortunately, not long after their arrival in London, the housekeeper at Claridge's helped her to find a new maid—a young woman—named Ellen Bird, who would accompany them back to America aboard the *Titanic*. By now Ida was wary, noting, "I have engaged a nice English girl now but as with the other do not know whether I can count on her."[40] But Ellen Bird proved quite satisfactory and took over her duties, allowing Marie to return to Cap Martin to marry her barber.

Despite a busy schedule, Isidor also found time to keep up with the news and even pen a few letters himself. Jesse had kept him well informed about the political situation in America. Isidor had been particularly interested in Theodore Roosevelt's recent effort to be nominated by the Republican Party and would no doubt have supported his candidacy. As he had already learned from newspaper accounts, Jesse informed him that Roosevelt "was snowed under in his attempt to get the New York delegates. Uncle Oscar [nominated as a Roosevelt delegate] went down to defeat with the rest of the candidates."[41] Roosevelt lost the Republican nomination to the incumbent president, William Howard Taft. But Jesse enclosed an article from the *New York Times* of March 28, reporting a speech Roosevelt had made in Chicago, "in which he gives intimation that he may run on an independent ticket."[42]

Isidor had also kept up with any matters that might affect business at Macy's. Thus when he read in the *Daily Telegraph* about the efforts of a Rev. H. H. Redgrave, he wrote to the man on April 9, his last day in London, lauding his work in attempting to aid "the dire distress" and provide relief in the Pottery Districts, "with which my firm has been in business for almost half a Century" and enclosing a donation of fifty pounds drawn on the Manchester & Liverpool District Bank "to assist in the worthy work."[43] Many years later, on September 13, 1934, Redgrave mailed a copy of the letter to one of the Straus sons, suggesting it was most likely the last letter ever written by Isidor Straus. The day after it was written, Isidor and Ida would set sail for New York aboard the *Titanic*.

10

The *Titanic*

By 9:30 on Wednesday morning April 10, Ida and Isidor had already checked out of Claridge's Hotel, made their way to Waterloo Station, and waited on platform 12 to board their first class car on the White Star Line's boat train for Southampton. Once they were comfortably settled in their seats, upholstered in the suitably nautical colors of navy blue trimmed with gold braid, they had only a few minutes to wait. At 9:45 the train pulled out of the station, wove through the outskirts of London, and began to cut its way eighty miles south through the British countryside toward the coast. England was abloom with an early spring abundance of flowering cherry trees and almond blossoms, and the morning ride was pleasant as the train rushed through woodlands and fields, past the villages and streams of southern England. Less than two hours later they arrived on the track that ran parallel to the quay. There the *Titanic* lay berthed in the newly created White Star Dock, which encompassed sixteen acres of water that opened onto the River Test.[1]

As Isidor and Ida stepped from the train into the brisk 50-degree April air and approached the dock, they were impressed by the sheer immensity of the vessel waiting there. She loomed splendidly against the cloudless sky as high as an eleven-story building. Around her hull gleamed the bright gold band that marked all the ships of the White Star Line. In comparison to the *Saint Louis*, the ship Isidor remembered so well from his boyhood, the *Titanic* was a leviathan. The newly constructed ship was almost 900-feet long, more than three times the length of the *Saint Louis*. Her nine decks would have dwarfed the two-decked steamer of his youth. Instead of one funnel, she had four of enormous proportions, twenty-two feet in diameter and rising sixty-two feet above the deck. Large gold letters on her bow splendidly announced her name—*Titanic*—and on her mainmast the red White Star pennant flapped in the breeze.

This much-touted maiden voyage promised to be spectacular in every way. Those lucky enough to be boarding knew they were participating in what was being ballyhooed as the voyage of the century. Neither Isidor nor Ida could help but be infected by the excitement that surrounded them once they stood on deck, looking down at the hundreds of people on the dock waving enthusiastically and awaiting the historic moment when *Titanic* would cast off. They must have noticed with a sense of satisfaction that the ship's band was playing tunes from the popular operetta, *The Chocolate Soldier*, written four years earlier by Isidor's relative, a second cousin once removed, the Viennese composer, Oskar Straus, whose father had left Otterberg in 1860 to avoid military service.[2] They would enjoy the little five-piece band many times during the next four days.

In short, although Isidor's main objective was to get back to New York as soon as possible, he certainly had no reason to regret his choice of carriers. They would be very comfortable and well entertained on the *Titanic*, the largest and most luxurious ship in the world. He knew she was considered virtually unsinkable because of her unique hull design, with its fifteen interior bulkheads that created sixteen "watertight" compartments. And she was said, like the *Great Eastern* that had attracted his attention so many years ago, to be the wonder of the age.

Just before noon, to announce its impending departure, the ship's crew ran up on its fore yardarm the maritime flag known as the Blue Peter and sounded its whistle three times. Strong-armed sailors cast off the lines that connected the ship to the dock. Before the departure Isidor had already escorted Ida to their Regency

Style parlor suite on the first-class C Deck, where they found a beautiful floral arrangement of roses and carnations, compliments of the Sir Richard Burbridges, whom they had seen in London, where Sir Richard was manager of Harrods Department Store.[3]

As Ida admired the flowers and settled in, Isidor returned to the deck, where he now stood beside a friend, Col. Archibald Gracie, to watch the activity below.[4] Five tiny tugboats strained at the hull to guide the ship into the River Test and toward the open sea. As her propellers began to turn, the *Titanic*'s forward motion created a suction that disturbed the tranquility of two vessels side by side in their harbor berths, the *Oceanic* and the *New York*. Suddenly the force lifted the outside ship, the *New York*, from its mooring and snapped seven of its cables as easily as if they had been rubber bands. As passengers watched in horror, the stern of the smaller vessel swung out into midstream and threatened to strike the port side of the *Titanic*.

For the captain of the brand-new ship, Edward J. Smith, and his pilot, George Bowyer, the moment must have been like a flashback to the previous September off the Isle of Wight, when the two of them had been in charge of setting sail on the *Olympic*, the *Titanic*'s sister ship. As it moved from its moorings, the *Olympic* had created a similar suction, pulling a British cruiser, H.M.S. *Hawke*, into its path. The two ships had collided, causing considerable damage to both and taking the *Olympic* out of service for six weeks of repairs.[5]

This time Captain Smith was more accustomed to navigating the larger vessels and acted quickly, giving an order of "full astern" in an effort to diminish the pull of the *Titanic*'s wake. At the same time the captain of one of the tugboats, the *Vulcan*, managed to secure a line to the runaway vessel and tow it out of harm's way just in time before it could strike the larger ship's hull. But the two ships came within four feet of one another, while all those aboard held their breath, expecting an imminent collision.[6]

The incident created quite a flurry of excitement among the passengers. But no harm was done, and it would give them all something interesting to talk about once they reached America and to recount to the passengers who would be joining the ship at its scheduled stops at Cherbourg and Queenstown.

As the passengers began to relax, Isidor told Col. Gracie the story of his own experience with the *New York*. It seemed but a few years ago that he had been a passenger on her maiden voyage, when she was said to be the "last word in shipbuilding."[7] Now as they looked down on the *New York*, dwarfed beside the *Titanic*, Isidor commented wryly to Col. Gracie on the progress made since then.[8]

When he returned to the cabin, he reported the near accident to Ida, who mentioned it in the letter she wrote that afternoon to Lilian Burbridge to thank her and her husband, Sir Richard, for "the exquisite basket of flowers."[9] Ida indicated that Isidor "was on deck when the start was made" and told her that "it looked painfully near to the repetition of the Olympian's [sic] experience on her first trip out of the harbor." She was happy to report to Mrs. Burbridge that "the danger was soon averted and we are now well on our course across the channel to Cherbourg." The Strauses' quarters definitely met with their approval, and Ida was enthusiastic about the *Titanic*. "[W]hat a ship!" she wrote. "So huge and so magnificently appointed. Our rooms are furnished in the best of taste and most luxuriously as they are really rooms and not cabins."[10]

Like the other passengers, the Strauses admired the ship's luxuries and expected the maiden voyage of the *Titanic* to be one of the social events of the season, with no lack of human interest and variety. During their first hours at sea, Ida and Isidor, like the other passengers, began to learn their way around the ship and strolled the deck, encountering some of the people who had boarded with them in Southampton. Three members of the

Widener family included George Dunton Widener, heir to the largest fortune in Philadelphia, was traveling with his wife, the former Eleanor Elkins, and their twenty-seven-year-old son Harry, already well recognized as a collector of rare books.[11] Lucy Noël Martha Dyer-Edwardes, the Countess of Rothes, accompanied by her cousin, Gladys Cherry, was on her way to join her husband, the Earl of Rothes, who had gone to America to look over a citrus farm in Florida he was thinking of buying.[12] Nineteen-year-old Daniel Warner Marvin, the son of the founder of Biograph Pictures, and his young bride were returning from their honeymoon in Europe. Also aboard were J. Bruce Ismay, chairman and managing director of the White Star Line, and Thomas Andrews, managing director of Harland & Wolff, who had overseen the design and building of the ship. It promised to be an elegant crossing, with the crew working especially hard to provide Mr. Ismay, Mr. Andrews, and the other first-class passengers a perfect sailing.

Also among the Southampton passengers were the three Lamson sisters, Caroline Brown, a widow whose husband had been managing director of the publishing house of Little, Brown and Company, and her sisters, Malvina Cornell and Charlotte Appleton. They were returning to America after the sad task of attending the funeral in England of their sister, Lady Lily Drummond.[13] Col. Gracie was frequently at their side, for they were all "old friends" of his wife, and as a gentleman traveling alone, he had offered his services and assistance to the three sisters during the voyage. As a youth, he had also been a friend of Charlotte Appleton's husband at St. Paul's Academy. These sisters, too, would be among the people with whom the Strauses would spend a great deal of time in the next few days.[14]

The incident with the *New York* caused an hour-long delay in departure and hence a late arrival near dusk in the Norman port of Cherbourg. By the time *Titanic* dropped anchor, it was already

6:30 P.M. Because of her size, the vessel was compelled to pause in the harbor off the Grande Rade, the world's largest man-made breakwater, while the White Star tenders, the *Nomadic* and the *Traffic*, transported 274 new passengers and their luggage to the ship. Twenty-two "cross-channel" passengers debarked at Cherbourg, and the tenders took them back to the dock. A band was playing on the quay as a crowd gathered to admire the magnificent vessel anchored offshore, silhouetted against the setting sun, and to wait for her to set sail once more. By the time she did so, it was after 8:00 P.M. and dinner was already being served on the ship.

One of the new passengers who boarded at Cherbourg was struck not only by the ship's size but by its smooth sailing as the vessel steamed toward its next stop in Queenstown, Ireland, "[W]e could not believe she was moving: we are less shaken than in a train....The sea is very smooth, the weather is wonderful. If you could see how big this ship is! One can hardly find the way back to one's cabin in the number of corridors."[15]

Among those who joined the trip in Cherbourg was Edith Corse Evans, a traveling companion and niece of the bereaved Lamson sisters. John Jacob Astor, one of the wealthiest men in New York, also boarded the ship with his eighteen-year-old pregnant bride, Madeleine, who was a year younger than Astor's son. The couple had married on September 9, 1911 and were returning from their extended honeymoon touring Egypt and France. Traveling with their party was Margaret (later widely known as "The Unsinkable Molly") Tobin Brown.

Benjamin Guggenheim and his mistress, Madame Léontine Aubart, a French singer, also boarded the ship at Cherbourg, as did Mr. and Mrs. John Borland Thayer, with their seventeen-year-old son, Jack. The renowned American painter and writer, Francis Millet, was among them, accompanied by Major Archibald Butt, President Taft's military aide, who was returning from a trip to

Rome as the president's emissary to the Vatican. Certainly there would be no lack of interesting people for the crossing.

In addition to the social interaction, there was a great deal to do on the *Titanic*. As they wandered through the oak-paneled corridors of the ship, the Strauses would discover its saltwater swimming pool, the first on any ocean liner, its Turkish bath, and a squash court, which they would not likely use, but which would surely keep the younger folks occupied. They would, however, make use of the four-passenger elevators and the delightful palm veranda where the orchestra played each evening after dinner. They explored "the smoking room with its inlaid mother-of pearl—the lounge with its green velvet and dull polished oak—[and] the reading room with its marble fireplace and deep soft chairs and rich carpets of old rose hue."[16] And like all the other passengers at mealtimes, they would find their way to the elegant first-class dining room with its grand staircase and its fine cuisine. There was even the special touch of the Café Parisien. Their first luncheon had offered among its many choices fresh lobster, roast beef, potted shrimp, Virginia and Cumberland ham, and Galantine chicken.[17]

Following an even more lavish dinner, they most likely joined their fellow passengers in the lounge to listen to selections from *The Tales of Hoffman* and *Cavalleria Rusticana* played by the White Star orchestra. Finally, as the ship steamed toward Ireland, Ida and Isidor settled for the night into their well-appointed suite on C deck, consisting of cabins 55 and 57. Ida's new maid, Ellen Bird, was in a smaller inner cabin across the hall, C-97 and Isidor's valet, John Farthing, occupied the adjacent cabin C-95.[18] The Wideners, the Countess of Rothes, Col. Gracie, and the Lamson sisters were all among their neighbors on C Deck. Their paneled cabin was elegant, not so lavish as the two extravagant "millionaire's suites" on B deck, which were no doubt already booked by the time Isidor finally made the decision to sail on the

Titanic rather than the *Olympic*, though in all likelihood he would have thought them ostentatious.

The following morning, April 11, at 11:30 A.M., after a good night's sleep for the Strauses, the *Titanic* arrived for its second stop in Queenstown. One of the passengers described their approach. "The coast of Ireland looked very beautiful as we approached Queenstown Harbour, the brilliant morning sun showing up the green hillsides and picking out groups of dwellings dotted here and there above the rugged grey cliffs that fringed the coast."[19] This was not, in fact, the first time the ship had sailed in Irish waters. She had been constructed in Belfast at the Harland & Wolff shipyards, where her builders had watched her slide into the water for the first time on May 31, 1911, though she would not be completed and delivered to her owners until early April 1912. Bruce Ismay had been at the initial launch with his father, Thomas Ismay. Lord Pirrie, chairman of Harland & Wolff, joined them for the festivities and the American financier, J. P. Morgan, whose shipping trust, the International Mercantile Marine, held controlling interest in the White Star Line.[20] The next day the *Irish News and Belfast Morning News* ran a story that proudly described the ship in some detail, including its sixteen watertight compartments "practically making the vessel unsinkable." An editorial in the same issue questioned the peculiar naming of the ship for the deities known as the Titans who challenged Zeus in a war that led to their ruin. In Greek mythology, it said, the Titans "symbolized the vain efforts of mere strength to resist the ordinances of the more 'civilized' order established by Zeus." Perhaps, it concluded, the ship was named in "the spirit of contradiction."[21] Bruce Ismay was the only one of those particular dignitaries present at the launch event who was also on board for the maiden voyage.

As she approached Queenstown, the vessel, once again too large for the harbor, anchored off shore to take on 113 new passengers and 1,385 sacks of mail, which were brought to the ship on the tenders *America* and *Ireland,* while seven people debarked to remain in Ireland.[22] Most of the new passengers were young immigrants traveling third class and on their way to make new lives in America. Their boarding created less of a stir among the first-class passengers than those among the elite who had boarded at Cherbourg. Nevertheless, it was their last stop before they headed across the North Atlantic, and by 1:30 P.M. the ship was under way again.

Throughout the rest of the day they steamed along the Irish coast until finally, by late afternoon, the land receded into the distance.[23] Passengers could finally settle down for the relaxing cruise and the comfortable routine they had all looked forward to on this majestic ship. No doubt the Strauses and most of the other first-class passengers shared the enthusiasm expressed by Archibald Gracie for the elegant and leisurely life aboard the *Titanic.* "I enjoyed myself as if I were in a summer palace on the seashore, surrounded by every comfort."[24]

While Ida played bridge and chatted with the Lamson sisters and another new friend, a native of Germany named Emma Schabert, Archibald Gracie and Isidor strolled the deck together exchanging war stories.[25] During their "daily talks" Isidor told Gracie about his "early manhood in Georgia" and how he had come to run the blockade and spend the war years as an agent in London with the Georgia Import and Export Company. The two men discussed Isidor's special friendship with President Cleveland and the honors Cleveland had bestowed upon him. Although they no doubt talked of many other things during their days together on the *Titanic,* as Gracie declared, those were the "topics of daily conversation that interested me most."[26] Early in the voyage, Gracie had loaned Isidor a copy of his new book, *The Truth about Chickamauga,* which he read, determined to finish it before the end of the trip. And on Sunday, April 14, he returned it with his compliments to the author.

It was an exciting day for the Strauses. Before noon they made arrangements to send a message on the Marconi to their son Jesse and his wife Irma aboard the passing ship *Amerika*. Though they could not actually see or talk to Jesse, Irma or little Beatrice, sending such a ship-to-ship personal message, still a novelty at the time, was almost as good, and they were delighted with this possibility.[27] Making their way to the inquiry office on the starboard side of the deck toward the bow, they had written out the message to be sent, limiting it to only nine words, which cost them 12 shillings sixpence. Despite the brevity of the telegram, it conveyed their high spirits and the pleasures they were enjoying aboard the *Titanic* and asked for news from their children: "fine voyage fine ship feeling fine what news."

The telegraph officer was busy much of the day sending messages for other passengers as well who were enjoying the relatively new miracle of the Marconi at sea. In fact, the telegraph operator was so busy sending messages from passengers that he even became testy toward some of the more official messages that began to come in as early as 9 A.M. warning of ice along the *Titanic*'s route. Not long after the Straus's telegram had been sent, at 1:45 P.M. a message arrived from the telegraph officer of the *Amerika*, requesting that it be relayed on to the hydrographic offices in Washington: "Amerika passed two large icebergs in 41°27' N., 50°08' W., on the 14th April."[28] It was only one of many iceberg sightings that the telegraph operator received that day.

The warnings came in from many ships, with one of the last from the nearby *Californian*, at 10:55 P.M.: "We are stopped and surrounded by ice." The irritated telegraph operator, Jack Phillips, who was scheduled to be relieved at midnight and who had been working hard and uninterrupted for many hours receiving and transmitting passengers' personal communications, replied with the abrupt message: "Shut up! I am busy. I am working Cape Race."[29]

Less than one hour later, the *Titanic* struck an iceberg at latitude 41°46′ longitude 50°14′ latitude, quite likely the very one, about 400 miles east of Newfoundland, that had been reported by the *Amerika*, and relayed by *Titanic*'s own dispatch. It had drifted only slightly to the northwest. The closest vessel to them that night was the *Californian*, about ten miles away, where unfortunately, shortly after receiving Phillips's angry message, the telegraph operator had cut off his system and gone to bed.[30]

There are two contradictory accounts of the Strauses' whereabouts at the moment the *Titanic* struck the fatal iceberg. Both are attributed, at least in part, to Ida's maid, Ellen Bird. One, published in the *New York World* on April 20, 1912, is based on an interview with Sylvester Byrnes, who claimed to have gotten the story from Ellen Bird. That version indicates that the couple was strolling on the deck at the moment the event occurred. It was already close to midnight. If that account were correct, Ida and Isidor would have lingered a very long time over their ten-course dinner in the first-class dining room, choosing among appetizers and entrées that included oysters, salmon, filet mignon, sauté of chicken Lyonnais, lamb, roast duckling, and sirloin of beef.[31] After dinner they might have joined other passengers over coffee in the palm court, listening to the music and chatting with their table companions. According to that account, at the moment the ship struck the iceberg, the "were walking arm and arm on the upper deck."[32]

The second and more plausible account was reported in a letter to Percy Straus written on April 24, 1912, by the Macy's grocery buyer, John Badenoch, who had been a passenger aboard the *Carpathia*, which had been the first vessel to arrive at the scene. The *Carpathia* had just started picking up *Titanic* survivors, including Ellen Bird, about 3:45 "just as the day was breaking" on the morning of April 15. Badenoch, realizing that the Straus family would be extremely anxious, pieced together from "statements of eight or ten of the survivors" including Ellen, and presented to Percy the version he considered "most accurate."

According to Badenoch's account, the Strauses were already in bed at the time of the incident and were awakened by a grinding noise and the slight lurch of the ship. They were seen soon afterwards "in the companion-way in bath robes." Other passengers as well were milling about trying to find out what had happened. They found a ship's officer and learned they had struck an iceberg and might wish to don their life jackets as a precaution. Ida and Isidor knocked on Ellen Bird's door to alert her to the danger. Although there seemed to be no immediate cause for alarm, this account indicated that Ida "seemed to realize the danger, and prepared to dress, requesting your Father to do likewise." She sent Ellen to get Isidor's valet Farthing "to assist him in dressing." Given their ages, it is far more plausible that, at midnight, they would have already retired for the night. And Ellen Bird would surely have remembered helping Ida dress. Her recollections, later shared with the family, even included what Ida put on to face the outside cold.

When they appeared on the deck, both were fully dressed. They "mingled with the other passengers and discussed the danger in a perfectly calm and collected manner. No one seemed to believe that there was any great danger of the ship sinking."[33] The sea was calm. There was no moon, but the stars shone, reassuringly bright.

Isidor must have felt the tender pressure of Ida's hand on his arm. Although he could not see her fingers through her leather gloves, she wore no jewelry except for her engagement and wedding rings. Beneath her coats, however, she had brought with her a little jewelry pouch that contained not only her pearls, but also special gifts from Isidor, among them the little gold purse encrusted with diamonds and emeralds he had bought her in Paris. One might imagine that she had chided him good-naturedly at the expense, but she loved his gifts and wasted no time in expressing delight to her children about the little purse.

As they stood on the deck, it seemed at first that everything would be all right. Lights still gleamed throughout the ship. Music from the lounge played on. And passengers resumed their nightly strolls, looking out at the calm sea, some picking up chunks of ice they found on the deck or pointing back toward the iceberg that had already disappeared in the darkness as the ship moved on.

Little by little, however, passengers began to feel a slight tilt on the deck, and, shortly thereafter, they heard the engines stop. After a time, a white-coated steward began to approach those on deck, informing them that "as a precaution" passengers who weren't currently wearing lifejackets should do so, and assemble on the Boat Deck above. Some were enjoying a bit of brandy at the bar, while others were playing cards, taking coffee in the Palm Court, or listening to the light-hearted music the little orchestra played each night. Why bother? Everyone knew the *Titanic* was unsinkable.

Ellen Bird had already joined the Strauses three levels above their cabins on the forward side of the Boat Deck. The sixteen boats had all been uncovered and stood ready, as passengers began to load. Some were refusing to enter the boats, but the Strauses, who were seasoned travelers well familiar with the dangers of the sea, were less reluctant. They stood waiting as the boats were filled and lowered.[34] Nearby were the Astors, the Lamson sisters with Edith Evans, Col. Gracie, and three other gentlemen Ellen did not know.[35]

Their decision to wait on the port side of the ship would prove to be a crucial factor in all that happened next. On the port side, where the even-numbered boats were located, Second Officer Charles Lightoller was adhering strictly to the captain's orders of women-and-children-first. On the starboard side, however, where

First Officer William Murdoch was in charge, lifeboats were filled with women and children first, but when no more stood waiting to board, men were allowed to board as well.

Some passengers still refused to believe the seriousness of their situation, feeling safer on the dry, lighted deck than in the dark, icy water below. But the urgency on the faces of the ship's officers, who by now understood the extent of the damage, suggested that the situation was indeed grave. The lifeboats had become much more than a mere precaution.

Ida and Isidor waited patiently beside boat 8, the second boat portside to be loaded. Among those climbing into the boat was the Countess of Rothes, as well as a number of other women they had encountered on the ship. When it came their turn to take a place, Isidor reached out to help Ida aboard. She started to climb in, assuming he would follow her. However, as she put her foot into the boat, Isidor stepped back.

"Aren't you coming, Isidor?" she asked.

"No," he replied. "I can't. It is impossible." He had heard the captain's order and seen the strictness with which Lightoller was enforcing it. At his words, Ida scrambled out of the boat again, this time without assistance, and rushed to her husband's side.

"Where you are, Papa, I shall be," she told him, rushing back into his arms.

With Isidor at her side, she turned to her maid, Ellen. "You go," she said. "I must stay with my husband." Briefly removing her life preserver, she took off her fur coat and handed it to her maid. "I won't need this anymore," she said. "You take it."[36]

Finally, realizing that Ida Straus had no intention of boarding, "several men passengers lifted Miss Bird into the boat, which was lowered with all haste."[37]

In fact, there was plenty of room in the boat for all of them. The regulation capacity of the wooden lifeboats was 65. Boat 8 was lowered at approximately 1:10 A.M. with a total of only 39 aboard.[38]

The Strauses watched the boat as it was lowered, swinging slightly away from the vessel, which was listing to port. After it touched the oily water, they could see crew members, who seemed to have little idea about what to do, trying awkwardly to row away from the ship, although at first one of them did not even have the oars in the oarlock.[39]

Without her fur coat Ida shivered in the icy night air. Isidor led her down one level to the glassed-in Deck A, where it was less chilly. They found deck chairs and sat for a time, watching the hubbub around them.[40] Another lifeboat was being lowered and paused adjacent to the Deck A windows, where Second Officer Lightoller proposed to load the boat. However, as yet, no one had opened the windows.

Passengers stood about waiting for assistance. Among them were John and Madeleine Astor, Eleanor and George Widener with their son Harry, and Marian and John Thayer. They waited quietly and patiently for crewmembers to open the windows. Beyond the glass they could see some of the lifeboats already afloat, looking so tiny and vulnerable compared to the mammoth vessel that still rode high in the water, though it dipped ever lower at the prow.

Finally, crewmen pried open the windows and began to load the boat. A steamer chair was placed under the window opening so that passengers could climb aboard more easily. One family, the Ryersons, had two daughters and a thirteen-year-old son. As they began to board, one of the officers said, "That boy cannot go."

His father, Arthur Ryerson, a Chicago lawyer with a commanding voice, said with authority, "Of course that boy goes with his mother; he is only thirteen."[41] Ryerson was not about to allow his wife Emily to lose another son. The family was rushing back from a European vacation to arrange for the funeral of their eldest son had just been killed in an automobile accident. Thus, with her two daughters, Emily and Suzette, and her son Jack, Mrs. Ryerson boarded lifeboat #4, while her husband stepped back.

When it came time for Mrs. Astor to board, John Jacob Astor, moved forward to help his pregnant young bride into the little vessel. He quietly asked Officer Lightoller if he might join her in light of her "delicate condition," but the second officer told him in no uncertain terms that no men were allowed until all women and children were loaded. Without argument, Astor assured the distraught Madeleine that he would join her later and he too stepped back.

Crewmen Jack Foley and Sam Parks were struggling to free lifeboat 4 from a sounding spar just below, when Madeleine Astor caught sight of Ida Straus standing in the background beside her husband.

"Here is a place for you, Mrs. Straus," she called out, patting the seat beside her.[42]

Ida shook her head, and Col. Gracie, who was also assisting with the loading of boat 4, heard her say, "I will not be separated from my husband; as we have lived so will we die together." [43]

"You can both go. There's room for both," urged a voice from the lifeboat.

"As long as there is a woman on this vessel I will not leave," Isidor responded with quiet dignity. "When they are safe then come the men."

"You are an old man, Mr. Straus," a voice urged him to reconsider.

"I am not too old to sacrifice myself for a woman."[44]

Ida stood beside him, fully understanding his code of honor, and equally firm in her refusal to leave him.

Finally, weary of persuasion, some of the sailors grasped Ida's arm and pulled her away from her husband and toward the boat.

"Isidor!" she cried out, stretching her hands toward him.

As they approached the lifeboat, Ida clutched the rail, refusing to let go, as several of the women, already seated in the wooden vessel, reached out to try to pull her aboard. Finally, as she continued to resist, the sailors shrugged and gave up the struggle. There were others to assist.

Those standing around, even Lightoller, anxious to launch the little vessel, urged Isidor to get in the boat. They would, given his age, make an exception to the "Women and children first" rule.

"No," he replied. "I do not wish any distinction in my favor that is not granted to others."

Time was running out. The water rose higher and higher. After number 4, no more wooden boats would be left on the ship's port side. Only a few collapsible rafts were still to be launched. The *Titanic* was sinking and passengers realized that there were not enough lifeboats for the many people still left on board. There was no time to waste.

Isidor took Ida in his arms, stroked her head, and begged her to save her own life, "Please dear, please go into the boat."[45]

Those watching the drama played out on deck remember Ida's loving defiance of her husband's wishes as she argued her own point of honor and loyalty, "Isidor, my place is with you. I have lived with you. I love you, and, if necessary, I shall die with you."

Finally the crewmen freed the lifeboat from the spar. They could wait no longer. Everyone realized by now that efforts to persuade Ida to leave her husband were useless. If they forced her into the boat, she would merely jump out again. Back in Isidor's arms, Ida felt safe. There and only there would she stay, and whatever happened to him would happen to her. She was not afraid as long as he was by her side. She smiled up at him. He patted her arm and smiled back, gazing for a long moment into her eyes. Both were weeping.

"I have lived with you for forty years," Ida said to her husband. "I have loved you, and I would rather die with you than live without you."[46] He had always been sure of her love, but never more than at that moment.

As number 4 was being lowered, crew member Jack Foley heard Mrs. Straus say to her husband, "We are as safe here as anywhere, and I am happy to be with you wherever you are."

Now in the water, the lifeboats glided across the still darkness as their passengers gazed back at the leviathan they had left. It looked so grand, even now, lit like a tilting palace against the night sky. The stalwart band, still on deck, played various lively tunes and at the last, a popular song of the day, "Songe d'automne," to calm the frightened passengers.[47]

Many of those in the little lifeboats reported still seeing the Strauses standing alongside the rail, holding each other and weeping quietly. At that moment the couple must have recognized the fullness of their love for one another and what they were about to face together.[48] A Newark man, Charles E. Stengel, who had witnessed the initial efforts to get Ida into a lifeboat before he entered one himself, gave this account: "The last thing I saw as we pulled away in the boats was the woman in whose gentle heart was a heroism greater than I have ever witnessed, standing clasped in her husband's arms while the water mounted about them."[49]

Their final moments on the *Titanic* were recounted by Archibald Gracie, who, like the Strauses, went down with the ship, but had the good fortune to be rescued. As he described the scene, "when the ship settled at the head the two were engulfed by the wave that swept her."[50] His was the last reported sighting of the Strauses.

One can only imagine their deaths. The cold of the north Atlantic must have struck Ida with full force, shocking her frail heart into silence. Isidor, afloat in his life jacket, no doubt clung to Ida's body as he clung to life. But overcome with hypothermia, as his hands grew numb in the icy water and his own life slipped away, he was compelled to let her go. The last sounds he heard were the heart-rending cries of those still alive around him, calling for help that did not come in time.

EPILOGUE:

STRAUS PARK

On April 15, 1915, three years to the day after the sinking of the *Titanic*, mourners gathered once more in New York's upper west side to remember the lives of Ida and Isidor Straus. All six of Ida and Isidor's children were present, as well as both of Isidor's brothers and their wives, his sister Hermine, and various members of the Blun family. The event was held to rededicate a tiny triangle of land formerly known as Bloomingdale Park and located near the site of the old Straus family home at Broadway and 105th Street.

Much had changed since the Strauses' deaths. Only ten days after Isidor's funeral, their house had been sold to a real estate developer named Harry Schiff, who, by the following fall, had demolished the structure and filled the site with an upscale, thirteen-story apartment building called The Clebourne.[1]

In terms of the family business, Isidor's brother Nathan was no longer a partner in Macy's. The year after his brother's death, he sold his interest in the store to Jesse, Percy, and Herbert, while his sons took over the family firm of L. Straus & Sons. Nathan himself retired from business altogether, choosing not to work without Isidor, but rather to devote the rest of his life to philanthropic service. It was no doubt a better arrangement for the younger generation, for Nathan's surviving sons were more than a decade younger than Isidor's and might well have felt dominated by their older cousins who had so much more experience at Macy's than they did.[2] On June 8, 1913, five months before the two families went their separate ways in business, they had come together as partners one more time to join 5,000 employees at a ceremony held in Macy's restaurant to commemorate the lives of Ida and Isidor and to unveil a bronze plaque that contained a bas-relief image of the couple and the inscription "Their lives were benevolent, and their teachings glorious."[3]

Now afternoon shadows stretched across the little park, as a single sparrow fluttered down and paused on the granite coping around the brand-new reflecting pool. Hundreds of people gathered around, listening to speakers and gazing toward the pool's south end, where a reclining bronze statue of a beautiful woman cast her eyes downward as though watching the tiny bird. The occasion was the formal dedication of the new Straus Park, which had been proposed not long after the *Titanic* disaster and had been funded by donations from citizens throughout the world. The park was a small oasis of tranquility in the midst of buzzing traffic where Broadway merged with West End Avenue between 106th and 107th Streets. The people—men in top hats, family, friends, children, and members of the press--had come together to celebrate the lives and remember the deaths of Ida and Isidor. As the dedication of the park continued, a reporter watched as other sparrows joined the first bird, until finally, he observed, "a colony of them was splashing in the pool" as though it had all been arranged especially for them.[4]

For half an hour prior to the ceremony seventy-five musicians from the Beethoven Musical Society played funeral marches and other appropriately somber selections by Beethoven, Chopin, and Grieg. The actual ceremony began at 4:30 P.M. when a hundred children from the Educational Alliance marched past the monument and placed there a large wreath of roses and lilies, casting other flowers upon the water.[5] New York Supreme Court Justice, Samuel Greenbaum, who had replaced Isidor as president of the Educational Alliance at his death, presided over the event and made opening remarks in which he described the Strauses' deaths as demonstrative of "the highest love between man and woman."[6] It was above all that love and their rich, full lives that the occasion commemorated.

The second speaker, New York's mayor, John Purroy Mitchell, paid tribute to the Strauses for their "fidelity, simplicity and courage and the elevation of these attributes even above life itself," and he described the monument being dedicated as "a symbol of those high qualities of American citizenship and personal character which these two so splendidly exemplified."[7]

The completed monument was the result of a competition for artists to create a design that would "reflect the unostentatious but purposeful character" of the Strauses, neither of whom had ever sought self-aggrandizement. The committee further ruled "that any features that might be termed loud or spectacular should be avoided." It was to be primarily an "object of beauty, without necessarily containing an allegorical expression of any particular theme or subject."[8] The $10,000 first-place award had brought fifty-nine entries into the stiff competition. The winners, announced in March 1913 were the team of sculptor Augustus Lukeman and architect Evart Tracy.[9]

They had followed instructions well, with Lukeman selecting as his model a true "object of beauty," a woman who has been called the "American Venus." Her name was Audrey Munson, and in 1915, when the statue was unveiled, she was twenty-three years old and at the peak of her career. Ironically, her life and death would provide a stark contrast to those of the Strauses. While they lived quietly and never sought personal glory, Audrey's image and, whenever she could arrange it, her name were in the public spotlight. The same year the Straus memorial was dedicated, she was chosen by Alexander Stirling Calder to be the "model of choice" for the Pacific International Exposition, and approximately three-quarters of the sculpture at that event depicted her image. She had also modeled for dozens of other statues at various locations in New York, among them the Firemen's Memorial on Riverside Drive, erected in 1913, a cause for which Isidor had given much of his time as chair of the Firemen's Memorial Fund Committee, which raised more than $90,000 to honor the firemen who gave their lives in the line of duty.[10]

Audrey had posed at various times as the personification of Beauty and Peace, and now she was the evocation of Memory, the title given to Lukeman's sculpture honoring the Strauses. The beauty of the statue was incontestable. It was also undeniably sensual—the figure reclining, her head resting upon one hand, the other hand playing indefinitely about her mouth and chin, her arms bare, her body draped from neck to ankle in folds of fabric that followed the curves of her body, one leg dangling nonchalantly over the edge of the plinth. She gazed into the waters of the fountain and pool as though in contemplation.

The year after the statue's unveiling, its model would move to California to become an actress and the first woman ever to appear fully nude on screen.[11] By 1919 she was back in New York, living in a boarding house owned by a man named Walter Wilkins. Wilkins was later convicted and sentenced to death for murdering his wife, allegedly because of his love for Audrey. He hanged himself in prison before his sentence could be carried out. The scandal tainted the young woman's life, and by 1920, still only twenty-nine years old, she was unable to find work anywhere.[12] She attempted to commit suicide and was eventually committed to what became the St. Lawrence State Hospital for the Insane in Ogdensburg, New York, where she lived for the next seventy-four years. She died at the age of 105 and was buried in an unmarked grave.[13]

Although most visitors to Straus Park today have no idea who the statue's model was and know nothing of her life, they might find even more to reflect upon if they did know. One is struck at first by the incongruity of the lives of the model and those it honors, but upon further consideration, it seems absolutely right, for it invites reflection not only upon memory, but an even more provocative reflection about what is really important in life. It speaks to the fleeting nature of physical beauty, the consequences of human choices, and the lasting quality of inner beauty. The committee, a distinguished group of New Yorkers, had determined early in the process that they did not want statues of Ida and Isidor, who were modest and unassuming and would likely have been discomfited by such images of themselves, but rather something that would evoke contemplation about their lives and their deaths.[14]

The result was brilliant in ways the committee could not have foreseen, for it reflects not their human form, but rather the inner fineness of the two people it was intended to celebrate, the memory of their mutual love, honor, and their enduring legacy. The lives they led were amazing in so many ways. Rare were their days that were not replete with productive activity, support of worthy causes, concern for others, and family affection. Although their bodies have vanished, like all that is purely physical in this world, in their wake they have left a trail of goodness, productivity, love, and faithfulness in a story that will not be forgotten. In their deaths, neither thought of self, but of others. He would not leave the ship as long as women and children were aboard; and she would not leave him behind. They would be remembered throughout the world for their noble sacrifice and the profundity of their love. And they were last seen locked in one another's arms, bravely awaiting death. The park is fittingly a place of peace in the midst of a city's busy-ness and turmoil, and the plaque on their monument contains a simple but fitting quotation from 2 Samuel 1:23: "Lovely and pleasant were they in their lives and in their deaths they were not divided."

For all her physical attractiveness, Audrey Munson never found such love or earned such admiration. Abandoned by her family, she lived out in an asylum the long and lonely life that she had once sought to end. By contrast, the love and devotion of Ida and Isidor and their concern for others, captured in the synecdoche of their final moments together, lived well beyond their lifetime, not just for their family but even for those who never knew them.

Eleven years after Straus Park was dedicated, in 1926, their three sons donated to their alma mater, Harvard University, $300,000 to build a Business School dormitory to house underclassmen. It was called Straus Hall in honor of their parents.[15] Even as late as 1958 Public School No. 198 in Manhattan, was renamed in their memory the Isidor and Ida Straus School by the city of New York.[16]

As a final tribute to their parents, Jesse, Percy, and Herbert executed on May 4, 1928, a deed for land to build a Straus family burial site on Myosotis Street in Woodlawn Cemetery in the Bronx. On December 22, 1930, the monument was complete. The bodies of Isidor and unnamed twin daughters of Herbert and Therese, who had died at birth on April 5, 1908, were moved from their previous burial places and interred at Woodlawn.[17] The monument's final design, executed by James Gamble Rogers, consisted of three mausoleums, one for the family of each of the Strauses' sons (The daughters would be buried with their husbands' families), linked together by a common courtyard.[18] In the front and center of the courtyard stood a special sarcophagus built in the shape of an Egyptian funeral barge to contain their father's body. It would also serve as a cenotaph for Ida and is dedicated to the memory of them both. As in Egyptian funerary art it would transport their spirits together to eternal rest. On its side is carved an inscription taken from the *Song of Solomon*. More than any other verse from the Jewish scriptures, it characterizes the indestructible beauty of the affections between Ida and Isidor: "Many waters cannot quench love—neither can the floods drown it."

Bibliography

Manuscript and Private Collections
Flowers Collection, Duke University Library, Durham, North Carolina
Gus Kaufman Collection, Macon, Georgia
Laurette Rothschild Rosenstrauch Collection, Columbus, Georgia
Macy's, Inc. Archives, New York City
Mike Buckner Collection, Junction City, Georgia
Muscogee County Deed Books, Columbus, Georgia
Nathan Straus Papers, New York Public Library
Oscar S. Straus Papers, Library of Congress, Washington, D.C.
Oscar Solomon Straus Papers, Columbia University Rare Book & Manuscript
    Library, Archival Collection, New York City
Rare Pamphlet Collection, Georgia Historical Society, Savannah, Georgia
Straus Historical Society Collection, Long Island, New York
Straus Family Papers, New York Public Library, New York City
Record Group 41, Nova Scotia Archives, Halifax, Nova Scotia

Periodicals
Atlanta Constitution
Atlanta Journal
Belfast Telegraph
Brooklyn Eagle
Brooklyn Standard Union
Christian Science Monitor
Columbus Enquirer
Columbus Enquirer-Sun
Denver News
Denver Times
Halifax Evening Mail
Jewish Georgian
Matilda Ziegler Magazine for the Blind
Memphis Daily Bulletin
New Outlook
New York American
New York Evening Globe
New York Evening Post
New York Herald

New York Morning Advertiser
New York Sun
New York Times
New York Tribune
New York World
Newark Morning Star
North American Review
Savannah Daily Morning News
Spokane Review
Straus Historical Society, Inc. Newsletter
Tammany Times
Trenton New Jersey Times
Washington Post
"wholedamfam" Straus Family Newsletter

Online Sources
http://www.ancestry.com/tree/2513075/family [Francell Family Tree (A)]
http://www.encyclopedia-Titanica.org/
http://www.geocities.com/corklh/Titanic.html
http://jwa.org/encyclopedia
http://www.ncjwla.org
http://www.thepeerage.com/
http://www.titanic1.org/
http://www.titanichistoricalsociety.net/
http://www.wso.net/ga/education.html
http://www.wso.net/ga/talbotcom.html

Published Secondary Sources
Anbinder, Tyler. *Five Points: The Nineteenth-Century New York City Neighborhood That Invented the Tap Dance.* New York: The Free Press, 2001.
Beatty, Jack. *Age of Betrayal: The Triumph of Money in America, 1865-1900.* New York: Vintage, 2008.
Beesley, Lawrence. *The Loss of the S. S. Titanic: Its Story and Its Lessons.* Boston: Houghton Mifflin, 1912: reprinted First Mariner Books, 2000.
Bethell, John T. *Harvard Observed: An Illustrated History of the University in the Twentieth Century.* Cambridge: Harvard Magazine, 1998.
Blaustein, David. *Memoirs of David Blaustein: Educator and Communal Worker,* arranged by Miriam Blaustein. New York: McBride, Nast & Co., 1913.

Blun, Henry. *Reminiscences of My Blockade Running* (n. p., 1910?), Rare Pamphlet Collection, Georgia Historical Society.

Birmingham, Stephen. *"Our Crowd": The Great Jewish Families of New York.* New York: Harper & Row, 1967.

Carnegie, Andrew. "Wealth," *North American Review,* 148/391 (June 1889): 653, 657-62.

Davidson, William H. *A Rockaway in Talbot: Travels in an Old Georgia County.* West Point, Georgia: Hester Printing, 1983 (4 vols.), vol. 1.

Documents of the Assembly of the State of New York. Albany, New York: J.B. Lyon Company, 1902. v. 16.

Eaton, John P. and Charles A. Haas. *Titanic: Triumph and Tragedy.* New York: Norton, 1986.

_____. *Titanic: Destination Disaster: The Legends and the Reality.* New York: Norton, 1996.

_____. *Titanic: A Journey Through Time.* New York: Norton 1999.

Geller, Judith B. *Titanic: Women and Children First.* New York: W.W Norton, 1998.

Geyer, Andrea. *"Queen of the Artists' Studios"—The Story of Audrey Munson. Intimate Secrets of Studio Life Revealed by the Most Perfect, Most Versatile, Most Famous of American Models, Whose Face and Figure Have Inspired Thousands of Modern Masterpieces of Sculpture and Painting.* Commissioned and published by Art in General, 2007.

Gracie, Archibald. *Titanic: A Survivor's Story.* Chalford-Stroud, Gloucestershire: History Press, 2008. Originally published under the title of *The Truth about Titanic.* New York: M. Kennerley, 1913.

Grippo, Robert M. *Macy*s: The Store. The Star. The Story.* Garden City, New York: SquareOne Publishers, 2009.

Haas, Charles. *Titanic: Triumph and Tragedy.* New York: Norton, 1995.

Howells, Richard. *The Myth of the Titanic.* London: Macmillan, 1999.

Hower, Ralph M. *History of Macy's of New York 1858-1919: Chapters in the Evolution of the Department Store.* Cambridge, Mass.: Harvard University Press, 1943.

Johnson, Curtiss S. *America's First Lady Boss: A Wisp of a Girl, Macy's and Romance.*Silvermine: Norwalk, Conn., 1965.

Jones, Jacqueline. *Saving Savannah: The City and the Civil War.* New York: Knopf, 2008.

Kaufman, Gus B. "A Jewish Family's Time in a Small Georgia Town." *The Jewish Georgian* 6/1 (January-February 1996): 16-17.

Kauffman, Reginald Wright. *Jesse Isidor Straus: A Biographical Portrait.* New York: Privately Published, 1973.

Korn, Bertram Wallace. "American Judaeophobia: Confederate Version," in *Jews in the South,* edited by Leonard Dinnerstein and Mary Dale Palsson. Baton Rouge: Louisiana State University Press, 1973.

Langley, Henry G. *San Francisco Directory for 1878.* San Francisco: Commercial Steam Presses, S. D. Valentine & Sons, 1878.

Lord, Walter. *The Night Lives On.* New York: William Morrow, 1986.

Marcus, Geoffrey. *The Maiden Voyage.* New York: Viking, 1969.

Marshall, Logan. ed. *Sinking of the Titanic and Great Sea Disasters.* 1912 (n.p., 1912).

McCash, June Hall. "The Last Rebel," *Georgia Backroads.* 9:1, spring, 2010. 16-21.

Misulia, Charles A. *Columbus, Georgia 1865: The Last True Battle of the Civil War.* Tuscaloosa: University of Alabama Press, 2010.

Nason, Henry Bradford. *Biographical Record of the Officers and Graduates of the Rensselaer Polytechnic Institute 1828-1886.* Troy, New York: William H. Young, 1887.

Order of Prayer for Divine Service. Revised by Dr. L. Merzbacher, rabbi of the Temple "Emanu-el" (1855), third edition, revised and corrected by Dr. S. Adler (1864), printed by M. Thalmessinger & Co.

"Packer's Business College," *Scientific American.* 43:25, December 1880, 383-88.

Painter, Nell Irvin. *Standing at Armageddon: The United States 1877-1919.* New York: W. W. Norton & Co., 1987.

Real Estate Record. Brooklyn, New York: C.W. Sweet & Co, 1868-1884, vols. 7 and 8.

Report on the Loss of the S. S. Titanic. New York: St. Martin's Press, 1990; originally printed 1912 and "Presented to Both Houses of Parliament by Command of His Majesty."

Ridgely-Nevitt, Cedric. *American Steamships on the Atlantic.* Newark: University of Delaware Press; London and Toronto: Associated University Presses, 1981.

Rozas, Diane, and Nita Bourne Gottehrer. *American Venus: The Extraordinary Life of Audrey Munson Model and Muse.* Los Angeles: Balcony Press, 1999.

Shurz, Carl. *The Autobiography of Carl Shurz,* ed. Wayne Andrews. New York: Charles Scribner's Sons, 1961.

Eugene W. Smith, *Passenger Ships of the World Past and Present.* Boston: George H. Dean, 1978.

Steinebrei, Hans. *History of the Jews of Otterberg: An Example of the History from the Palatinate in the 19th Century.* New York: Straus Historical Society, inc. 2008.

Straus, Isidor. *The Autobiography of Isidor Straus*. Privately published, 1955.

Straus, Lina Gutherz. *Disease in Milk, The Remedy Pasteurization: The Life Work of Nathan Straus*, 2nd ed. New York: E. P. Dutton, 1917.

Straus, Oscar S. *Under Four Administrations: From Cleveland to Taft*. Boston: Houghton Mifflin, 1922.

Strouse, Jean. *Morgan: American Financier*. New York: Random House, 1999.

Sullivan, Buddy. *Early Days on the Georgia Tidewater*. Darien, Georgia: Published by the McIntosh County Board of Commissioners, 1990.

Szold, Henrietta, ed. *American Jewish Year Book 5668, September 9, 1907 to September 25, 1908*. Philadelphia: Jewish Publication Society of America, 1907.

Viener, Saul. "The Political Career of Isidor Straus" Master's thesis, West Virginia University, 1947.

Wade, Wyn Craig. *The Titanic: End of a Dream*. New York: Penguin Books, 1986.

Watterson, Henry. *History of the Manhattan Club: A Narrative of the Activities of Half a Century*. New York: privately printed for the Manhattan Club, 1915.

Wilson, James H. *Under the Old Flag*, 2 vols. New York: Appleton's, 1912.

Wise, Stephen R. *Lifeline of the Confederacy: Blockade Running During the Civil War*. Columbia: University of South Carolina Press, 1988.

Notes

Prologue

[1] Percy wrote his parents on 9 February. "Yesterday we decided to take the apartments on Seventy-Eighth Street and Park Avenue. I have the lease in my pocket now." [Percy] to Papa and Mamma. The letter is dated 12 February 1912, but he had written this part of it on 9 February. Straus Family Collection, New York Public Library (hereafter referred to as NYPL). That they were staying at the time in his parents' home is made clear by a letter he had written them two weeks before, indicating mother-in-law's arrival on Thursday evening, 25 January, from Dallas, Texas, where there was an epidemic of spinal meningitis. His physician brother-in-law "Dick [Weil] advises us it would be dangerous....We have therefore engaged a room for her at Bretton Hall," where she would change her clothes take a disinfectant bath, have a shampoo and spend the night. "Her trunks and clothes will be taken to 71 St. to be fumigated. She probably won't like it." Later he writes. Mrs. A. [Marose Abraham] "was not overjoyed...[but] she bowed to what she realized was necessary. I think she will return to 105ᵗʰ Street this morning." [Percy] to Papa and Mama, 26 January 1912. Straus Family Collection, NYPL. Portions of this letter were written earlier. There is no indication in any of the correspondence that they moved into the new apartment, which they were likely refurbishing, before the sinking of the *Titanic.*

[2] Stephen Birmingham lists the Strauses, along with the Seligmans, Lehmans, Goldmans, Sachs, and Loebs as one of "the great Jewish families of New York" in *"Our Crowd": The Great Jewish Families of New York* (New York: Harper & Row, 1967) endpapers.

[3] Where newspaper citations within the text make the source clear, I have not added additional footnotes.

[4] The headline of the *Christian Science Monitor* was "Passengers Safely Moved and Steamer Titanic Taken in Tow." It even included a special bulletin that "The New Haven railroad will send a special Pullman train to Halifax to accommodate the passengers of the Titanic." The details of the "rescue" are very specific, even giving the time, "at 2 o'clock this afternoon," that passengers had been transferred to the *Parisian* and the *Carpathia,* while the floundering vessel was "being towed to Halifax by the *Virginian* of the Allan line."

[5]All wireless messages and letters cited herein are located within the Straus Historical Society, Inc. collection, henceforth given as SHS, unless otherwise indicated. Where senders, recipients, and dates are made clear within the text, no additional documentation is given.

[6]Jacob H. Schiff, to C. S. Mellon, 15 April 1912. SHS.

[7]EHP to [Jacob H. Schiff?], 15 April 1912. SHS. The writer indicates that "Mr. Mellon's Secretary telephones from New Haven, that Mr. Mellon has received Mr. Schiff's telegram; that their General Passenger Agent, Mr. Cole, is going to Halifax on the same train that Mr. Straus is going up on; that they are making special arrangements to bring the passengers down from Halifax."

[8]These early numbers reported in the press are exaggerated and optimistic. All sources do not agree on the number of survivors, but they range from 701-713, far below the number first reported.

[9] Telegrams from Oscar S. Straus to Hon. Charles D. Hillis [sic], Secretary to President, to Secretary Meyer, Navy Department, to Right Hon, R. L. Bordon, all sent 16 April 1912, copies in SHS.

[10] Telegram from Charles D. Hilles to Hon. Oscar S. Straus, 17 April 1912, SHS; R. L Borden to Hon. Oscar Straus, 18 April 1912. SHS.

[11]John Badenoch to Percy Straus, 24 April 1912. SHS.

[12]At Percy's request, Badenoch later committed all his information to writing. John A. Badenoch to Dear Mr. Percy, 24 April 1912. SHS.

[13]*Trenton New Jersey Times*, 20 April 1912.

[14] Reported in the *New York Evening Post*, 20 April 1912.

[15] *New York Times*, 22 April 1912.

[16]*New York World*, 22 April 1912.

[17]For example, the Daughters of Jacob decided on April 22 to name a hospital ward for her in the new home being constructed for the poor, aged and infirm.

[18]In Atlanta, for example, in recognition of the family's Georgia roots, a movement had begun for some type of memorial, and as far away as Jerusalem, sixty thousand Jews were said to be mourning the Strauses. *Brooklyn Standard Union*, 23 April 1912; *New York Sun* 24 April 1912; *Brooklyn Eagle*, 26 April 1912.

[19]*New York Times*, 24 April 1912; *New York Tribune* 24 April 1912.

[20]*Halifax Evening Mail*, 30 April 1912.

[21]Copy of Mackay-Bennett description in SHS.

[22]The description presumably provided by the family to the White Star line (contained in SHS) describes him as follows: "Medium height, slim build.

Head bald in center. Hair gray. Beard and whiskers short, reddish gray. Many teeth filled with gold. Gold mounted spectacles. Hands and feet very finely formed. Possibly wears a truss." It indicated that he was dressed in "Underclothing marked 'I.S.' Underclothes, silk & wool. Day shirt, day suit, boots (high shoes). Black over coat, fur (seal) lined, with seal collar. Grey tweed cap. Life belt." They also supplied "supplementary marks of identification" indicating that his shirt would "most likely bear the identification marks as coming from Jas. W. Bell, Son & Co, the N.Y. Tailors." He would also be carrying "a split second Smith & Jurgenson watch, either on a platinum chain or a fob with an ancient gold coin." Finally they indicated that he had "a fairly large mole in the center of his back, a little to the right."

[23]This description of Ida was provided to rescuers along with that of Isidor (above). Among the "supplementary marks of identification" given for Ida were also her wedding ring, which "might bear the mark 'July 12, 1871,' and the additional small ring would bear 'July 12, 1896,'" evidently one that Isidor had presented to her on their twenty-fifth wedding anniversary.

[24]An undated telegram sent by Percy provides this information: "Maid with us since arrival Carpathia Forced by Mother leave Titanic early knows very little...." Family stories indicate that Ellen Bird tried to return to Sara Straus Hess a coat that Ida had given to her on the night of the tragedy and at the moment she herself entered a lifeboat. Sara refused the coat, telling her to keep it as a gift from her mother. Ellen Bird eventually took a job in Tuxedo Park with the Frederick Spedden family, friends of the Strauses, who had survived the sinking of the *Titanic*.

[25][Percy Straus] to My dear Pat, 30 April 1912. SHS.

[26]A typewritten document containing this description and the announcement that a "Liberal reward will be paid for the recovery of the body of Mrs. Isidor Straus, lost on the Titanic" is located in SHS. Concerning the purchase of the handbag from Noury's, see Ida to Dear Children, April 4, 1912. SHS.

[27]*Halifax Evening Mail*, 30 April 1912. Many of those reburied were said to be bruised or mangled beyond recognition; in truth the *Mackay-Bennett* had inadequate supplies and embalming facilities for the overwhelming number of bodies they found. When the *Minia* arrived, the sea burials ceased. It is possible that Farthing's body was one of those buried at sea. It is unlikely, however, that Ida's was among them, as her body could have been easily identified from the initials in her undergarments. See on-line *Encyclopedia-Titanic*, Mackay-Bennett entry.

---

[28]*New York Sun*, 3 May 1912.

[29]Herbert [Scheftel] to Strauss [sic], R. H. Macy, n.d., SHS; Percy to Scheftel, Majestic Hotel, Paris, 27 April 1912, SHS.

[30]*Brooklyn Eagle*, 8 May 1912; *New York Evening Globe*, 8 May 1912.

[31]*New York Times*, 9 May 1912.

[32]*New York Sun*, 9 May 1912.

[33]*Denver Times*, 26 April 1912. Nathan did not, in fact, return to New York until 29 May aboard the *Caronia*. See *New York Evening Globe*, 30 May 1912.

[34]Isidor Straus to Charles W. Eliot, 19 September 1909. Included in *The Autobiography of Isidor Straus* (n.p.1955), privately published by his daughter Sara Straus Hess. A-23-A-24.

[35]*Brooklyn Standard Union*, 23 April 1912; *New York Sun,* 24 April 1912; *Brooklyn Eagle*, 26 April 1912. According to the newspaper account, these Jews mourned him as their benefactor who had funded a soup kitchen with $10,000 a year for three years in order to feed 500-700 people a day. It is likely that these fasting Jews had confused Isidor with his brother Nathan, who had definitely opened soup kitchens in Jerusalem and was well known for his benefactions in the Holy Land. Other tributes, too numerous to mention, took place. Among them, on Saturday, 27 April 1912, 250 blind men and women assembled at the office of the *Matilda Ziegler Magazine for the Blind* to send a letter to the Straus family. "Mr. and Mrs. Straus had been greatly interested in a department for the sale of goods made by the blind, inaugurated in the R. H. Macy department store two years ago." *New York Herald*, 29 April 1912. And a memorial service was held on 28 April at the Temple Ohab Zedek attended by an estimated 2,000 persons, with many more "turned away at the doors for lack of room." *New York Sun*, 29 April 1912.

[36] Seventeen months later Gaynor would die unexpectedly of his injury. A former New York Supreme Court Justice, he had come into the mayoral office with the support of Tammany Hall. Once in office, however, he disappointed the Tammany machine by appointing expert and competent people to office rather than the party hacks they proposed. When Tammany Hall refused to support him for a second term, he was quickly nominated as an independent, though he never had the chance to run again. It was no doubt the man's integrity that endeared him to Isidor Straus. Isidor wrote his brother Oscar of Gaynor's shooting and the extent of his wound: "rumor has it that he is a very much damaged man; that his vocal chords are paralyzed, and that while he is physically able to be about he is far from being his

normal self in other respects." Isidor to Dear brother Oscar, 15 August 1910 and 22 September 1910. Straus Family Papers, NYPL.

[37]Andrew Carnegie, "Wealth," *North American Review*, 148, no. 391 (June 1889): 653, 657–62.

[38]*New York Times*, 13 May 1912; Andrew Carnegie to Oscar Straus, 22 April 1912, Straus Family Papers, NYPL.

[39]*New York Times*, 1 December 1913.

[40]Isidor was also an admirer of Miss Richman. He wrote a letter to Mayor Gaynor on 23 June 1911, recommending her in glowing terms: as "a woman of exceptional capacity, originality, energy, intelligence, courage. She has ideas of what is needed and cannot be 'bluffed' from expressing them, no matter who may be the opponent. I know her well!" (Straus Family Papers, NYPL). He never names her in the letter, but it is clear that he is writing of Miss Richman.

[41]On Ida's service as a board member, see the web site of the Jewish Women's Archive at http://jwa.org/encyclopedia/article/settlement-houses-in-united-states. In 1913, one chapter of the National Council of Jewish Women founded the Ida Straus Nursery for children of working women of all nationalities. See The web site of the NCJW Los Angeles at http://www.ncjwla.org/about/history.php.

[42]*New York Times*, 13 May 1912; *New York Tribune*. 13 May 1912, *New York World*, 13 May 1912; *New York American*, 13 May 1912. Julia Richman was an extraordinary woman, who shared the ideas of Isidor and Ida that the Jewish immigrants coming into America must adapt to their new country and learn American ways. Her efforts toward this end were evident in her interest in the Educational Alliance, her work on the National Council of Jewish Women, and even in her goals for education. She died only six weeks after making her speech in memory of Ida. Sailing for France to spend the summer improving her French, she took ill on the vessel, was taken to the American Hospital in Neuilly upon arrival, and, despite emergency surgery, she died on 24 June 1912, of peritonitis.

[43]The letters cited below were all published at the end of Isidor's Autobiography, A-1-A-10. Copy in SHS.

[44]*New York Times*, 15 October 1912. More specifically they estimated the estate at $3.5 to $4 million. A later estimate, cited in the *Atlanta Constitution* 10 August, 1913, sets the amount of Isidor's estate at $4,565,106, and Ida's at $325,578.

[45]A copy of Isidor's final will is contained in SHS. He lists the location of their summer home as Deal, New Jersey. The home is actually in Elberon, in

close proximity to Deal Beach. In terms of the legal deed, it may well have listed the site as Deal, but there is no question that he was referring to the house in Elberon. See chapter 5.

[46]This letter, written at their summer home in Elberon, New Jersey, on 18 July 1904. is contained in Straus, *Autobiography*, A-3-A-4.

[47]The letter to his sons, written on the same day as the letter to his wife (see above) are in Straus, *Autobiography*, A-5-A-9.

[48] Isidor Straus to "my Dear Children," Straus, *Autobiography*, A-1. He goes on to say "Be quick to forgive, ready to forget, eager to acknowledge when you have been in the wrong. Stubbornness is a grievous fault."

[49]This information is contained in the letter to his sons in Straus, *Autobiography*, A-7. The gifts he made to employees, "should [they] be still in my employ," included those to his former secretary and now Macy's general manager, Sylvester Byrnes ($5,000); a Mr. Pitt, whose employment is unspecified but referred to, unlike all the others, as "service" ($5,000); Macy's head cashier, Miss [Abigail] Golden ($2,500); the Straus coachman, Patrick McDermott ($1,000), whom Isidor mentions first; a Miss Blair and Mr. Fitzhugh, Macy's chief accountant, ($1,000 each).

[50]Foreword by Sara Straus Hess to Straus, *Autobiography*. All subsequent quotations attributed to Straus's autobiography are from this volume. In a letter written more than two decades earlier, Ida had already noted Jesse's "reverence for everything concerning our early days. Mama to My dear Isidor, Tuesday morning 1890. SHS.

Chapter 1

[1]"Introduction," Straus *Autobiography,,* no page number. The number of pages is based on this edition. It has, in addition, a 35-page appendix, which contains letters and newspaper clippings.

[2]Oscar went on to note that his "chief aim and purpose" was "to cast…light upon our country's development and upon events in which, in public and private life, I have been permitted to take part." Oscar S. Straus, "Preface," *Under Four Administrations: From Cleveland to Taft* (Boston: Houghton Mifflin, 1922) viii.

[3]Straus, *Autobiography*, 1.

[4]The ship was built by Jacob Westervelt and Company.

[5]See Cedric Ridgely-Nevitt, *American Steamships on the Atlantic* (Newark: University of Delaware Press; London and Toronto: Associated University Presses, 1981) 175-77, 274-75.

[6]Ridgely-Nevitt, *American Steamships*, 274-75. Fairly large for the time, the *Saint Louis* was 270 feet long and weighed 1,621 tons, slightly more than her sister ship, the *Sonora*.

[7]On the name of the maid, see the *New York Times* report on the ship's arrival and the original ship's manifesto, where the names are inconsistent, one giving her last name as Faruz. Copy in SHS.

[8]Details of the voyage and of Isidor's early life are contained in Straus, *Autobiography*. Sara and Lazarus had a fifth child, Jacob Otto, who was born in 1849 and died in 1851, the year before his father left for America. Sara Straus, the daughter of Soloman and Joanna Weil Straus and Lazarus's first cousin, was Lazarus's second wife. He had been married first to Fannie Levi Straus, who had died in 1843, leaving behind one daughter, Karoline, born in 1838. Information contained in an unpublished "Straus Genealogical Miscellany," copy in SHS.

[9]See decree concerning the Jews, dated 17 March 1808, signed by Napoleon Bonaparte and the ministre secretaire de l'Etat, H. B. Maret, Straus Family Papers, NYPL.

[10]Carl Shurz, *The Autobiography of Carl Shurz*, ed. Wayne Andrews (New York: Charles Scribner's Sons, 1961), 13. Shurz would later come to America and play a significant role as a Union Army General in the Civil War. He was also the first German born American to serve in the U.S. Senate.

[11]*Straus Historical Society, Inc. Newsletter*, I/1 (August 1999): 5.

[12]Oscar Straus in his memoirs, *Under Four Administrations,* commented that the men who struggled in the Revolution of 1848 did so "for constitutionalism and democracy... basically for American principles. They were Americans in spirit...even before they arrived" in America. Cited in Reginald Wright Kauffman, *Jesse Isidor Straus: A Biographical Portrait* (New York: Privately Published, 1973) 19.

[13]Hand-written document in the collection of Mike Buckner, Junction City, Georgia. See also Kauffman, *Jesse Isidor Straus*, 21.

[14]This information about the early life and background of Isidor Straus is derived largely from the Straus, *Autobiography*, 1-6, and from the *Straus Historical Society, Inc. Newsletter* I/1 (August 1999): 5.

[15]On the success of the Seligmans in the South, see Stephen Birmingham,"*Our Crowd,*" 36-45.

[16]See Birmingham, "*Our Crowd,*"46-47.

[17] Information about the early days of the Kaufman brothers in Georgia comes from Gus B. Kaufman, "A Jewish Family's Time in a Small Georgia Town," *The Jewish Georgian* (January-February 1996), pp. 16-17.

[18]Quoted Kauffman, *Jesse Isidor Straus*, 22.

[19]Straus, Autobiography, 3-4.

[20]Straus, Autobiography, 4.

[21]Straus, Autobiography, 3-4.

[22]Marx Kaufman to his family, 15 December 1850. Translated copy provided by Laurette Rothschild Rosenstrauch, German original in the Leo Baeck Institute, New York City.

[23]Marx Kaufman to his family, 15 December 1850.

[24]Straus, *Autobiography*, 4.

[25]The Franklin House Hotel was built by William P. McKeen but at the time Lazarus moved to Talbotton, it was owned by the estate of Peter Fournoy Mahone, who had purchased it in May 1840 but died in 1850. In December 1855, Peter Dennis and William Spain purchased the hotel and changed its name to the Dennis House, a name it would retain until 1860, when it was sold to James P. Miller of Geneva. It burned in 1870 and was replaced by the Thornton House. Next door to the hotel when Lazarus came to Talbotton was Joseph Wynn's shoe store.

[26]Straus, Autobiography, 7-8.

[27]Isidor spells the name "Ferbach" in his autobiography.

[28]Some sources give 29 August.

[29]The news from the crossing of the *St. Louis*, including all the details cited herein, were published in the *New York Times*, 13 September 1854. The iceberg sightings were made as the ship crossed a latitude of 46 degrees 20' and a longitude 48 degrees.

[30]Straus, *Autobiography*, 9.

[31]For descriptions of the hurricane and yellow fever epidemic of 1854, see Jacqueline Jones, *Saving Savannah: The City and the Civil War* (New York: Knopf, 2008) 54.

Chapter 2

[1]Straus, *Autobiography*, 9. Essentially the same information is contained in "Oscar Straus Reminiscences," p. 8, from the collection of Mike Buckner. On the yellow fever epidemic of 1854 in coastal Georgia, see Buddy Sullivan, *Early Days on the Georgia Tidewater* (Darien, Georgia: Published by the McIntosh County Board of Commissioners, 1990) 163.

[2]The stagecoach line was run by William Batts Spain, who also owned a livery stable and blacksmith shop in Talbotton. On business in early Talbotton, see Carol Johnson and Lea L. Dowd, "Early Life: Talbotton," at: http://www.wso.net/ga/talbotcom.html.

[3]Straus, *Autobiography*, 10.

[4]A photograph of the house has been published in *"wholedamfam":
Straus Family Newsletter* , 1/1 (January 1983): 5. There is also a photograph of
the house in the *Atlanta Constitution*, 23 March 1927. It was still standing
when two of Isidor's sons paid a visit to Talbotton that week.

[5]Oscar S. Straus, *Under Four Administrations: From Cleveland to Taft* (New
York: Houghton Mifflin, 1922) 12. The Straus's first house in Talbotton was
demolished about 1930, but the site is indicated today by a historical marker
erected at the lot on the corner of Monroe Street and Jefferson Avenue by the
Georgia Historical Commission. For the text of the marker, see William H.
Davidson, *A Rockaway in Talbot: Travels in an Old Georgia County* (West Point,
Georgia: Hester Printing, 1983) I, 169.

[6]See footnote 2 above.

[7]Straus, *Autobiography*, 11.

[8]Straus, *Autobiography*, 12.

[9]See Bertram Wallace Korn, "American Judaeophobia: Confederate
Version," in *Jews in the South*, edited by Leonard Dinnerstein and Mary Dale
Palsson (Baton Rouge: Louisiana State University Press, 1973) 147, n. 35.

[10]Oscar Straus, "Reminiscences," 9; see also Kauffman, *Jesse Isidor Straus*,
26.

[11]The school closed during the Civil War, and its owner David Seay,
along with most of the teachers and many of the older students, enlisted in
the Confederate army. In 1878 Collingsworth Institute merged with LeVert
Female College to become a coeducational school called LeVert College. (See
Carol Johnson and Lea L. Dowd, "Early Schools: Early Talbot County
Educational Centers," http://www.wso.net/ga/education.html.

[12]Johnson and Dowd, "Early Schools."

[13]Copies of his report cards are contained in SHS.

[14]Straus, *Autobiography*, 38.

[15]Oscar Straus, "Reminiscences," 12.

[16]Oscar Straus, "Reminiscences," 13.

[17]Oscar Straus, "Reminiscences," 13.

[18]Volunteer units commonly elected their officer in the Confederate
army.

[19]Straus, *Autobiography*, 13.

[20]Straus, *Autobiography*, 14.

[21]Straus, *Autobiography*, 14.

[22]Oscar Straus, "Reminiscences," p. 10.

[23]*Savannah Daily Morning News*, 16 September 1862. Information on "Judaeophobia" in the Confederacy comes from Korn, "American Judaeophobia,"135-55.

[24]See letter from Huldah A. (Fain) Briant Papers, 14 April 1863, Santa Lucah, Ga., in the Flowers Mss. Collection, Duke University Library, Durham, N. C. and *Memphis Daily Bulletin*, 28 April 1863.

[25]*Savannah Daily Morning News*, 16 September 1862.

[26]Straus, *Autobiography*, 15-16. Evidently Julius Kaufman had moved to Columbus prior to this incident in October 1862. On May 30, 1863, he wrote to his parents that he was living in Columbus and that "we have been living here for already 8 months." Copy provided by Laurette Rothschild Rosenstrauch, German originals in Leo Baeck Institute, New York City.

[27]Julius Kaufman to My dear good parents, 30 May 1863, written in Old German, translated by Gus Kaufman, Jr., Collection of Laurette Rothshild Rosenstrach. "Where we are now living (Columbus) is a city of 18,000 inhabitants 10 hours from Talbotton."

[28]On Isidor's visit to Georgia, see Isidor to Dear Brother Oscar, 8 February 1889, where he indicates his intention to visit Talbotton. On Oscar's visit, see *The Columbus Enquirer*, 7 April 1908. Oscar tried to get Isidor to accompany him on his trip to Georgia, but Isidor declined because of other commitments. See Isidor to Dear brother Oscar, 30 March 1908, Straus Family Papers, NYPL. Nathan's visit is recorded in the *Atlanta Constitution*, 13 January 1915. Isidor's sons, Jesse and Herbert, visited Georgia in March 1927 for the opening of the new Davison-Paxon store, an affiliate of Macy's. They were honored at a dinner at the Biltmore Hotel on March 21. Representatives of both Talbotton (A. P. Persons) and Columbus (J. Ralston Cargill) welcomed them. Following their visit to Atlanta, they visited their father's childhood home in Talbotton, where they were fêted with a reception and barbecue. See *The Atlanta Journal*, 23 March 1927, and the *Atlanta Constitution*, 23 March 1927.

[29]Newspaper clipping containing a notarized list of participants, dated 17 June 1863, from unidentified source, noted as being from the Blackmar scrapbook, collection of Gus Kaufman.

[30]Isidor to Uncle Emanuel, 19 September 1863. SHS.

[31]Isidor to Homefolks, 18 June 1963. SHS.

[32]I am grateful to Kevin J. Foster for this information. For general information on blockade-running vessels, see Stephen R. Wise, *Lifeline of the Confederacy: Blockade Running During the Civil War* (Columbia: University of South Carolina Press, 1988).

[33]Isidor Straus to Dearest Ones at Home, 22 June 1863. SHS. He makes clear that the "dearest ones at home" include "Pa, Ma, Sister, Brothers, Julius, Lazarus & Joe."

[34]Straus, *Autobiography*, 18-19.

[35]Isidor reported this number in his letter to his family of 22 June 1863. SHS.

[36]The *Alabama* was in the end sunk by the U. S. Frigate *Kearsage* in the summer of 1864.

[37]Straus, Autobiography, 20.

[38]Isidor gives the date of his arrival in New York as "July 5th or 6th." Straus, *Autobiography*, 20.

[39]Straus, *Autobiography*, 20-21.

Chapter 3

[1]Straus, *Autobiography*, 28.

[2]Isidor to Dear Ones at Home, 22 June 1863. SHS.

[3]None of his letters written between June 22 and July 29 has survived.

[4]Simon Frank Rothschild was born 14 June 1861 in Eufaula, Alabama; his brother, Elias, was born 25 January 1863. He would not, however, live to see his first birthday, dying on 25 August 1863. Information on the Rothschild family comes from Ancestry.com, Francell Family Tree (A). I am grateful to Thomas Francell for sharing this information.

[5] Straus, *Autobiography*, 21.

[6]Eugene W. Smith, *Passenger Ships of the World Past and Present* (Boston: George H. Dean Co., 1967) 109-110.

[7]Straus in his *Autobiography* remembers the date of the ship's scheduled departure as "about July 22nd," but he cautions his children, for whom he wrote the memoir, "all the dates [are] from memory, hence I say about." In fact, the *New York Times* of 10 July 1863 carries an advertisement for both the *Great Eastern* and the *City of Baltimore*, reporting the departure dates of 21 July and 11 July respectively.

[8]A detailed account of these events was carried in the *New York Times* of 14 July 1863.

[9]Straus, *Autobiography*, 21.

[10]Straus, *Autobiography*, 21-22.

[11]Straus, *Autobiography*, 23.

[12]Isidor to Dear Ones at Home, 29 July 1863, Straus Historical Society. SHS.

[13]Isidor to Dearest Ones at Home, 18 August 1863. SHS.

[14]Straus, *Autobiography*, 22-24. The exclamation point is the punctuation mark he used.

[15]Isidor to Dearest Ones at Home, 18 August 1863. SHS.

[16]Capt. Henry Blun returned to Savannah to reenter the Confederate Army and take charge of a company of home guards. When the Union army entered the city, he was briefly taken prisoner. At the war's end, he took the required oath of allegiance to the Union. The information on Henry Blun is contained in his pamphlet, *Reminiscences of My Blockade Running*, Georgia Historical Society. It is interesting to note that Henry Blun, a Jew like Isidor, converted to Catholicism when he married Catherine Ann Savage in Savannah in 1861.

[17]Straus, *Autobiograhy*, 22.

[18]Isidor to Dearest Ones at Home, 18 December 1893. SHS.

[19]Isidor to Dear Ones at Home, 24 June 1863. SHS.

[20]Isidor to Dear Ones at Home, 12 December 1863. SHS.

[21]Isidor to Dearest Ones at Home, 18 December, 1863. SHS.

[22]Isidor to Dearest Ones at Home, 19 December, 1863. SHS.

[23]Isidor to Dearest Ones at Home, 26 December, 1863. SHS.

[24]Isidor to Dearest Ones at Home, 16 January 1864. SHS.

[25]Isidor to Dearest Ones at Home, 29 February, 1864. SHS.

[26]Isidor to Dearest Ones at Home, 2 April 1864. SHS.

[27]Isidor to Dearest Ones at Home, 2 July 1864. SHS.

[28]Isidor to Dearest Ones at Home, 2 July 1864. SHS.

[29]Isidor to Dearest Ones at Home, 20 October 1864. SHS.

[30]Isidor to Parents, 20 October 1964. SHS.

[31]Straus, *Autobiography*, 26.

[32]Straus, *Autobiography*, 27-28.

[33]Straus, *Autobiography*, 28.

[34]Straus, *Autobiography*, 28-29.

[35]Straus, *Autobiography*, 28-30.

[36]Straus, *Autobiography*, 33.

[37]Isidor to Mother and Sister, 16 June 1865. SHS.

Chapter 4

[1]Charles A. Misulia, *Columbus, Georgia, 1865: The Last True Battle of the Civil War* (Tuscaloosa: University of Alabama Press, 2010). The phrase occurs in the title.

[2]Lee surrendered formally to General Grant on 9 April 1865. The battle of Columbus took place one week later on Easter Sunday, 16 April.

---

[3]See James H. Wilson, *Under the Old Flag*, 2 vols. (New York: Appleton's, 1912) II, 266.

[4]Misulia, *Columbus, Georgia*, 69. He appointed Col. Leon Von Zinken as field commander to assist in the effort. Ironically, Cobb had been elected governor in 1852 as the Union candidate, dedicated to preserving the Union. He would later identify himself as a Democrat. Cobb was at the time commander "of the Department of Tennessee and Georgia, as well as Georgia's Reserve Force." See Misulia, 35.

[5]Misulia specifies the Franklin Street Bridge, but some sources name it the 14th Street Bridge. His is the most thorough and most recent recounting of the Battle of Columbus.

[6]Oscar Straus recalled the Confederate defenders as "mainly superannuated men and schoolboys." See Oscar Straus, *Under Four Administrations: From Cleveland to Taft* (New York: Houghton Mifflin, 1922) 19. One of the men Isidor had met in Savannah not long before he ran the Union blockade out of Charleston, Charlie Lamar, was the last man killed in that battle. On the battle and Lamar's death, see June Hall McCash, "The Last Rebel," *Georgia Backroads*, IX: (spring, 2010): 16-21.

[7]Based on an account of the battle from the *Columbus Enquirer-Sun*, 27 June 1865. Union troops seized all munitions, cannons, and commissary stores and destroyed gunboats, fifteen locomotives, two hundred and fifty train cars, the railroad and foot bridge across the Chattahoochee, 115,000 bales of cotton, paper mills and four cotton factories, as well as the navy yard and armory.

[8]Oscar Straus, *Under Four Administrations*, 19.

[9]See [Joan Adler],"Nathan Straus, 1848-1931," *"wholedamfam": Straus Family Newsletter* 6/1 (February, 1998): 4.

[10]Lazarus Straus to Dear Jacob, 7 July 1865, Philadelphia. SHS. The original letter is written in German. Translations provided by SHS. Lazarus spells the last name of the firm as "Nordlinger," though the firm letterhead spells it "Nirdlinger."

[11]Lazarus Straus to Dear Mother-in-law, 17 July 1864. SHS. Lazarus's letter to his in-laws are also originally in German.

[12]Straus, *Autobiography*, 35.

[13]The house in question was built in 1857 by Dr. Samuel A. Billings "as a wedding gift for his bride, the widow of General Daniel MacDougald. Frank Rothschild and his older brother Simon moved there from Eufaula, Alabama and purchased the house in 1862 from Billings for $8,200. They sold it two years later to Col. George Parker Swift from Thomaston, Georgia, "for

$50,000 Confederate dollars and a quantity of osnaburg (a heavy duck material) manufactured in his cotton mill." [Deed Books L57 and M105, Columbus, Muscogee County.] The source of this information is a copy of a nomination form to get the house on the National Register of Historic Places, provided to me by the late Laurette Rothschild Rosenstrauch. The house still stands today.

[14]According to his war record, Frank Rothschild was taken to Washington on 26 January 1864, and was released the following month by order of the Military Governor of Washington, D.C., General John H. Martindale. I owe this information to Thomas Francell, a descendent of Amanda and Frank Rothschild. Frank and Simon Rothschild both served in Chapman's Company (under Capt. F. S. Chapman), organized in 1861 as part of the 17th Regiment of Georgia Volunteer Infantry, Company C. These designations changed at various times. It was originally known as the 9th Battalion, which consolidated with the 3rd Battalion of Georgia Volunteers to form the 37th Regiment of the Georgia Volunteer Infantry.

[15]This account is based on a letter from Alfred Redgis (formerly Rothschild), the son who was born to Frank and Amanda on 1 July 1864. According to his account the trip in the covered wagon did not take place until September 1864. Alfred Redgis to Elsa [Blun Long], 28 April 1957. Copy provided by Laurette Rothschild Rosenstrach.

[16]Their daughter, Hermine, and her new husband, Lazarus Kohns, would join them in New York.

[17]The partners in this firm were Simon W. Arnold, Ernst Nusbaum, and Jacob Nirdlinger. It was located in 1861 at 55 N. 3rd Street in Philadelphia.

[18]Lazarus Straus to Dear Mother-in-law, 17 July 1865, Philadelphia. SHS. He writes in lieu of his wife Sara, because her arm has still not recovered from her stroke. She did recover briefly in the summer of 1871 and wrote a letter to her parents in her own name on 19 September 1871. Sara [Straus] to "My dear good Parents!" SHS. In that letter she wrote, "I feel, thank God, so much stronger, like many years ago." Unfortunately that strength would not last through the winter months.

[19]Straus, *Autobiography*, 35.

[20]Oscar Straus, *Under Four Administrations*, 21-22.

[21]Oscar Straus, *Under Four Administrations*, 21.

[22]L. Straus to Dear mother-in-law, 17 July 1895. SHS.

[23]We know that he had not returned by 17 July but did return before 6 September, when the family received a letter from Sara's parents, which had followed them from Philadelphia to New York. It is likely that at least a week

would have passed since his arrival and the move to New York, for which some arrangements, even the purchase of the new family home, would most likely have been made. See L. Straus to Dear Parents-in-law, 12 September 1865. SHS. The letter was originally written in Yiddish and translated into English by Lily Cohen. Lazarus knew at least four languages: English, German, Yiddish, and Hebrew.

[24]Straus, *Autobiography*, 35.

[25]Straus, *Autobiography*, 35.

[26]The family of Nathan Blun lived at 20 West 38th Street.

[27]Oscar Straus, *Under Four Administrations*, 21. The house was "long since" demolished in 1922, as Oscar notes in his book published that year.

[28]Straus, *Autobiography*, 40.

[29]Straus, *Autobiography*, 41.

[30]Straus, *Autobiography*, 41.

[31]L. Straus to Dear mother-in-law, 17 July 1867. SHS.

[32]Established in 1858, under the name of Bryant, Stratton & Packard's Mercantile College, this school was part of a chain of institutions, which would eventually include fifty such business schools in large cities in the United States and Canada. In 1867 S. S. Packard acquired the Bryant & Stratton interest in the New York College, and changed its name to Packard's Business College. "Packard's Business College," *Scientific American*, 43/25 (18 December 1880): 386. Nathan had already received more advanced education than Isidor when he studied Hebrew for a year in Montgomery, Alabama, with a rabbi friend of his father's.

[33]L. Straus to Dear mother-in-law, 17 July 1865. SHS.

[34]Oscar Straus, *Under Four Administrations*, 22.

[35]Oscar Straus, *Under Four Administrations*, 23.

[36]According to Jesse's biographer, when the family first arrived New York, the Bluns lived at Matilda Terrace on 24th Street, in one of a group of "English Villas," known as London Terrace, which allegedly belonged to Clement Clarke Moore, author of the poem popularly known as "The Night Before Christmas. See Kauffman, *Jesse Isidor Straus*, 45. He provides no source for this information, and I have been unable to verify its accuracy.

[37]The passenger manifest of the *Seine* voyage from Le Havre to New York indicates their arrival on 15 August 1851. The passengers included in the manifest are Mine Blun, Amanda Blun, Elias Blun, Louis Blun, Augusta Blun, Ida Blun, and Isaac Freudenberger [sic]. A copy of this manifest is contained in SHS. Although family stories indicate that Nathan Blun arrived with his family, he is not listed on the passenger manifest.

[38]As noted above, Sara Straus's hand recovered briefly in the summer of 1871, so that for the first time in many years, she was able to write herself to her family. But by March 1872, Lazarus was once again writing the letters in German to his in-laws: "My wife's hand, which improved so very much last summer in the spa, that she was able to write fluently, returned this winter to its old condition, so that she now can again not write and goes this summer again to the spa." L. Straus to My dear Parents-in-law, 27 March 1872. SHS.

[39]There has been some confusion about the date of Ida's birth, with her grandson, Robert K. Straus, concluding as a result of his genealogical inquiries, that she was born, on 9 February. This date was based on a misreading of her German birth registration, which was in fact recorded on February 9. However, the document itself clearly states that she was born at her parents' home three days earlier, on 6 February. Copy of original document at SHS.

[40]See Straus, *Autobiography*, 42. There the lease was $6,000 per annum. As the Straus firm grew, so did the Blun operation, as Nathan Blun took his two sons, Louis and Elias, into the family business. On 3 January1871, Nathan Blun, designated a "special partner," put up $75,000 in cash to establish a 3-year limited partnership with his two sons, under the name of H. N. Blun & Company. Their company was responsible for "manufacturing, selling and dealing in clothing for men and boys." See *Real Estate Record*, (Brooklyn, NY: C.W. Sweet & Co, 1868-1884), vols. 7 and 8, pp. 15, 31, 48 72, and 84.

[41]Straus, *Autobiography*, 45. The firm of Helbing & Straus would later be succeeded by Straus, Kohnstamm & Company.

[42]This trip is described on pp. 46-47 of his *Autobiography*.

[43]Straus, *Autobiography*, 46.

[44]Isidor to Dear Cousin Gabe, 25 April, 1871. Straus Family Papers, NYPL.

[45]L. Straus to My dear good In-laws, 28 April 1871. SHS. Either he misdated the letter or he was not told of the engagement until the 27th. As noted above, Sara Straus was unable to write because of her earlier stroke. In a letter from Lazarus to his in-laws written on 5 April 1871, he wrote "This evening I will give her [Sara] your letter to read. She regrets as always that she cannot write. She says sometimes that she would know more to write about than I do." SHS.

[46]Straus, *Autobiography*, 46, emphasis his.

[47]Straus, *Autobiography*, 46. Nathan Blun became a U.S. citizen on 17 April 1872. Copy of his certificate of citizenship in SHS.

[48]Alfred Redgis (formerly Rothschild) to [Elsa Blun] Long, 28 April 1957. Copy provided by Laurette Rothschild Rosenstrauch.

[49]This is one of the more conservative estimates of the dead.

[50]The details of this and subsequent births of their children are recorded in *The Order of Prayer for Divine Service,* rev. by Dr. L. Merzbacher, rabbi of the Temple "Emanu-el" (1855), third edition, revised and corrected by Dr. S. Adler (1864), printed by M. Thalmessinger & Co. Copy in SHS. The handwriting appears to be that of Isidor. There he records the day, date, time, and address where the birth took place. All subsequent births and their details come from this family record.

[51]Their move also made room for Ida's brother, Louis, to bring his bride, Jenny Levy, whom he married in January 1875, to his father's home. It is likely that Louis would choose to begin his married life, as Ida and Isidor had done, in his father's home, for he and his father were close and Louis apparently worked more closely with Nathan in the family business. As Nathan Blun made clear in his will, he included no specific legacy for Louis, "not from any lack of my love and affection for him but for the purpose of equalizing in some degree my benefactions among my children, he having been benefited freely to that extent by reason of my early association [of] him with me in business." After his father's death, Louis was given the responsibility of running Blun & Co. He was also named as co-executor, with Isidor Straus, of his father's estate. See Nathan Blun's will, Collection of Laurette Rothschild Rosenstrauch.

[52]Minnie would be their last child.

[53]Even after their marriage Nathan made annual buying trips to Europe, but as his family grew, he felt the need to spend more time at home and began to cast about for ways to reduce his travels.

[54]The comment appears on an extensive genealogy of the descendents of Nathan Blun contained in SHS.

[55]Straus, *Autobiography,* 50.

[56]Straus, *Autobiography,* 50.

[57]Straus, *Autobiography,* 59.

[58]Straus, *Autobiography,* 50

[59]Isidor underscored this point in the letter he left for Ida to be read in case of his death (copy at the end of his published *Autobiography*). Although she never had the opportunity to read it, she was no doubt well familiar with his philosophy and shared his positive outlook.

[60]On 30 July 1868, her four-month-old daughter, Flora Caroline Kohns, died and was buried at Salem Field cemetery in Brooklyn. The following

year, on 26 December 1869, her first daughter, Clara Louisa Kohns, died at the age of 3 years and 7 months. Fortunately, her only son, born in Columbus in the midst of the Civil War on 1 September 1864 and named for Robert E. Lee, would live to adulthood. On 11 May 1871 she gave birth to another daughter, Irene.

[61]Straus, *Autobiography*, 51. Isidor incorrectly gives the date as 1878.

[62]The details of his death and burial are recorded in the Strauses' *Order of Prayer for Divine Service.* Copy in SHS.

[63]Information about Abraham Blun's brief life and death are found in *Biographical Record of the Officers and Graduates of the Rensselaer Polytechnic Institute 1828-1886*, ed. Henry Bradford Nason (Troy, New York: William H. Young, 1887) 435. He had graduated with a B.S. degree from the College of the City of New York and entered Rensselaer in 1870. In 1876 he joined his father's firm and became a partner. The notice of his death and funeral, which took place at the home of his brother-in-law, E. Eising, at 6 E. 66th Street on 11 September 1881, appears in the *New York Times*, 11 September 1881. The only child of Abraham and Lucie died in 1884. Lucie remained a widow for eight years, living with Nathan and Lina Straus. In about 1890 she returned to her home in Mannheim to care for her ailing mother. There she met Edward Mammelsdorff who became her second husband. His name is spelled variously Mamelsdorff and Mammelsdorff.

[64]All these births are recorded in the Strauses' copy of the *Order of Prayer for Divine Service,* in SHS.

[65][Joan Adler] "The Women in the Family: Part Two," *"wholedamfam": Straus Family Newsletter* 4/2 (August 1996) 7.

Chapter 5
[1]Straus, *Autobiography*, 47.

[2]Jesse rhymed: "Mamma can you recollect when we were all petite, / The various kinds of medicines you used to make us eat? / My earliest recollection is that Caster Oil was king. / If I had a headache, prickly heat or mumps, it was the only thing./ To it ipecac succeeded / Twenty drops was all prescribed. / But mamma gave a pint for full measure / And despite it all we survived. / Well, all those cures have had their sway / And straight and tall we grew. / But it was love and care that won the day / And reared this healthy crew." Punctuation and capitalization are Jesse's. "Jesse Isidor Straus, 40th Anniversary Poem to Isidor and Ida Straus, 1911," Source: Paul A. Kurzman and Peter Kurzman, Copy in SHS.

[3]The 1880 census shows them living with their first four children at 26 Madison Avenue, but, if they lived there, it was only temporary, for in 1881, their son Herbert was born at 26 East 55th Street.

[4]Kauffman, *Jesse Isidor Straus*, 56-57.

[5]See [Joan Adler], "2745 Broadway: The Home of the Isidor Straus Family," *Straus Historical Society, Inc. Newsletter*, 8/1 (August 2006): 9.

[6]Tyler Anbinder, *Five Points: The Nineteenth-Century New York City Neighborhood That Invented the Tap Dance* (New York: The Free Press, 2001), 331. The prisoner in question was an associate of Boss Tweed named Harry Genet.

[7]*New York Times*, 23 December 1873.

[8]Straus, *Autobiography*, 47.

[9]Kauffman, *Jesse Isidor Straus*, 41-47.

[10]Straus, *Autobiography*, 47.

[11]Isidor made it clear that "Ida would not hear of having a housekeeper." Isidor to Dear Brother Oscar, 13 September 1910.

[12]Ida wrote to him in August 1890, for example to tell him "what to take out of the cedar closet." Mama to My darling papa, [between 21-24] August, 1890. SHS. Ida referred to his packing for Isidor. Mama to My darling papa, 4 September 1890, SHS.

[13]Concerning Patrick and the six household servants, see Kauffman, 58-61. One of the servants (possibly the gardener) was named Jerry. Information concerning Fraulein is drawn from various letters in the Straus correspondence, and the two tutors are referred to by Joan Adler in "Jesse Isidor Straus," *Straus Historical Society, Inc. Newsletter* 6/1 (August 2004): 3. Fraulein also accompanied them on family trips to Lower Saranac Lake.

[14]The hallway is described in Kauffman, *Jesse Isidor Straus*, 48.

[15]On Ida's membership, see *The American Jewish Year Book 5668, September 9, 1907 to September 25, 1908*, ed. Henrietta Szold (Philadelphia: Jewish Publication Society of America, 1907) 58. Both of Isidor's brothers were members, as was his son Jesse, but not Isidor.

[16]Kauffman, *Jesse Isidor Straus*, 57.

[17]Virginia Brooks McKelway, letter to the editor, *New York Times*, 22 April 1912. On Mrs. McKelway's completion of the "Woman's Law Class" at New York University, see *New York Times*, 31 March 1899.

[18]Quoted in Kauffman, *Jesse Isidor Straus*, 65.

[19]Christopher Gray, *New York Times*, 23 August 1998. This description of the house is otherwise based on Kauffman, *Jesse Isidor Straus*, 46-49, and [Adler], "2745 Broadway."

[20]Isidor to Dear Brother Oscar, 8 February 1889, Oscar S. Straus Papers, LC.

[21]Isidor to Dear Brother Oscar, 8 February 1889, Oscar S. Straus Papers, LC.

[22]Isidor to Dear Brother Oscar, 8 February 1889, Oscar S. Straus Papers, LC.

[23]Isidor to Dear Brother Oscar, 8 March 1889, Oscar S. Straus Papers, LC. Isidor indicates in this letter that he had selected a beautiful piece of cut glass, "which Ida had filled with the choicest flowers and orchids," which the two of them delivered to Cleveland's hotel "[o]n account of their great courtesy to me and my wife while in Washington last." This occurred on 8 March during Cleveland's visit to New York.

[24]Isidor to Dear Brother Oscar, 6 March 1889 [continued and mailed 8 March 1889], Oscar S. Straus Papers, LC. Henry Grady was a prominent journalist, editor and part-owner of the *Atlanta Constitution* and promoter of the concept of the New South. Isidor would return to Atlanta in November 1895 when he attended the Atlanta Exposition as a member of a New York Committee invited to attend. Isidor to C. R. Breckinridge, 29 November 1895. Straus Family Papers, NYPL. See also Isidor to "My Dear Friend" [W. L. Wilson], 3 December 1895. Straus Family Papers, NYPL. In the latter letter, he indicates that he passed through Washington on the way back from Atlanta and then arrived home in time for Thanksgiving with his family. There is no indication that he visited Talbotton or Columbus during this trip.

[25] See Isidor Straus to Henry Blun, 10 May 1992. Straus Family Papers, NYPL.

[26]See Birmingham, *"Our Crowd,"* 141-50.

[27]Ida wrote to Isidor near the end of July 1889, evidently speaking of the incident: "Was that not a terrible [calam]ity in the Adirondacks[?] I am afraid of the effect it will have on Nathan. Pa prophecies that he will not remain up there and that he will not care to go back another year." Ida to My darling papa, 21 [?] July 1889. SHS.

[28]Mama to My darling papa, 23 January 1890. SHS. In that same letter she noted that "Nathan is so full of his hotel project that he does nothing else but talk of it. An entire scrapbook (Scrapbook 14) of clippings, advertisements, and articles about the Lakewood hotel is contained in the Nathan Straus Papers, NYPL.

[29]Isidor to Dear Brother Oscar, 18 June 1887, Oscar S. Straus Papers, LC.

[30]Papa to My Dear Mama, 1 August 1886. SHS.

[31]Isidor to Dear Brother Oscar, 28 July 1887. Oscar S. Straus Papers. LC.

---

[32]Ida to My darling papa, 21[?] July 1889. SHS.

[33]"This is the most wonderful place," she wrote. "I am almost entirely rid of my cough and Sara has not coughed since we came here." Mama to My darling papa, 26 June 1891. SHS.

[34]Jesse, Percy, and Herbert all attended Sachs Collegiate Institute, which had been founded by the well-known botanist Julius Sachs and was modeled on the German gymnasium. It was located on West 59th Street between Fifth and Sixth Avenues, overlooking Central Park. The school was strict and rigorous in its expectations, and it usually prepared its students to enter Harvard earlier than the traditional age. Jesse was seventeen when he entered Harvard as a freshman in 1889. Over time the name and location of the Institute changed to the Franklin School and later, Dwight School, as it is called today. It is also located farther uptown (at West 89th Street) than when the Straus sons attended.

[35]Papa to My dear Percy, 5 October 1893. SHS.

[36]Daughty [Sara] to My dear Papa, 27 August 1890. SHS.

[37]Mama to My darling papa, 4 July 1891. SHS.

[38]Aside from the published copies of these poems, which occurred later, a typewritten copy is in the Straus Family Papers, NYPL, on which someone else, most likely Percy, noted that it was written during the time of the Russian pogroms in the 1880s.

[39]On their relative language skills, see Kauffman, *Jesse Isidor Straus*, 65. Although Jesse struggled with French, he was later glad he had been compelled to learn it when he was named ambassador to France by Franklin D. Roosevelt and served from 1933-1936.

[40]Once, in fact, while Isidor's partner Charley Webster was in Italy, his parents complained that "Ida and her friends…forced him to go out to gayteies [sic] theatres, etc., which pulled him down…instead of building him up." Oscar to Dear Bro. Isidor, 12 July 1889. Straus Family Papers, NYPL. No doubt Ida was trying merely to include him in her many social activities, which he could have refused. She also often took the children to the theatre, reading Shakespearean plays (i.e., *As you Like It*) with them ahead of time in order to prepare them to understand the theatrical experience. (Mama to My darling papa, Thursday afternoon [n.d.]. SHS.

[41]He was enrolled in French 6 the second semester of his freshman year and was told by the professor that he should be satisfied as a freshman making a C in a junior/senior level course. However, the professor indicated that "if I kept on as I was doing I would get a B on the finals." Herbert Straus to My dear Mother, 2 February 1900. SHS. Isidor bought her "a yearly seat at

the theatre" in 1899, knowing that she would enjoy it but that it was something she was not likely to buy for herself. Isidor to My Dear Ones, 29 May 1899. Straus Family Papers, NYPL.

[42]Herbert Straus to Dear Mama, N.D. [October 1899], SHS. Ernest Sachs was the son of Julius Sachs, who founded and taught at the Sachs Collegiate Institute, where Herbert had attended preparatory school prior to coming to Harvard. The Strauses also made certain that their children had superior musical instruments once they had gained adequate proficiency. As Herbert told his parents, "After the rehearsal a fellow came up and asked me what kind of cello I had. He said he noticed its sweet and sympathetic tone and wondered what it was. On my telling him, he said he could well understand, and thought I was mighty lucky to have such an instrument. I agreed with him entirely." Herbert to My Dear Mother, 17 October 1899. SHS.

[43]The word "casino" was frequently used during this period of time as a pavilion for games, which included bowling, a shooting range, a tennis, squash, or rackets court and other kinds of indoor activities for the amusement of family and friends. It does not refer necessarily to a gambling location.

[44]Knollwood has been well preserved and has hosted many distinguished visitors. In fact, Alfred Einstein was a guest at Knollwood on the day he heard of the dropping of the atomic bomb on Hiroshima.

[45]Ed. Mammelsdorf to Valued Mr. & Mrs. Isidor Straus, 19 August 1890. SHS. This is presumably the Edward Mammelsdorf, who would marry Lucie Gutherz, Lina's sister and the widow of Ida's brother, Abraham.

[46]Mama to My darling Isidor, 26 August 1890. SHS

[47]Mama to My darling Papa, 27 August 1890. SHS.

[48]See Kauffman, *Jesse Isidor Straus*, 42-43.

[49]Kauffman, *Jesse Isidor Straus*, 60.

[50]Mama to My darling Papa, 25 June 1891. SHS.

[51]Mama to My darling Papa, 25 August 1890. SHS.

[52]Mama to My darling papa, 4 September 1890. SHS.

[53]Jesse to Papa, 5 September 1890. SHS. Guides identified were Warren Bryan and a man named Perly.

[54]See letter from Mama, Pete, Sara, and Percy Selden S. to My darling papa, 13 September 1890. SHS. They all send New Year's greetings for Rosh Hashanah, and below Percy's signature are the words "(new name)." Many such name changes were made in order for individuals to sound less Jewish. There is no indication of Percy's motive.

[55]Mama to My darling papa, 31 August 1890. SHS.

---

[56] Mama to My darling papa, 2 September 1890. SHS.

[57] Mama to My dear papa, 8 September 1890. SHS.

[58] Mama to My darling papa, 9 September 1890. SHS.

[59] Daughter [Sara?] to My dear Papa, 5 August 1891. SHS

[60] They were married on 4 June 1895, at the Nathan family's home, Fairlawn, located on North Broadway in New York. *New York Times,* 5 June 1895.

[61] Ida to My darling papa, 15 September 1890. SHS.

[62] Mama to My darling papa, 9 September 1890. SHS. "Your two letters written on Saturday reached me yesterday and the pleasure they gave me was tinged with an alloy of regret at your inability to carry out your design of coming up this week, and also at your having to stand the great heat of the city while we are all here."

[63] Mama to My darling papa, 13 September 1890. SHS.

[64] Ida to My darling papa, 18 September 1890. SHS.

[65] Ida to My dear papa, 15 September 1890. SHS.

[66] "Daughty" [Sara] to My dear Papa, 17 September 1890. SHS.

[67] M.D. to My dear Papa, 16 September 1890. SHS.

[68] This comment is preceded by the following: "I return [to] you the note of Miss Doree with an explaining note by Mr. Kuppenheimer, which makes me very suspicious. Your sending it to me was probably a blind, you hardly knew that there would be anyone up here who will know an actress." The actress in question was most likely Nadage Doree, a comely young woman popular at the time.

[69] Mama to My darling papa, Thursday afternoon [n.d.]. SHS. Tony Pastor was a well known variety performer in minstrel shows, circuses (he worked for a while for P.T. Barnum), and various comic routines. He was also a singer, a songwriter and an impresario, who is credited with having been one of the forces behind the founding of vaudeville.

[70] Mama to My darling papa, 4 July 1891. SHS.

[71] Mama to My darling papa, 2 September 1890. SHS

[72] Jesse to My dear papa, 18 July 1891. SHS.

[73] Percy to Dear Papa, [21 July 1891?]. SHS.

[74] Mama to My own darling papa, [21 July 1891], SHS.

[75] Ida quotes from his letter in her own on 22 July 1891. See following note.

[76] Mama to My own darling papa, 22 July 1891. SHS.

[77] Mama to My own darling papa, 31 July 1891. SHS.

[78] Mama to My own darling papa, 4 August 1891. SHS.

[79]Mama to My own darling papa, 7 august 1891. SHS.

[80]Mama to My darling papa, 24 June 1891. SHS.

[81]Mama to My darling papa, [3 (?) July 1891]. SHS.

[82]Mama to My darling Isidor, 26 August 1890. SHS.

[83]Mama to My darling papa, 27 August 1890. SHS.

[84]Mama to My darling papa, 24 June 1891. SHS. They had added an ice house since the previous season.

[85]Jesse to Dear Mamma, 19 July 1891. SHS.

[86]Mama to My own darling papa, 20 July 1891. SHS. Note that Ida often spells Lina's name "Lena."

[87]Lina to Dear Bro. Isidor, 24 July 1891. SHS.

[88]Jesse to My dear papa, 12 October 1893. SHS.

[89]Mama to My darling papa, [13 October 1893]. SHS.

[90]Mama to My darling papa, 14 October 1893. SHS. The house was rented that summer to someone named McCutcheon.

[91]Mama to My darling papa, 14 October 1893. SHS.

[92]Stephen Birmingham, *"Our Crowd"* 257-66.

[93]She would also later be a "feminist and a suffragette." [Joan Adler], *"wholedamfam": Straus Family Newsletter* 4/2 (August 1996): 7.

[94]Mama to My dear ones, 31 May 1901. SHS.

[95]Isidor to My Dear Brother & Sons, 31 May 1901. SHS. He was evidently speaking of Wolvercote Common located north of Oxford beside the river. It is also known as Port Meadow. I owe this information to my English friend, Rosemary Kew.

[96]Mama to My darling Papa and Daughter, 13 May 1901. SHS.

[97]Mama to My darling papa and daughter, 23 May 1901. SHS

[98]Jesse and Irma lived for 15 years at 49 East 74th Street in a house given to them by Max Nathan, Irma's father.

[99]*New York Times*, 13 October 1904. After the death of the Strauses, Dr. Hess would go on to do groundbreaking studies in the role of nutrition in scurvy and rickets.

[100]*New York Times*, 31 May 1905.

Chapter 6

[1]It should be noted, however that there were two serious economic downturns during the three decades prior to the turn of the century. One occurred in 1873 and another, more serious, one began in 1893 and affected business for several years thereafter. Overall, however, New York and the business environment grew by leaps and bounds.

[2]Straus, *Autobiography*, 47.

[3]Straus, *Autobiography*, 45. Helbing and Straus had by 1878 been succeeded by Straus, Kohnstamm & Company and later Straus, Bloom & Company, which also specialized in crockery. See Henry G. Langley, *San Francisco Directory for 1878*. (San Francisco: Commercial Steam Presses, S. D. Valentine & Sons, 1878).

[4]This first meeting is described in Robert M. Grippo, *Macy*s: The Store. The Star. The Story*. (Garden City, New York: SquareOne Publishers, 2009) 40, 43.

[5]Ralph M. Hower, *History of Macy's of New York 1858-1919: Chapters in the Evolution of the Department Store* (Cambridge, Mass.: Harvard University Press, 1943) 221. They also had a concession in Wechsler & Abraham, which would later become Abraham & Straus.

[6]The entire article (no source indicated) appears in Grippo, *Macy*s*, 41.

[7]Hower, *History of Macy's*, 123-124.

[8]Grippo, *Macy*s*, 43. Grippo bases his statement on entries in the diary of Margaret Getchell, then Macy's store superintendent and allegedly the "first American woman to hold an executive position in retailing" (Grippo, *Macy*s*, 33, caption).

[9]Obituary in the *New York Times*, 31 March 1877.

[10]Obituary in the *New York Times*, 31 March 1877. Abiel LaForge had married Margaret Getchell. Her biographer has dubbed her "America's First Lady Boss." While that label is not entirely accurate, she was one of the first women in corporate America to hold an executive position in such a major firm as Macy's. She began as a cashier in the early 1860s and worked her way up to store superintendent, where she had a significant influence on Macy's success. See Curtiss S. Johnson, *America's First Lady Boss: A Wisp of a Girl, Macy's and Romance* (Silvermine: Norwalk, Conn., 1965).

[11]See Grippo, *Macy*s*, 46-47.

[12]Grippo, *Macy*s*, 47.

[13] *New York Times*, 16 February 1879.

[14]*New York Times*, 26 February 1879.

[15]For additional information on the rift between Webster and Wheeler, see Grippo, *Macy*s*, 49-51.

[16]See Hower, *History of Macy's*, 204 and 213. Charles Webster's interest in Martha Toye may have resulted from disappointment in his own marriage. Oscar Straus contended that Charley's wife "does everything she knows how for Charley's comfort," but she "lacks the finer feelings that are inborn in Charley." Oscar to Dear Bro Isidor, 12 July 1889. Straus Family Papers, NYPL.

[17]Isidor to Oscar, 15 October 1887. Oscar S. Straus Papers, LC.

[18]Isidor to Oscar, 18 November 1887. Oscar S. Straus Papers. LC.

[19]Nathan to Oscar, 10 December 1887. Oscar S. Straus Papers, LC. This conversation took place one week after the agreement between Webster and Wheeler. Nathan tells his brother in the letter in question that "About four weeks ago Charley bought out Jerome's interest...Just three weeks ago Charley was at my house for dinner."

[20]See Hower, *History of Macy's*, 223.

[21]Isidor to Oscar, 9 December 1887. Oscar S. Straus Papers, LC. Concerning the purchase of Wheeler's share and details of the financial arrangements, see Hower, *History of Macy's*, 223. He notes that the money was borrowed from L. Straus & Sons, which served as "a kind of private bank or family treasury into which all members of the Straus family paid their surplus cash and from which they drew money to meet business or personal requirements" (223).

[22]Lee [Kohns] to Dear Uncle Oscar & Aunt Sarah. Oscar S. Straus Papers, LC. It is Lee who records the date of the signing in family correspondence.

[23]*New York Times,* 3 January 1888. Concerning Wheeler's "western interests," he owned at least three banks, all of which failed in the economic recession of 1893. See Isidor to Dear Brother Nathan, 21 July, 1893. Straus Family Papers, NYPL.

[24]Isidor to Dear Brother Oscar, 7 January 1887 [sic, 1888]. Oscar S. Straus Papers, LC. Note that the date is incontestably 1888, but Isidor mistakenly dates the letter 1887, as many people do early in a new year.

[25]Isidor to Oscar, 24 December 1887. Oscar S. Straus Papers, LC.

[26]Oscar Straus, *Under Four Administrations*, 37.

[27]Nathan to Dear Brother Oscar, 19 February [1882]. Oscar S. Straus Papers, LC.

[28]Oscar Straus, *Under Four Administrations*, 29.

[29]Oscar Straus, *Under Four Administrations*, 28, 33. Five manuscripts of poems are located in the Oscar S. Straus Papers, 1869-1947. Archival Collection of the Rare Book & Manuscript Library, Columbia University.

[30]Oscar Straus, *Under Four Administrations*, 31.

[31]Oscar Straus, *Under Four Administrations*, 37-38.

[32]Oscar Straus, *Under Four Administrations*, 38, 41.

[33]Oscar Straus, *Under Four Administrations*, 43-46.

[34]Henry Ward Beecher to Grover Cleveland, 12 February 1887. Oscar S. Straus Papers, LC.

[35]Oscar Straus, *Under Four Administrations,* 46. Oscar points out on this same page that Keiley had earlier been nominated as minister to Italy, but the Italian government had let it be known that he was unacceptable because of a speech he had made "denouncing King Victor Emmanuel for his treatment of the Pope." Oscar believed that the underlying reason for his refusal by Austro-Hungary was that they did not want to offend another member of the Triple Alliance by accepting him. In his opinion, the stated "religious grounds" were believed to be less offensive.

[36]T. F. Maynard to Oscar S. Straus, 26 March 1887. Oscar S. Straus Papers, LC. It is interesting to note that Oscar had set out to assume his post in Constantinople in April 1887, although the appointment did not receive Senate confirmation until 21 December. See Isidor to Dear Brother Oscar, 24 December 1887. Oscar S. Straus, Papers LC.

[37]Isidor to Dear Brother Oscar, 29 October 1887. Oscar S. Straus Papers, LC.

[38]Nathan to Dear Brother & Sister, 11 June 1887. Oscar S. Straus Papers. LC.

[39]Isidor to Dear Brother Oscar, 18 June 1887. Oscar S. Straus Papers, LC. The salary changed over time, but was never higher than $10,000 per annum.

[40]Isidor to Dear Brother Oscar, 29 October 1887. Oscar S. Straus Papers, LC.

[41]Isidor to Dear Brother Oscar, 12 November 1887. Oscar S. Straus Papers, LC.

[42]Isidor to Dear Brother Oscar, 21 October 1887. Sarah also recorded in her diary both Oscar's criticism and her own feelings of loneliness and uselessness in her unfamiliar role. See especially her entries for 25 and 26 September, 1887. Sarah Lavanburg Straus Diary, SHS.

[43]Lee [Kohns] to Oscar and Sarah Straus, December 1887, Oscar S. Straus Papers, LC.

[44]Oscar to Dear Brother Isidor, 22/24 April 1888. Straus Family Papers, NYPL.

[45]Isidor to Dear Brother Oscar, 18 March 1888. Oscar S. Straus Papers, LC.

[46]Nathan Straus to Dear Brother Oscar & Sister Sarah, 10 December 1887, and Nathan to Dear Brother Oscar, 26 January 1888. Oscar S. Straus Papers, LC. Although Jerome may have treated Charley "shamefully," Nathan notes that "he treated almost every-one else very nicely."

[47]Nathan Straus to Dear Brother Oscar & Sister Sarah, 10 December 1887, Oscar S. Straus Papers, LC.

[48]Virginia Brooks McKelway, Letter to the editor, *New York Times*, 22 April 1912.

[49]*New York Times*, 22 April 1912.

[50]Isidor to Dear Brother Oscar, 14 January 1888. Oscar S. Straus Papers, LC.

[51]Isidor to Dear Brother Oscar, 14 January 1888. Oscar S. Straus Papers, LC.

[52]Isidor to Dear Brother Oscar, 25 February, 1888. Oscar S. Straus Papers, LC.

[53]The Manhattan Club, located at the time on the corner of Fifth Avenue and 15th Street, would move in 1890 to the marble mansion of A. T. Stewart at the corner of Fifth Avenue and 39th Street. For the club's evolution, see Henry Watterson, *History of the Manhattan Club: A Narrative of the Activities of Half a Century* (New York: privately printed for the Manhattan Club, 1915); *New York Times*, 10 October 1915. Both Isidor and Nathan Straus were club members, and Isidor gave each of his sons a lifetime membership in the Manhattan Club when they came of age.

[54]Oscar to Dear Bro Isidor, 12 July 1889. Straus Family Papers, NYPL.

[55]Isidor to Dear Brother Oscar, 25 February, 1888. Oscar S. Straus Papers, LC.

[56]Financing for this purchase came, not from L. Straus & Sons, which Ralph Hower has referred to as the "family bank," but rather, in part at least, from the United States Trust Co, which loaned the firm half a million dollars on a six-months loan, with three renewals at 5%. See Straus, *Autobiography*, 37.

Chapter 7

[1]Fitch was a Democrat who had resigned to accept the post of comptroller of the city of New York.

[2] Cleveland named William S. Bissell as Postmaster General instead of Isidor.

[3]*Washington Post*, 13 February 1894.

[4]Straus, *Autobiography*, 53.

[5]The goal of the Reform Club, which first met in the home of Theodore Roosevelt on 10 October 1882, is taken from the minutes of that meeting cited in *New Outlook*, 126 (1920): 368.

[6]*The Tammany Times*, 6 January 1893, 2.

[7]Straus, *Autobiography*, 50.

[8]Their protest was addressed to Edward L. Hedden, Collector of Customs, SHS.

[9] Witnesses included Oliver A. Gager, Samuel L. McBride, and Charles A. Welling.

[10] He was from the firm of McBride & Co in Atlanta, Georgia, and testified on 31 December 1885.

[11]Testimony to the City, County, and State of New York, sworn on 31 December 1885, "In the Matter of the Re-appraisements per 'Belgerland' and 'Nordland,'" Case Nos. 22231 and 15564. SHS.

[12]Straus, *Autobiography*, 50.

[13]Quoted in [Joan Adler] "Hon. Isidor Straus: House of Representatives 1894-1895," *Straus Historical Society Inc. Newsletter* 4/1 (August 2002) 3.

[14]Jesse to Papa, 16 September 1890, SHS. See also article [Adler], "Hon. Isidor Straus: House of Representatives 1894-1895," 3.

[15]Nell Irvin Painter, *Standing at Armageddon: The United States 1877-1919* (New York: W. W. Norton & Co., 1987) 116-17, 129; Jack Beatty, *Age of Betrayal: The Triumph of Money in America, 1865-1900* (New York: Vintage, 2008) 360-61. Painter also points out (p. 116) that the 1890 failure of Baring Brothers, a London banking house, had brought about a withdrawal of European capital from the United States, thus reducing the money supply.

[16]Painter, *Standing at Armageddon*, 129.

[17]Isidor to Nathan Straus, 5 July 1893, SHS.

[18]Isidor to Nathan Straus, 5 July 1893. SHS.

[19]Isidor to Dear Brother Nathan, 4 August 1893. Straus Family Papers, NYPL.

[20]Wilson would also serve as Postmaster General under Grover Cleveland from 1895 until the end of his term.

[21]Fitch served in Congress as a Republican from 1887-1889, but in his bid for re-election he ran as a Democrat and was elected for three more terms, resigning his seat in 1893.

[22]*New York Tribune*, 9 January 1894.

[23]Quoted in *New York Herald*, 11 January 1894.

[24]Isidor to Hon. W. L Wilson, 19 December 1893, SHS.

[25]*The Tammany Times*, 27 January 1894, 3.

[26]*The Tammany Times*, 27 January 1894, 3.

[27]*New York Sun*, 10 January 1894.

[28]These are the numbers in the official vote count from the published "Statement of the Board of County Canvassers of the County of New York" for the election of January 30, 1894, SHS. Numbers differ slightly, given as

15,396 and 10,528 respectively, in "A Biographical Sketch sent to F. M. Cox," Clerk of Printing Records United States Senate and cited in Saul Viener, "The Political Career of Isidor Straus" (Master's thesis, West Virginia University, 1947) 33.

[29]Isidor to Carl Schurz, 12 March 1894, Carl Shurz papers, LC.

[30]Isidor to My Dear Mamma, 11 July 1894. SHS.

[31]Isidor to My Dear Mamma, 7 August 1894, SHS. In that same letter, he relates his social evenings with friends, recounting an evening when Congressman Wilson cancelled a prior dinner invitation to dine with Isidor. "After dinner we were joined in my room by Secy Gresham and Mr. Breckinridge and after chatting for an hour and a half W & B went to see the President and I took an hours [sic] drive with the Secretary."

[32]Ida to Isidor, 1 July 1893. SHS.

[33]Isidor was no doubt fond of Senator Gorman, who had been associated with his brother Oscar in Grover Cleveland's campaign in 1884 and who had pushed for Oscar's nomination as U. S. Minister of Turkey. See Straus, *Autobiography,* 51. Cleveland later intended to appoint Isidor ambassador to Holland, but he was elected to Congress instead, where the President felt he could do even more good.

[34]Isidor to My Dear Mamma, 13 August 1894. SHS.

[35]Isidor to My Dear Mamma, 15 August 1894. Straus Family Papers, NYPL.

[36]Commencement address given by Isidor Straus at Washington and Lee University, 18 June 1902. SHS.

[37]Jean Strouse, *Morgan: American Financier* (New York: Random House, 1999) 343. Strouse's account of the negotiations between the President and the Secretary of the Treasurer, among others, and Morgan and August Belmont explores the negotiations in detail. For her account of the entire matter and all involved, see 339-60.

[38] Viener, 41.

[39]Straus, Commencement speech. Straus Family Papers, NYPL.

[40]Isidor felt close enough to President Cleveland to invite him to the wedding of his son Jesse the following November. Cleveland was unable to attend "owing to the pressure of time on account of his message to Congress," but he sent "a beautiful letter and Mr. and Mrs. Cleveland's photographs, signed and dated, which as you can well imagine pleased the young couple immensely." Isidor to My dear friend [C. R. Breckinridge], 29 November 1895. Straus Family Papers, NYPL.

[41]Papa to My dear Mamma, 18 July 1894. SHS.

[42]*New York Times*, 26 July 1894.

[43]Although their father, Lazarus, still lived, his name no longer appeared on the L. Straus & Sons letterhead by 1896. See the scrapbook of newspaper clippings in the Straus Family Papers, NYPL.

[44]Papa to My dear Percy, 20 January 1897, Straus Family Papers, NYPL.

[45] Straus, Commencement address. See note 36.

[46][Joan Adler], "Hon. Isidor Straus, House of Representatives, 1894-95," 8.

[47]Richard Croker was at the time a powerful political force. He had also endorsed Isidor in February 1893 for the office of U. S. Postmaster-General. For various senatorial endorsements of Isidor, see, for example, *The Globe* (New York), 22 March 1911, and an editorial in the *New York Evening Journal* of 17 March 1911. Twenty pages of clippings of these endorsements are contained in a scrapbook at SHS. Democrat James A. O'Gorman was elected Senator from New York in 1911.

[48]*New York Times*, 10 October 1894. "There was a great deal of talk yesterday about the possible nomination by Tammany [Hall] of Nathan Straus for Mayor."

[49]It was also a year in which strong anti-Tammany forces were at work. There were serious divisions within the Democratic Party and there was even a fusion ticket with names of both Republicans and Democrats. For details on Nathan's public service, see [Joan Adler], "Nathan Straus, Public Servant," *Straus Historical Society Newsletter* 4/2 (February 2003): 5. In the end, after a great deal of behind-the-scenes maneuvers, no reconciliation was in order. Democrats and the Democratic Reform ticket ran two separate slates, both of whom went down in defeat. The mayor elected in 1894 was William L. Strong and the governor Levi P. Morton, both Republicans. See also articles in the *New York Times*, 12 October 1894, 13 October 1894, 14 October 1894, and 19 October 1894. An article of 8 November 1894 in the *New York Morning Advertiser* congratulated Nathan for his "extraordinary foresight that enables him to see around the block." However, the ordeal of even considering a run for mayor had been a "nervous strain" on Nathan's health, and on October 24, the *New York Times* reported that "he has taken his physician's advice to go abroad." He subsequently resigned as a member of both the Park Commission and the Forestry Commission. He would, however, eventually accept a position as President of the Board of Health. But in January 1898, he wrote to Isidor announcing his new responsibility and noting, "I did not seek the office and did not want it, and I will relinquish it just as soon as I see my

way clear to do so." (Nathan to Isidor, 7 January 1898. SHS). He would serve in that capacity only three months, resigning on 4 March 1898.

[50]Isidor Straus to President McKinley, 8 April 1898. SHS.

Chapter 8

[1]Kauffman, *Jesse Isidor Straus*, 86.

[2]Kauffman, *Jesse Isidor Straus*, 86-91.

[3]Grippo, *Macy*'s, 65-66.

[4]Interestingly enough, it would later be Jesse, not Percy, who would enter the diplomatic corps as Ambassador to France.

[5]*New York Times*, 15 January 1898. A typewritten copy of this elaborate news release is in the Straus Family Papers, NYPL.

[6]Hermine to Ida and Isidor, 7 January 1898. SHS. See also *"wholedamfam": Straus Family Newsletter* 7/1 (February 1999). In this same letter, she informs Isidor that she had gone with Nathan on January 1 to city hall "to see him sworn in as Health Commissioner."

[7]Jesse to parents, 7 January 1898. SHS.

[8]Percy to Dear Papa, 14 January 1898, SHS. Hermine's name was spelled officially with an *e*, but pronounced as though there were an *a* at the end. Thus, some family members took to writing it with an *a*. It has an *e* on her tombstone.

[9]Irene Kohns to Isidor Straus, 21 January 1898. SHS.

[10]Oscar to Isidor, 20 January 1898, SHS.

[11]Sarah Straus to Isidor, 21 January 1898. SHS. All of the letters relating to Lazarus's death and its aftermath are summarized in *"wholedamfam": Straus Family Newsletter* 7/1 (February 1999).

[12]Sarah [Lavanburg Straus] to Dear Ida and Isidor, 21 January 1898. SHS.

[13]Irene Kohns to My dear Uncle Isidor, 21 January 1898. SHS. The funeral service was held at the Temple Emanu-El.

[14]Oscar to Dear Brother & Sister, 20 January 1898. SHS.

[15]Percy to My dear Papa, 18 January 1898. SHS.

[16]Grippo, *Macy*'s, 63.

[17]Kauffman, *Jesse Isidor Straus*, 38.

[18]By 1898 Macy's had approximately 3,000 employees. See Hower, *History of Macy's*, 305.

[19]Grippo, *Macy*'s, 65; Hower, *History of Macy's*, 305,

[20]*New York Times*, 18 April 1909.

[21]Hower, *History of Macy's*, 264.

[22]Grippo, *Macy*s*, 66.

[23]Grippo, *Macy*s*, 76. Grippo contends that the Siegel-Cooper agent offered to sell them the land at the price he had paid, but evidently it came with strings attached and the Strauses refused on principle.

[24]For details on the building of the new store, see Grippo, *Macy*s*, 69-77.

[25]See *Documents of the Assenbly of the State of New York*, v.16. (Albany, New York: J.B. Lyon Company, 1902) 3; Ida was also active as a supporter of the J. Hood Wright Memorial Hospital, and by 1903 she was third vice-president of the Ladies Association, *New York Times*, 8 January 1903.

[26]Kauffman, *Jesse Straus*, 38-39.

[27]Testimonial from the Board of Trustees of the Educational Alliance, presented to Honorable Isidor Straus, New York, April 15th, 1899. Straus Family Papers, NYPL.

[28]Mamma to My dear children, 28 May 1899. Straus Family Papers, NYPL. All quotations in his paragraph are from this letter.

[29]Oscar to Dear Bro & Sister, 25 May 1899. SHS.

[30]Sarah to Dear Ida, 5 November 1898. SHS. Sarah elaborates, tongue in cheek. "Your son Percy is really overworking himself. He goes to the office as early as ten o'clock comes back at one & works as hard as possible at horseback & passing tea for the rest of the afternoon. We have nicknamed him the horse back attaché."

[31]Although in the correspondence, the young woman is referred to as "Sissie," Joan Adler, executive director of the Straus Historical Society, suggests that it "is a pet name for Oscar and Sarah's oldest child, Mildred, and not Nathan and Lina's daugher, whose actual name was Sissie." *See Straus Historical Society Inc. Newsletter* (February 2011): 12-2, p. 1. There is no question that Mildred was in Constantinople at the time, for she returned with Ida and Isidor. Her younger siblings, Roger and Aline, were also present.

[32]"Mama & Papa have decided to spend the summer on the Bosporus as Uncle Isidor and Aunt Ida will perhaps be with us even before July ..." Aline Straus Diary, 11 April 1899. SHS. "Aunt Ida, Uncle Isidor as well as Aunt Milly & Uncle all spent some time with us especially the former." Aline Straus Diary, 3 December 1899. They would visit a second time in 1910, during Oscar's last year as ambassador.

[33]It had rained from September 9-14. See *New York Times*, 20 September, 1899.

[34]Mama to My dear children, 24 September 1899. Straus Family Papers, NYPL.

[35]Mama to My dear children, 24 September 1899. Straus Family Papers, NYPL. Ida comments particularly on a Hoffman engraving entitled "Let him who is guiltless cast the first stone," and "the companion piece of Christ as a boy of about 12 before the rabbis in the temple."

[36]The sole female guest listed in the *Times* account of the event was Miss Julia Richman, who would later be a speaker at the Straus memorial given by the Educational Alliance. *New York Times*, 13 January 1907.

[37]Herbert A. Scheftel died very young on 12 September 1914, leaving Vivian with two sons, Stuart and Herbert Jr., nicknamed "Buzzie." Herbert Sr. is often referred to (inexplicably) as a physician, but there is no question that he was instead a banker and stockbroker. Three years after his death Vivian married George A. Dixon, Jr. and would have a daughter they called Vivian. They lived in Paris for many years.

[38]Isidor to Dear Brother Oscar, 18 December 1906 and 29 December 1906, Oscar S. Straus Papers, LC.

[39]The attestation about Vivian's beauty comes from [Joan Adler], "The Women in the Family-Part Two: Isidor and Ida's Daughters Sara, Minnie and Vivian." *"wholedamfam,": Straus Family Newsletter* 4/2 (August 1996): 4.

[40]*New York Times,* 16 January 1907.

[41]Isidor to Dear Brother Oscar, 31 December 1906. Oscar S. Straus Papers, LC. Nathan's nervous condition is well documented, and in 1910 he had a serious nervous breakdown. His secretary wrote dozens of letters to people in January and February to explain why Nathan could not respond to their correspondence. He blamed the nervous collapse on "the hard fight he has been making to keep the poor children at the Cleveland Preventorium in Lakewood." Folder G.C. 1. Jan.-15 Feb. Nathan Straus Papers, NYPL. Lina Straus, who canceled his appointments right and left, wrote openly of "my poor husband's nervous breakdown." For example, see Lina Straus to My dear Mr. Stokes, 15 January 1910. Nathan Straus Papers, NYPL. By early March he was much better and preparing to leave for Europe on March 12. Lina Straus to My dear Miss Golden, 8 March 1910. Nathan Straus Papers, NYPL.

[42]Isidor to Dear Brother Oscar, 6 February 1907. Oscar S. Straus Papers, LC.

[43]Vivian to My dear Uncle Oscar, 5 February 1907, Oscar S. Straus Papers, LC.

[44]Morris Loeb would die in October 1912. He and Isidor shared many characteristics—their lack of vainglory and their interest in the betterment of Jews in America. Both had at one time served as members of the American

---

Jewish Committee. Isidor was still serving in that capacity at the time of his death. See *American Jewish Yearbook,* v. 15 (New York: Jewish Publication Society of America, 1913-1914) 451.

[45]Isidor to Dear Brother Oscar, 19 February 1907. Oscar S. Straus Papers, LC.

[46]Isidor to Dear Brother Oscar, 10 March 1907. Oscar S. Straus Papers, LC.

[47]Cablegram to Oscar Straus, 20 April 1907. Oscar S. Straus Papers, LC.

[48]Edward Hamelsdorf to Hon. Oscar S. Straus, 29 April 1907, Oscar S. Straus Papers, LC.

[49]*New York Times,* 17 July 1907.

[50]Jesse and Irma had vacationed at Deal Beach in June 1907. All these coastal areas, Elberon, Long Branch, and Deal Beach are in close proximity in Monmouth County, New Jersey. Hermine and Lazarus Kohns also had a house at Elberon, to which an ailing Lazarus was bought to summer with his family in 1910. He had been comatose for some time. Isidor wrote to Oscar on 3 June 1910 that "Lazarus was removed Thursday to his Elberon home. He was absolutely oblivious to his surroundings and it is not likely that he knows anything about his removal. They had a special car and from a telephonic message I learned that the trip was without detriment." Letter in SHS. According to his obituary, published in the *New York Times,* 4 December 1910, he was at his home on 23 West 56th Street at the time of his death on 3 December.

[51]Alfred Rothschild changed his name to Alfred Redgis.

[52]Ida Straus to Alfred Redgis, 17 October 1907, SHS. According to the letter, Amanda had been out for her "accustomed walk" when she began to feel faint and stopped in the garden of a Mr. Hamershlag, who spotted her from the porch, and brought her a chair and "a stimulant." She asked to lie down, than closed her eyes in what appeared to be sleep. Ida's son-in-law, Dr. Richard Weil, was called, but he arrived too late.

[53]Isidor to Dear Brother Oscar, 8 October 1907 and 10 October 1907, Oscar S. Straus Papers, LC.

[54]Isidor Straus to Dear Brother Oscar, 29 October 1907. Oscar S. Straus Papers, LC.

[55]Isidor to Dear Brother Oscar, 29 October 1907. Oscar S. Straus Papers, LC.

[56]Isidor to Dear Brother Oscar, 12 November 1907. Oscar S. Straus Papers, LC.

[57]Isidor to Dear Brother Oscar, 8 October, 1907, 10 October, 1907. Oscar S. Straus Papers, LC. Rosendale was, like Isidor, an anti-Zionist.

[58]Isidor to Dear Brother Oscar, 17 June 1907. Oscar S. Straus Papers, LC. Oscar had said, in the presence of an employee, and in the midst of a discussion, "'I won't discuss this matter with you,' and left in a huff." Lee was, according to Isidor, "sore and mortified."

[59]Lee to Dear Uncle Oscar, 21 June 1907. Oscar S. Straus Papers, LC.

[60]Oscar to Dear Ones at Home, 20 March 1888. This letter was written on letterhead from Shepheard's Hotel in Cairo. Straus Family Papers, NYPL.

[61]After Isidor's death, the Educational Alliance building would be renamed Straus Memorial Hall.

[62]The poem, "To the Czar," was reproduced the following month in the *Jewish Chronicle* (7 June 1912): 11. The full quotation of the last sentence states that it sheds "additional light on the character of one who on the ill-fated Titanic preferred death to parting with her husband..." For reasons of narrative, I have omitted the last part of the sentence. A manuscript copy of this poem is also located in the Straus Family Papers, NYPL.

[63]David Blaustein, *Memoirs of David Blaustein: Educator and Communal Worker*, arranged by Miriam Blaustein (New York: McBride, Nast & Co., 1913) 237-239. These comments were included in a eulogy he gave for the Strauses at the memorial meeting at the Educational Alliance on 11 May 1912.

[64]Jacob H. Schiff to Hon. Oscar S. Straus, 4 October 1907. Oscar S. Straus Papers, LC. See also *New York Times,* 28 July 1907 and 23 August, 1907

[65]Isidor to Dear Brother Oscar, 8 Oct. 1907. Oscar S. Straus Papers, LC.

[66]Nathan to Dear Brother Isidor, 1 November [1907]. Oscar S. Straus Papers, LC. Emphasis his.

[67]Your affectionate sister to My dear Brother Oscar, 8 December 1907. Oscar S. Straus Papers, LC. This is one of only two known surviving letters written by Hermine.

[68]Oscar to Dear Brother Isidor, 23 December 1908, Straus Family Papers, NYPL.

Chapter 9

[1]Isidor to Oscar, 17 September 1909. SHS.

[2]Jesse to My dear Papa, 9 September 1909. SHS.

[3]Isidor to Oscar, 17 September 1909. SHS.

[4]Isidor to Jesse. 13 September 1910. Straus Family Papers, NYPL. He announced his intent to take rooms at the St. Regis in a letter to Oscar on 17 September 1909. Straus Family Papers, NYPL. The Strauses later moved into

an apartment at 524 Fifth Avenue. Other family members used the house at 105th Street, rather than leave it empty. Oscar's daughter, Aline, moved in as did her parents at a later date. See Isidor to Dear Brother Oscar, 13 September 1910. "Aline is making arrangements to move into our 105th Street house and I understand that you are going to live with her. As I finally concluded that it would be unwise for us to move in, as Ida would not hear of having a housekeeper, I concluded that Aline and you had better have the use of it that to leave it standing empty." Percy would be staying there at the time of his parents' death. See prologue.

[5]Jesse to Dear Papa, 20 September 1909. Straus Family Papers, NYPL.

[6][Joan Adler] "Jesse Isidor Straus: 1872-1936," *Straus Historical Society Newsletter* 6/1 (August 2004): 4.

[7]Oscar served under Democratic and Republican presidents alike. Once asked by an admirer to declare his party, he explained simply that he had served under presidents in both parties. He had shifted his affiliation as the issues changed. Most historians today consider him a Republican. Taft was the fourth president under whom Oscar had served.

[8]Percy S. Straus to Dear Papa and Mamma, 19 March 1910 and 21 March 1910. SHS. Unfortunately, there are no extant details from this trip.

[9]Letter from The Cunard Steamship Co., Ltd to Mr. Isidore Strauss [sic], 10 November 1911, SHS.

[10]Percy(?) to Papa and Mamma, 22 January 1912, SHS. The letters in this series are unsigned copies from the Macy's letterbook; however, based on the style and content of the letters, it is usually possible to discern which of the sons wrote them. Often, one brother can be eliminated as a possible writer, but not both. In the text I have made a best guess as to which brother wrote a given letter. Where there is any doubt, however, I have included a question mark after the name in the notes.

[11]This letter is quoted in an unidentified newspaper article entitled "Comfort for Oscar Straus" contained in SHS.

[12]Son to Mother and Father, 6 February 1912. SHS.

[13]Isidor Straus to Oscar Straus, 3 June 1910, Straus Family Papers, NYPL.

[14]Lina Gutherz Straus, *Disease in Milk, The Remedy Pateurization: The Life Work of Nathan Straus*, 2nd ed. (New York: E. P. Dutton, 1917) 147-48. It is interesting to note that, although Lina found Ida not in the best of health, the letters that she and Isidor sent home always reassured the family that they were both in good health. Like her sister Amanda, she never wanted to worry her children with such concerns.

[15]Percy (?) to Papa, 12 February 1912, Straus Family Papers, NYPL.

[16]Percy (?) to Father and Mother, 20 February 1912, Straus Family Papers, NYPL.

[17]Percy to Papa and Mamma, 18 March 1912. Straus Family Papers, NYPL. Although the letter is dated 18 March, the contents had been written on various days. The comments quoted were dated 16 March.

[18]Frank H. Tabor to Isidor Straus, 17 November 1909. Straus Family Papers, NYPL.

[19]Percy (?) to Papa on 1 March 1912, SHS.

[20]In fact, the April 24 sailing would also be canceled when the ship's firemen went on strike, refusing (following the *Titanic* disaster) to sail without adequate lifeboats. The *Olympic* would not sail to New York again until May 15, arriving on May 22.

[21]Wyn Craig Wade, *The Titanic: End of a Dream*. (New York: Penguin Books, 1986).

[22]Isidor to Oscar, 12 March 1912. SHS.

[23]Percy (?) to Papa and Mamma, 25 March 1912. Straus Family Papers, NYPL.

[24]Percy to Papa and Mamma 27 March 1912, Straus Family Papers, NYPL.

[25]Isidor to Oscar, 12 March 1912. SHS.

[26]Isidor to Oscar, 12 March 1912. SHS.

[27]Grandma to Beatrice, 18 March 1912. SHS.

[28]Ida to Rose Abraham, March 30 1912. SHS. It is uncertain whether "Rose" Abraham is the same person as Marose Abraham. I have listed them separately in the index.

[29]Ida to Rose Abraham, 30 March 1912. SHS

[30]Ida to Children, April 4 1912. SHS The children did not receive the letter until April 15.

[31]See her letter of April 4, note 29.

[32]Jesse to Herby, 28 March 1912. Straus Family Papers, NYPL.

[33]Jesse to Herby, 28 March 1912. Straus Family Papers, NYPL.

[34]Jesse to Papa, 29 March 1912. Straus Family Papers, NYPL.

[35]Jesse to Papa, 29 March 1912. Straus Family Papers, NYPL.

[36]Alfred Redgis to Dear Elsa [Elsa Blun Long], 28 April 1957. Copy provided to me by Laurette Rothschild Rosenstrauch.

[37]Ida to My dear children, 4 April 1912, SHS. Even on this final trip, as an example of their support of Jewish causes, Ida had requested that her sons send his Aunt Amena [?] $100, no small sum in 1912 as a donation for the

Beth-El Sisterhood, Mrs. Schulman's Sabbath School. See Jesse (?) to Papa, 2 February 1912. Straus Family Papers, NYPL.

[38]In addition to the Strauses and Mr. Brown, the guest list included Franklin M. Gunther, Reed Paige Clark, Mr. and Mrs. Robert P. Skinner, Mr. and Mrs. Charles Butler Rogers, Mrs. John Ridgely Carter, William P. Cresson, and Sheldon L. Crosby. The guest list was sent to the Straus family by Ambassador Reid. Copy in SHS.

[39]It is likely that the two couples spent some time together in London since the Burbridges later sent flowers to their cabin on the *Titanic*.

[40]Ida Straus to Rose Abraham, 30 March 1912. SHS.

[41]Jesse to Papa, 29 March 1912. SHS.

[42]In fact, Roosevelt founded a third party, the Progressive Party, also known as the Bull Moose Party, and ran for the presidency, outpolling Taft considerably. However, the election went to Democrat Woodrow Wilson.

[43]Isidor Straus to Rev. H. H. Redgrave, M.A., 9 April 1912. SHS. The letter was sent by Rev. Redgrave to an unidentified son of Isidor on 13 September, 1934. With the letter, he sent a note, which contained the following words: "For 22 years now I have kept secret from the world a matter in which the British public would have evinced the most profound interest, namely, the last letter which your beloved Father, Isidor Straus, wrote on earth, only the day prior to the day he and your saintly Mother joined their ship of destiny—The Titanic."

Chapter 10

[1]Geoffrey Marcus, *The Maiden Voyage* (New York: Viking, 1969) 24; John Eaton and Charles Haas, *Titanic: Triumph and Tragedy* (New York: Norton, 1995) 51-52. Marcus refers to the dock as Ocean Dock, but its name was not changed until 1922.

[2]Oskar Straus's father, Ludwig, was born in Isidor's hometown of Otterberg in 1841 but moved to Vienna in 1860. See Hans Steinebrei, *History of the Jews of Otterberg: An Example of the History from the Palatinate in the 19th Century*, (New York: Straus Historical Society, Inc. 2008) 84. One of the earliest books on the sinking of the *Titanic* attests to this particular music. See *Sinking of the Titanic and Great Sea Disasters*, ed. Logan Marshall, (n. p.:L.T. Myers: n.p. 1912) 32.

[3]The Strauses' suite is described in John P. Eaton & Charles A. Haas, *Titanic: Destination Disaster: The Legends and the Reality* (New York: W. W. Norton & Co., 1987) 81. See the following note for the source of detail about the flowers.

---

[4]Letter from Ida R. Straus to Mrs. Burbridge, 10 April 1912, copy in SHS. Isidor was standing on the deck with Col. Archibald Gracie who recorded his reaction. Gracie occupied Cabin C-51, just down the hall from the Strauses, which he verifies in his book, *Titanic: A Survivor's Story*, (Chalford-Stroud, Gloucestershire: History Press, 2008) 6-7, 9. Originally published as under the title of *The Truth about Titanic* (New York: M. Kennerley, 1913).

[5]For a fuller description of the incident and its aftermath, see Walter Lord, *The Night Lives On* (New York: William Morrow, 1986) 40-41.

[6]*New York Tribune*, April 15, 1912. The four-foot estimate is based on the testimony of Captain Gale of the tug *Vulcan*, who stated, "…we got hold of the *New York* when she was within four feet of *Titanic*." See John P. Eaton and Charles A. Haas, *Titanic: Triumph and Tragedy*, 76.

[7] The maiden voyage of the *New York*, then called the *City of New York*, was in 1888. See Eugene W. Smith, *Passenger Ships of the World*, 62. I am grateful to David Dearborn of the Maine Maritime Museum for verifying this information.

[8] Gracie, *Titanic*, 6.

[9]It is little wonder that Isidor Straus would have been friends with Richard Burbridge, who had turned Harrods into the world's most successful department store with his innovations. Lilian Burbridge was Sir Richard's second wife, whom he had married in 1910. It is possible but not probable that the letter, which is addressed only to Mrs. Burbridge could have been sent to the wife of Richard Woodman Burbridge, son of Sir Richard, who succeeded to his title at his father's death in 1917. If so, his wife's name was Catherine. However, the second baronet Burbridge was a generation younger than Isidor Straus, and it is far more likely that the senior Burbridge and Straus, both of whom were actively involved in managing a department store would have had more in common. (See http://www.thepeerage.com.)

[10]Ida Straus to Mrs. Burbridge, 10 April 1912. SHS.

[11]To his credit, Harry Widener had already acquired a Guttenberg Bible. After his death on the *Titanic*, his mother would donate funds to establish the Widener library at Harvard University in his memory.

[12]Judith B. Geller, Titanic: *Women and Children First* (New York: W.W Norton, 1998) 63.

[13]Gracie, *Titanic*, 12. The Lamson sisters had married, respectively, John Murray Brown, Robert C. Cornell, Daniel W. Appleton, and Victor Drummond.

[14]Gracie, *Titanic*, 12.

[15]Titanic Historical Society, Inc. Louise Laroche to My dear Dad, www.titanichhistoricalsociety.org.

[16]Impressions of a first-class passenger were published in the *Belfast Telegraph*, 15 April 1912.

[17]See the menu for first luncheon in Eaton and Haas, *Titanic*, 90.

[18]Cabin numbers, with the exception of Farthing's, are taken from the so-called Cave List, found among the personal effects of the drowned first-class steward, Herbert Cave. R.G. 41, Series C, vol. 76A, #218. Nova Scotia Archives. I am grateful to senior archivist Garry Shutlak for this information. The source of information concerning Farthing's cabin is from www.encyclopedia-titanica.org/titanic-biography/john-farthing.html.

[19]Lawrence Beesley, *The Loss of the S. S. Titanic: Its Story and Its Lessons* (Boston: Houghton Mifflin, 1912; reprinted First Mariner Books, 2000) 17.

[20]See Lord, *Night*, 21-26, for details on the original launching of the vessel.

[21]See Lord, *Night*, 26.

[22]County Cork Local History web site: http://www.geocities.com/corklh/titanic.html.

[23]See Beesley, *Loss*, 20.

[24]Gracie, *Titanic*, 3.

[25]*The Denver News*, 19 April 1912, quoted Mrs. Paul Schabert, whose name they gave incorrectly as Schubert: "Mrs. Straus, who had a stateroom near me, and with whom I had frequently talked, declared to me, when the ladies first order came, that in no circumstances would she leave Mr. Straus." Mrs. Brown attests to playing bridge with both the Strauses in a story reported in the *New York Sun*, 20 April 1912.

[26]Gracie, *Titanic*, 6-7.

[27]Gracie, *Titanic*, 7.

[28]*Report on the Loss of the S. S. Titanic* (New York, St. Martin's Press, 1990; originally printed 1912 and "Presented to Both Houses of Parliament by Command of His Majesty") 27.

[29]Richard Howells, *The Myth of the* Titanic (London: Macmillan, 1999) 108.

[30]Estimates of the *Californian*'s distance vary between five and twenty miles. The distance cited is based on that contained in the official British *Report*, 43-44.

[31]For their final menu, see Eaton and Haas, *Titanic: Triumph and Tragedy*, 133.

[32]This account of the Straus's whereabouts and actions at the time the *Titanic* stuck an iceberg and subsequent events is based on an interview with Sylvester Byrnes (who allegedly is repeating a narrative of Ellen Bird), reported in the *New York World* 20 April 1912, as well as in many other newspapers, among them the *New York Sun*, 20 April 1912, which reports the account from the perspective of Mrs. J. Murry Brown, and the *Baltimore Sun*, 21 April 1912.

[33] John A. Badenoch to Percy Straus, 24 April 1912, Straus Historical Society.

[34]Accounts of the loading of the lifeboats differ to some extent and some are inconsistent with one another and occasionally with the verifiable facts. It is completely understandable, given the excitement and confusion of the event, that memories would differ. I have made every effort to reconstruct the most consistent, probable, and logical sequence of events based on the various stories later told by passengers.

[35]The other three men were Clinch Smith, Hugh Woolner, and H. Björnström Steffanson. See Gracie, *Titanic*, 12-13.

[36]*New York World*, 20 April 1912. The detail about the coat is not included in Ellen Bird's account as it was reported in the *World*. However, after her rescue, Miss Bird attempted to return the coat to Ida's daughter, Sara Straus Hess, who refused to accept it, telling Ellen Bird that it had been a gift to her from their mother and that she must keep it. Information from Joan Adler, executive director of the Straus Historical Society.

[37]*New York World*, 20 April 1912.

[38]The number of those in this lifeboat differs in various accounts from 28 to 39. I have chosen to use the figures from the report that resulted from the British formal investigations that was originally printed in 1912. *Report,* 38. Some of the lifeboats took on additional passengers as they tried to rescue those in the water, which may sometimes explain the discrepancies.

[39]The crew members in boat 8 were so inexperienced at seamanship that the Countess of Rothes was compelled to take the tiller, while Ella (Mrs. J. Stuart) White had to inform one of the oarsman that the oar needed to go in the oarlock, and he confessed he had never rowed before; still another woman, Margaret (Mrs. Frederick J.) Swift, rowed "all the way to the *Carpathia*." See Ella White's testimony before the U.S. Senate (62nd Congress) Subcommittee on Commerce, Titanic Disaster, Washington 1912, 1008; quoted in Gracie, *Titanic*, 95-96.

[40]One of the passengers, identified as G. N. Stengel, indicated that the Strauses stood on Deck B. He was no doubt thinking of the Boat Deck (top

deck) as Deck A and the second deck down, where the Strauses actually were as the last lifeboat was launched, as Deck B. It was in fact Deck A. *New York Evening Globe*, 19 April 1912.

[41]Gracie, 124. *Titanic*, This testimony comes from the affidavit of Emily Ryerson, American Inquiry, 1107.

[42]The *New York World* account of 20 April 1912, which reports these words, suggests that Ellen Bird and Madeleine Astor were on the same boat, which was not the case. The account, supplied by Ellen Bird, is filtered through Sylvester Byrnes, general manager of Macy's. Other eyewitness accounts, however, place Ida Straus at both lifeboats 8 (Ellen's boat) and 4 (Mrs. Astor's boat). Boatside efforts get her to enter both lifeboats 4 and 8 are well documented in various accounts, which will be cited below. The account suggests that crewmen tried to get Ida into three lifeboats, but I can identify only boats 8 and 4 with certainty. If there was another boat, it would have to have been boat 6, the only portside boat to be lowered before boat 8. No survivors from boat 6 report any such incident.

[43]Gracie, *Titanic*, 16.

[44]Conversation based on *New York Sun*, 20 April 1912.

[45]Jack Foley and Sam Parks, members of the *Titanic* crew who were also saved, remembered Isidor's efforts to get Ida into boat 4. Their testimony was reported in the *Newark Morning Star*, 20 April 1912.

[46]Based on paraphrases and quotations from many sources, among them Gracie's account, the *Morning Star*, 20 April 1912; *Evening Mail*, 19 April 1912; *Spokane Review*, 21 April 1912. While the words may differ to some degree in the various accounts, and the order, based on the memories of those who witnessed their final moments together, is sometimes murky, the intent of the words and the emotions they express is always consistent.

[47]The legend that the band played "Nearer My God to Thee" as the ship was going down has been debunked by various authors, the first of whom, perhaps, is Gracie, 13. That the "Songe d'automne," composed by Archibald Joyce and then popular in England, was among the selections played by the band is based on several eyewitness accounts, who call it simply "Autumn," and on the fact that "Songe d'automne" was listed among the waltzes in the White Star Line's published repertoire of music selections, reproduced by Eaton and Haas, *Titanic: Triumph and Tragedy*, 132-33. One of those who reported that "Autumn" was what the band was playing when the ship went down was the Second Wireless Operator, Harold Bride, whose first interview from the *Carpathia* was reported by the *New York Times* on 19 April, 1912. Bride stated: "From aft came the tunes of the band. There was a rag-time

tune, I don't know what, and then there was 'Autumn.'" However the newspapers chose to interpret "Autumn" as the name of a hymn tune. See a full discussion by Lord, *Night,* 138-43 and Howells, *Myth,* 120-35. No band member survived the sinking.

[48]Based on account in *New York World,* 20 April, 1912

[49]*New York Evening Globe,* 19 April 1912. The *Globe* gives his name as G. N. Stengel, but Charles Emil Stengel was clearly the "Newark man" in question.

[50]*New York Evening Globe,* 19 April 1912. Ida was one of only five first-class female passengers who were not saved. Other than Ida Straus, they were Ann Elizabeth Isham, Edith Corse Evans, Bessie Waldo Allison, and her two-year-old daughter, Helen Loraine Allison.

Epilogue

[1] The Clebourne was designed by the architectural firm of Schwartz & Gross and is especially noted for its fine carriage entrance. The construction budget for the new park was set at $20,000. *New York Times,* 21 March 1913. Straus park was refurbished in 1997. The reflecting pool is now a bed of flowers and plants.

[2] Robert Grippo tells the story in his recent book on Macy's. Nathan's sons sought more responsibility at the store, while Isidor's sons thought they lacked sufficient experience. Jesse, Percy, and Herbert offered to sell their half to Nathan, who retired from business altogether after his brother's death. Nathan declined and proposed instead that he take over their share of L. Straus & Sons and relinquish to them his share of Macy's. Thus, Isidor's sons became the sole owners of Macy's in November 1913. See Grippo, *Macy*s,* 91-92.

[3] See Grippo, *Macy*s,* 90.

[4] *New York Tribune,* 16 April 1915.

[5] Although the *Tribune* account of 16 April indicates that the children cast the flowers into the pool, the *New York Herald* report of the same date states that they placed a wreath on the monument. Both accounts mention roses and lilies.

[6] *New York Herald,* 16 April 1915.

[7] *New York Herald,* 16 April 1915.

[8] *New York Times,* 21 March 1913.

[9] Funds for the construction of the park were all raised by citizen donations, according to the "Order of Exercises of the Dedication of Straus Park" (SHS). Lukeman's most ambitious work was the Civil War memorial

carving on Stone Mountain, Georgia, which remains, even though incomplete, a remarkable achievement.

[10] For the Fireman's Memorial forty thousand dollars had been allocated from public funds, and the committee raised the other $50,000. The original intent of the memorial had been to honor the recently deceased Fire Chief Charles W. Kruger, who had died in 1908 in the line of duty. But, as Isidor noted, the scope of the project had been enlarged to dedicate it "to all firemen of the uniformed force of the Greater City who have gone or will go to their deaths in the line of duty." Isidor Straus to the Honorable The Mayor and Members of the Board of Estimate and Apportionment." [October 1910], Straus Family Papers, NYPL. The designer of the memorial was Harold Van Buren Magonigle, and the sculptor was Attilio Piccirilli. In fact, on January 4, 1912, shortly before sailing Isidor had convened a meeting at his Manhattan apartment at 524 Fifth Avenue, where he and Ida were still living to lighten her load. Committee Resolution on 4 January 1912 at 5:30 P.M. Straus Family Papers, NYPL. Munson had also modeled for the sculptures on the granite arch at the foot of the Manhattan Bridge, the top of the Municipal Building, the front entrance to the New York Public Library, the fountain in front of the Plaza Hotel, and many others too numerous to mention.

[11] Munson's first film, *Inspiration*, depicts her as an artist's model.

[12] Audrey sought love desperately, even resorting to advertising for an ideal mate, which was quite unusual at the time. At one point she evidently thought she had found him, but when he allegedly jilted her, she tried unsuccessfully on 28 May 1922, to commit suicide by swallowing a solution of bichloride of mercury at her home in the town of Mexico in Oswego County, New York. See *New York Times*, 29 May 1922. She was committed in 1931 and remained in the asylum for the rest of her life. She died there in 1996.

[13] Audrey was buried in New Haven, New York. For a fuller exploration of her life, see her biography by Diane Rozas and Nita Bourne Gottehrer, *American Venus: The Extraordinary Life of Audrey Munson Model and Muse* (Los Angeles: Balcony Press, 1999) and, more recently, Andrea Geyer, "*Queen of the Artists' Studios"—The Story of Audrey Munson. Intimate Secrets of Studio Life Revealed by the Most Perfect, Most Versatile, Most Famous of American Models, Whose Face and Figure Have Inspired Thousands of Modern Masterpieces of Sculpture and Painting.* (Commissioned and published by Art in General, 2007).

[14] The jury consisted of Memorial Committee members Felix M. Warburg and Capt. Joseph B. Greenhut, with Supreme Court Justice Samuel

Greenbaum as an alternate, and members of the National Sculpture Society, Herbert Adams, Henry Bacon, and Karl Bitter. Bitter, a well-known sculptor, died only five days before the dedication as a consequence of being hit by an automobile in front of the Metropolitan Opera House (See *New York Times*, 11 April 1915). The full committee consisted of Henry Green, chairman, Herman Sieluken, treasurer, Jacob H. Schiff, Samuel Greenbaum, Adolph Lewisohn, William G. McAdoo, now U.S. Secretary of the Treasury; Felix W. Warburg, and Capt. Joseph B. Greenhut. The *Herald* article also lists among committee members: Dr. Cyrus Adler, E. C. Benedict, John Claflin, Robert W. DeForest, Henry Hentz, A. Barton Hepburn, Francis L. Leland, Louis Marshall, John J. Miller, Nathaniel Meyers, Adolph Ochs, George Foster Peabody, Leopold Plant, Isaac N. Seligman, Herman Siegel, W. A. Simonson, Louis Stern, Mayer Sulzberger, William Woodward, C. B. Webster, Louis Chamansky, and Benjamin Conroy. Many of these names are the same as those who helped to organize the memorial service at Carnegie Hall three years earlier.

[15] John T. Bethell, *Harvard Observed: An Illustrated history of the University in the Twentieth Century* (Cambridge: Harvard Magazine, 1998) 101.

[16] [Joan Adler], *Straus Historical Society Inc. Newsletter* 4:1 (August 2002), 12. In 1998 Lab School 77 was also incorporated into the building.

[17] I am grateful to Susan Olsen, Director of Historical Services at Woodlawn Cemetery for this information. Email message from Susan Olsen to June Hall McCash, 8 April 2011.

[18] Rogers, a well known designer for the cultural elite, is known for having designed such major works as Memorial Sloan-Kettering Hospital and the Sterling Memorial Library and the Harkness Memorial Tower at Yale, only two among the many structures he did for his alma mater.

Index